LIKE SODIUM IN WATER

Hayden Eastwood

Like Sodium in Water

A memoir of home and heartache

Jonathan Ball Publishers
Johannesburg & Cape Town

Published in South Africa in 2018 by
JONATHAN BALL PUBLISHERS
A division of Media24 (Pty) Ltd
PO Box 33977
Jeppestown
2043

ISBN 978-1-86842-854-0
ebook ISBN 978-1-86842-855-7

Every effort has been made to trace the copyright holders and to obtain their
permission for the use of copyright material. The publishers apologise
for any errors or omissions and would be grateful to be notified of any corrections
that should be incorporated in future editions of this book.

Twitter: www.twitter.com/JonathanBallPub
Facebook: www.facebook.com/JonathanBallPublishers
Blog: http://jonathanball.bookslive.co.za

Cover by Alexis Aronson
Design and typesetting by Nazli Jacobs
Set in Plantin

Printed by **novus print**, a Novus Holdings company

For Dan

When I was a child, I picked up a novel by Stephen Fry. The fore-word was by Hugh Laurie, and it went like this: 'It's very unfair. It took Joseph Heller seven years to write *Catch 22*. Stephen seems to have knocked this one off on a couple of wet Wednesday afternoons in Norfolk.'

I didn't know that twenty years later I'd look back and feel nothing but envy for Mr Heller. Seven years! How did he manage to write a book so quickly?

I knew I would tell this story when I was twenty-one, but it was only when I was thirty that I finally wrote it down. And I only did so because not writing it down was beginning to drive me mad.

I refer to real events and real people, but the account is written like a novel because it was easier to write like that. I have changed the names of some of the people and places involved, and one minor character is an amalgamation. I am reluctant to call this book a memoir because the word implies, at least to me, the existence of some certainty about what happened.

I don't have certainty, and I don't trust my memories (or my evaluation of them) enough to say, 'This is the truth.' As such, I make no claim that my descriptions and analyses are impartial, or that they present an accurate insight into my country or society. The events in this story should be understood for what they are: a catharsis of a time and place that boiled its way out of me.

I owe a big thank you to many people, but particularly Douglas Rogers, for introducing me to Jonathan Ball.

I received so many rejection letters from publishers that I planned to découpage a door with them. When just another email arrived, this time from Jonathan Ball, I almost sent it straight to the recycle bin without reading it. You are reading this story because I read that email.

Arrival

Chapter 1

Two large men in dark suits block access to First Class. The loud-speaker chimes. 'Ladies and gentlemen; esteemed members of the Politburo; Mai Grace Mugabe, Mother of Africa; and His Excellency, President and Head of State and Government, and Commander-in-Chief of the Armed Forces, Comrade RG Mugabe, welcome aboard this flight to Harare, Zimbabwe. Please fasten your seat belts for take-off.'

The thrust of the engines presses me into my seat. But the men in dark suits and sunglasses stand perfectly straight and still, as though they're immune to the equation $f=ma$, as though they're of another world. A passenger in a nearby seat mutters, 'Let's hope this thing can actually take off with all of Grace's shopping on board.' I open a copy of the *Journal of Chemical Physics* and read the summary section of an article on statistical thermodynamics.

'Good evening, ladies and gentlemen; esteemed members of the Politburo; Mai Grace Mugabe, Mother of Africa; and His Excellency, President and Head of State and Government, and Commander-in-Chief of the Armed Forces, Comrade RG Mugabe. Dinner will now be served.'

The man next to me removes a white-hunter's hat from his face. He sits up straight and rubs his eyes. The hostess taps him on the shoulder. 'Chicken or beef, sir?'

I turn my attention to the journal in my lap. It's the wrong reading material for a long flight; I put it away.

'Excuse me,' I say to the white-hunter man. 'Could I just squeeze out for a moment?'

'Toilet?'

'Yeah.'

'There's only one working,' he replies.

The queue of people stretches down the aisle. I edge closer to the door. The stench of urine grows stronger. A girl with bleach-blonde hair pushes past me. 'Excuse me, I really need to go,' she says.

I give up and return to my seat. I close my eyes and try to sleep but struggle to find a comfortable position in the cramped space.

Restless thoughts swirl around my head. What will I find when I return home? How much will life have changed this time? Will we even have water? And what about Blair Road? Will the old man have butchered all the trees? Will the roof and walls be crumbling yet?

When I open my eyes, the plane is below the clouds. The horizon glows a faint blue through the window. A hostess waddles down the aisle with a trolley.

The loudspeaker chimes. 'Ladies and gentlemen; esteemed members of the Politburo; Mai Grace Mugabe, Mother of Africa; and His Excellency, President and Head of State and Government, and Commander-in-Chief of the Armed Forces, Comrade RG Mugabe, welcome to Harare, Zimbabwe. Please fasten your seat belts for landing.'

Dry bush and derelict farmland glide past the window. The browns and beiges pierce me with their crispness. The plane jolts. We taxi along the bumpy runway. A long red carpet awaits us at the airport terminal. The airport building stands solitary and dirty and small against a perfect turquoise sky. Black Mercedes with tinted windows wait like columns of dead beetles. The brass of a military pipe band glints in the morning sun. Crowds of people wave pictures of the president above their heads.

His Excellency, President and Head of State and Government, and Commander-in-Chief of the Armed Forces, Comrade RG

Mugabe walks robotically down the red carpet. He shakes the white-gloved hand of what looks like a military general.

'Ladies and gentlemen, thank you for your patience. You may now disembark through the rear exit.'

Party supporters turn their heads and stare at me as I walk past them. They remain expressionless and silent, as though they're searching their memories for a section in the party handbook they once read, the bit that says, 'What to do if a bunch of dishevelled white imperialists exit the president's aeroplane immediately after he's said he doesn't like white imperialists.'

The customs man stamps my passport. I walk through the dim hall to the baggage collection area. I put my rucksack on a trolley and walk towards the glass doors. They open, and I put one foot into the arrivals hall. Mum stands on the other side waving at me.

I sense a tug on my shoulder. 'Excuse me, sir,' says a young man in an official-looking outfit. 'Would you mind stepping to one side, please?'

'This is just procedure,' he continues. 'I just want to make sure that you are not a security threat.' He puts my bags on a nearby table and unzips them. He pulls out some shirts and shoes and a PlayStation. He removes a pair of odd socks and some trousers. He removes a half-eaten chocolate bar, still in its wrapper, and a tennis ball. He pulls out my chemical physics journal. 'What is this?' he asks.

'It's a science journal,' I say. 'I need it for my research.'

'What kind of research?'

'Physical chemistry research. Or chemical physics. One of the two, I never know which.'

He pages his way through the equations and symbols as though studying them will somehow unveil a secret. He closes the journal and puts it on the table. He returns his hands to my rucksack and removes a British passport. He puts it on the desk next to my Zimbabwean one. Our eyes meet. My stomach turns. 'Wait here,' he says.

A woman with giant bosoms walks into the room. 'Come this way,' she says to me.

She leads me to a small office and seats me at a wooden desk, strewn with dog-eared papers. Her hair is in a bun, seemingly held in place with grease and glue, highly flammable. She studies me silently, her bosoms overflowing onto the table in front of her.

'What are you doing with two passports? Do you know that you are breaking the law?'

I say nothing.

'I have asked you a question!'

'Ma'am,' I reply. 'Technically I'm only using one passport. The other one is with me, but I've never used it.'

'No, no, no!' she shouts. 'Young man, you are breaking the law!'

'I'm sorry, ma'am,' I say. 'I really didn't think I was committing an offence.'

'Well, this is no longer a matter for me. This is a matter for the police.' She puts my passport to one side. 'Wait here.'

'If you're arresting me, could I please explain this to my mother? She'll have been waiting outside for the last while.'

'Yes, fetch your mother; I want to speak to her.'

A guard walks me to the arrivals hall. Mum waits there in bright-green tights and a big fluffy jersey with orange and yellow on it. Her hair is a shade she calls 'claret and carrot'. I want to scream, 'Mum, you complete dick! Why did you dress like Priscilla Queen of the Desert today? Why couldn't you have just worn some tragic floral blouse?'

The security guard escorts us to the interrogation room. The woman looks up from her desk and pauses before speaking, as though the sight of my mother dressed like a life-sized parrot has made her brain momentarily lose track of its thoughts, as though her customs-and-excise handbook doesn't specify what to do in the event of a white Rhodesian madam not wearing a tragic floral blouse. 'Do you know your son has broken the law?'

Mum seems shocked. 'Oh my goodness, what's he done now?'

'He has committed a serious offence. Carrying two passports. Very serious.'

Mum goes quiet for a moment and then takes a deep breath. 'I've been telling him for ages to get rid of that British passport! He's so disobedient! He never listens to me!'

The woman leans back in her chair. She chews something around in her mouth. 'Mrs Eastwood,' she finally says. 'I now sympathise with you. These young ones, they no longer listen to their elders. Young man, why do you not listen to your mother?'

'I'm sorry, ma'am,' I say.

'What is wrong with you young people nowadays, eh?'

'I promise I won't do it again, ma'am,' I say.

The woman leans forward and wags her finger close to my eyeball. I feel her warm breath on my face. A speckle of her spit lands on my cheek as she shouts.

'Sorry, ma'am,' I repeat.

'You know, Mrs Eastwood, sometimes my son is also disobedient. Sometimes he hangs around with unsavoury people who remain nefarious and unsophisticated.'

'Boys these days are a law unto themselves,' Mum adds.

The woman fixes me with a glare. 'You see, there is no respect young man. No respect!'

The woman leans back in her chair again. She seems to pause in thought for a moment. 'Okay, you may go,' she says, pointing at me. 'But from now on you must listen to your mother!'

The security guard standing nearby lifts the PlayStation from the desk. 'What about these things he failed to declare for duty?'

'Ah, not to worry,' the woman says as she gets to her feet. 'Mrs Eastwood, good day to you.'

I place my bags in the boot of the car. I breathe the dust and grass of the winter air into my lungs. We drive past a throng of people plodding along the airport road. 'There's the rent-a-crowd they bussed in this morning for your welcoming ceremony,' says Mum. 'Nice to see that they've been left to walk home on their Sunday.'

I study the people hitch-hiking into town. Moments ago they were party loyalists, now they are just pedestrians looking for a lift.

A motorbike carrying a man in military uniform overtakes us. He gestures for us to pull over. We wait at the side of the road with lines of other cars. Sirens and Mercedes and men with machine guns race past us in a blur of flashing lights. 'How's Beebs and Miley?' I ask.

'They're fine, really looking forward to seeing you. Miley came first in his hundred-metres race this week.'

'Have you got the ashes back from the crematorium yet?'

'Yes, I did, we're going to scatter them tomorrow.'

'I'm amazed they didn't throw them out. Amazed.'

'I know,' says Mum. 'Me too.'

'And have you visited Blair Road lately?'

'Ag, it's the same as ever. I don't visit unless I absolutely have to. It's filthy. Falling to pieces . . . Oh, that reminds me!' she says. 'Do you want to hear the good news or the bad news?'

'The—'

'The good news is that your father has emphysema. The bad news is that he's given up smoking.'

1987

Chapter 2

My class has lots of goodie-goodies in it. If the A-Team were here they would be really disappointed that nobody worked together to beat the teacher. Hannibal would sit next to me and smoke his cigar and look at the ground and stay quiet. And BA would fold his arms and show off his big muscles and frown his eyebrows. The guys in my class think they understand the A-Team just because they watch them on TV. But they actually have no clue who the A-Team are. I reckon I'm the only one in the whole world who understands the A-Team properly.

Bruce Bartlett puts his hand up and reaches high into the air and holds his breath until his face goes red. Then he says, 'Ma'am, Hayden's busy doing his homework.'

Then the teacher comes over to me with her big brown messy hair and goes, *'Ruff ruff ruff, rrrrruff, ruff . . .'* Then she says, 'Hands up who wants to take Hayden to Mr McLaren?'

Lots of guys always shout, 'Me, ma'am! Please me ma'am!'

Then she points to a big fat goodie-goodie called Scot McPherson. He's the kind of boy who writes really neatly and always brings shiny colouring crayons to school, the kind that say 'Staedtler made in West Germany' on them in silver. I wish I could write neatly like Scot but my writing always looks like a spider wrote it with broken legs. At least my writing is better than my brother Dan's. Dan irritates me like Murdoch irritates BA.

Even the boys who always get into trouble put their hands up. They know how scary it is to be in trouble, but they still want me to be in trouble. I hate people like that.

Goodie-goodie Scot McPherson takes me to Mr McLaren. In the secretary's office I smell the carpets and the heater and the flowers and then I want to wee.

I sometimes wonder which is worse, being beaten by Mr McLaren or dying by an injection like when Mum took the cat to the vet to die for weeing on her bed. At least if you die there's no pain.

But I know I'm lucky because I watched tell-tale Bruce go for a beating once and he came back all scared and told everyone not to tell his mum. I said, 'Bruce, why don't you want us to tell anyone?'

And then Bruce said, 'Because my dad will beat me again if he finds out.'

I am so lucky to have my dad. He never beats us.

After school I say bye to my friend Adrian with blond hair and skinny legs and ride home. The trees always look like tentacles from an octopus pulling on the houses to take them under the ground. I like it that sometimes the trees seem to be winning.

At home Emily the maid cuts onions in her special apron. She says, 'Hullo, Haydie,' and I say, 'Hi, Emily!'

I sit down at the kitchen table next to my little sister Beatrice. Mum walks in wearing her orange dress, the one where I always say, 'Mum, *jeez-like*, man, please don't wear that!'

Mum says, 'Hullo, darling. How was your day?'

'Fine, Mum,' I say. Then Dan puts his satchel down next to my one. Then Mum says, 'Hi, darling. Sit down, I've got some mince and rice for you.'

After lunch Dan and I always kick the rugby ball. Sometimes we wee on the plant outside the kitchen. Sometimes I'm nice to Dan but sometimes I punch him for being like Murdoch.

*   *   *

Sometimes I play at my friend Steve's house. Steve is short and has a pellet gun. I wish I had a pellet gun.

I hate spending the night at Steve's house because when he turns the lights off, the picture of the duck on his door looks like a snake-monster instead of a duck. And because Steve's carpet always smells like sweets and hospitals and I hate hospitals. And also because the light shining into his room from the window smells the wrong colour.

In the morning Steve's dad sings 'Onward Christian Soldiers' in the kitchen and makes us pray at breakfast. And then Steve makes me go to church.

Last time I went to church with Steve, the priest said, 'Hands up who's not a Christian.' And Steve put up his hand and said, 'Yeah, my friend Hayde here isn't.' And then the priest took me in front of everyone and made me into a Christian.

After we finish church stuff, old ladies with blue dresses give people tea. They always seem Christian-happy, which is extra-extra happy.

One time at church a man with a brown moustache gets on stage and says, 'Do you know what WASP stands for?'

Everyone stays quiet. Then he says, 'They're a pop group. Nobody here know what their initials mean?' Nobody says anything, so he says, 'Well, that's a good sign. WASP stands for "We Are Sexual Perverts".'

People behind me whisper to each other. Then he talks about some guys called Anti-Christ, Devil's Children.

In the car on the way home everyone stays quiet. Steve's dad says, 'Nicki and Heidi, you really ought to get rid of those Chris de Burgh tapes of yours.'

When I get home Dad sits in his special green chair, the one where he always reads his special pink paper called *Financial Times*.

Sometimes I sit on Dad's leg and he puts his paper down and pats me on the leg and says, 'Who's my big boy?'

I tell Dad about church. Dad says that I should stop going to church because Christians are right-wing.

Dad says that Hitler was right-wing and that right-wing people are dangerous. He says that right-wing people might even kill us one day like Hitler killed the Jews. At school my teachers tell me about Hitler. I think,

Hitler is bad,
Hitler is right-wing,
So being right-wing is bad.
Christians are right-wing,
Being right-wing is bad,
So being Christian is bad.

Dad thinks lots of things are right-wing. He even thinks *He-Man* is right-wing. I ask Dad who we are and he says left-wing. Left is opposite to right. If right is bad, then we're the opposite of that, which means we're good.

Chapter 3

At sunrise Mum plays my favourite song called 'Third movement of the Moonlight Sonata' on the piano. When her music plays I always see Zorro riding on his horse through a vlei. He rides in the daytime but the sky is dark like evening because a thunderstorm is coming. Zorro rides his horse while the wind blows the tall grass sideways. He rides to a girl tied to a bridge. He wants to set her free before the storm washes her away. His horse bucks against the sky and the tall grass blows sideways and the girl waits on the bridge with her long hair blowing in the wind. It's like a whole movie with just the sound of Mum's piano.

I put on my school clothes and run to my bike. Emily always shouts, 'Ay, you must eat your breakfast!' but I always shout back, 'No, I can't, I'll be late!' Then I jump on my bike and ride to school as fast as I can. The flowers are always red like lipstick.

At school I ask Adrian if I can borrow his homework. He always asks me why I didn't do it. And then I tell him that I was going to do it but then something got in the way, like building forts with Dan, so then I didn't.

When I grow up I want to be a fighter jet pilot so I probably don't need homework for that. Anyway, my dad always says that people who do well at school always do rubbish in life.

Then I tell Adrian to stop watching *He-Man* because it's right-wing. He says, 'What the hell is right-wing?' and then I tell him what Dad told me and he looks at me like he is sad, like he really wishes He-Man was actually left-wing like the A-Team.

* * *

I feel sorry for Steve when he comes over for dinner. Mum always says stuff like, 'Dear Lord, thank you for distributing the world's food so unfairly.'

And then Dan says stuff like, 'Rub-a-dub-dub, thanks for the grub.' And then Dad laughs and coughs smoke out of his mouth like he thinks it's funny.

Then Steve looks at me with his eyes wide open, like he's wondering if we're all going to go to hell. But the worst is when he goes to the toilet and sees all Dad's magazines with naked girls in them. Then I feel like saying, 'Sorry, Steve.'

At school a horrible guy called Mahenya Marumahoko always kicks me in the leg and then laughs and runs away. His teeth look extra white, so when he laughs after kicking you he looks extra happy.

Then Mr McLaren comes up to me and takes my hair in his hands and pulls it. Sometimes he lifts me off the ground by my tie and shouts until the veins in his neck stick out, 'Eastwood, I told you to cut your hair!'

We go into the hall and Mr McLaren waits for us on the stage. He wears his tight shorts made in Scotland. He has a big black beard. He says, 'You can sit down, gentlemen.'

We all say the Lord's Prayer. Then Mr McLaren says, 'Mr Merton has just handed me this plastic toy. Remember, gentlemen, toys are for home and not for school. I don't want to have to mention this again. Now, before I find its owner, what is this thing?'

He holds it up for everyone to see. A boy puts his hand up. Mr McLaren points to him and says, 'Yes, you over there.'

'Sir, it's a Teenage Mutant Ninja Turtle, sir.'

'A what?' says Mr McLaren.

'A Teenage Mutant Ninja Turtle, sir.'

'Speak up, I can't hear you.'

'Yes, sir. They're like turtles with special magic powers that can do ninja and stuff, sir.'

Mr McLaren looks at the turtle in his hand, and then looks at all of us and says, 'Gentlemen, the word is "ninya".' He stops and looks into the distance like he is actually a ninja himself. He says, 'The j is silent.'

I reckon Teenage Mutant Ninja Turtles are probably right-wing but sometimes it's difficult to know because the things you think are right-wing are actually left-wing, and also the other way round.

After assembly we go to Shona with vaShenje. He has a sticky-out tummy. Sometimes when he asks us what a word is I guess. I put my hand up and say, 'Yes, vaShenje, I know the answer.' Then I say, '*Makarangadugu*', or something, because Shona always sounds like you've made it up. Sometimes vaShenje says, 'Ahh, Haydie, how did you know that?' Other times he just goes, 'Ah-ah! You are talking rubbish now.' And then he laughs.

VaShenje is nice, except when you are naughty. If he catches you being naughty he calls you to the front of the classroom and says, 'Eh-eh, give me your hand.' Then he looks at you with his yellow eyes and laughs while he squeezes your knuckles in his big hand and breathes on you. 'Eh, eh, eh, you can shake my hand because you are my friend,' he says. And then your hand is really sore.

I used to be the best in Shona but now it's Richard Ross. He always speaks Shona on his farm. He speaks Shona like black people speak Shona.

Horrible Mahenya is next to me. Except now he is being nice instead of kicking me in the leg. He tells me his dad was run over by an army truck. He says the truck killed his dad on purpose. I would be so sad if my dad died. I say, 'Sorry, Mahenya, I wish your dad was still alive.'

* * *

Sometimes after school I go to Mum's room to be near her, but then she tells me to go away because she's painting pictures. So then I go to the kitchen to talk to Emily.

Emily likes to tell me about her favourite place in the whole world called Jo'burg. She says that you can get lots of toys and fancy things there. Things like Walkmans, and really nice bicycles and radios. She says Jo'burg is much better than Zimbabwe and Malawi.

I wish I could go to Jo'burg, but Dad says no because the government will put him in jail there.

Emily says that Jo'burg should stay with the whites because otherwise the blacks will take over and then mess it up.

I tell Emily that Jo'burg sounds like this place my dad told me about called Hamley's, which is a whole building full of toys in England.

Emily asks me about England and Germany. I tell her that Dad says that in England and Germany if you don't have a job then the government gives you money so you can buy food and live in a house.

Emily stops and puts her hands on her hips and says, 'Ah-ah . . . sure? An African will never do that for other Africans.'

At night time Dan and I sit down in the sitting room and play chess. Dan moves his knight and then I go 'swooosh', and knock it over with my castle.

Dan says, 'Wait! I didn't mean to do that. I was still checking to see if it was okay, and then you just took it!'

So I say, 'No ways, you made that move fair and square!'

Then Dan says, 'No, fuck you! I should be allowed to take that back!'

So I say, 'Come on, man, don't be such a dick. Fuck you!'

And Mum says, 'Hey, you boys, stop fighting!'

But I shout, 'Mum, Dan's being a spoilsport!'

'Ahh, I can't believe you're saying that!' says Dan. 'I let you take back the last move. I can't believe what an arsehole you're being!'

'Oh come on, Hayde,' says Mum. 'Why are you being horrible to Dan?'

'Mum, why do you think *I'm* always the one being horrible?'

Dan goes quiet. Then he says, 'Mum, what's that thing you're wearing on your neck?'

Mum turns on the TV and asks, 'When's Dallas on?'

Dan says, 'Mum, you're not listening! What's that thing on your neck?'

Mum says, 'Oh, it's just a neck brace. I think I've slipped a disk in my back playing the piano. I have to wear this until it gets better.'

Mum sits down on the couch with Beebs and watches *Dallas*.

Then Dad comes through the door and the dogs jump up and wag their tails. Dad walks to his chair and takes his smart blue jacket off. Dad is really tall. He has really black hair. He looks around the room and says, 'Who's going to pour me a drink?'

'Yes, me!' I say.

'Yes, me!' says Beebs.

'No, me!' says Dan.

Beebs jumps up first and goes to the drinks tray. Stupid Beebs. Dad sits down. 'Two fingers of gin please, Beebs.'

I ask Dad about work. He says, 'Christ, I don't want to talk about it.'

And then he asks Mum about her sore neck.

Mum tells him it's okay, but Dad says, 'Maybe we should send you off to Jo'burg.'

Then I say, 'Dad, why don't we ever go on holiday to Jo'burg? Emily always says that Jo'burg's the best place ever.'

I always ask Dad about going to Jo'burg, but he just says they'll arrest him.

I ask him why they're cross with him, but he just tells me I'm too young to understand. He says he'll tell me one day when I'm older. But I want him to tell me now because I'm already older than last time.

Dad takes out a cigarette from his pocket and puts it in his mouth. He opens his pink paper and starts reading. I wait for him to say something, but then he just turns the pages. I watch *Dallas* on TV. I think that maybe JR is right-wing and that Bobby is left-wing.

Then Dad says someone called Doris Lessing is coming for dinner next week. Dad says she tells really nice stories.

* * *

I hate Kuklinski. He is big and fat and horrible. And American. If he was in the movie *Karate Kid* he would be the horrible guy with blond hair who beats up Karate Kid. Except he is fat. I am like Karate Kid, except without karate skills.

Sometimes when we play rugby at breaktime Kuklinski punches me in the face when I try to tackle him. He probably wants me to hit him back so he can beat me up with his friends.

I wish that the A-Team would come to Zimbabwe. Then they could hide in the bushes by the far playing field and wait for the bullies to chase me there. And then just as I was about to get caught, Hannibal would come out from behind a tree and light his cigar. And then the bullies would all stop running after me and think, 'What the hell is Hannibal Smith doing here in Harare, Zimbabwe, at St Bartholomew's Preparatory School?'

And then before they could finish thinking about it BA would drop down from a tree and start laughing. And Hannibal would just spit his piece of cigar out and say, 'Well, well, what do we have here?' And then BA would take out a pencil case from one of the bullies' satchels and start laughing about their crappy pencils. And Face would say, 'Ha, ha, ha, they're not even made in West Germany. BA, show them what we do to scumbags like these.'

And then BA would smash up their pencil cases in front of them and make grunting sounds. And the bullies would run away while the A-Team and I folded our arms and laughed.

But then I think maybe I would kick one of them in the back while they ran away.

Mr Merton shouts, 'Eastwood, pay attention! How many times do I have to call your name?' Mr Merton sits at his desk looking at me like our dogs look at our chickens. I go to his desk and get my book. Mr Merton's knees stick out from his long shorts. He wears long blue socks that go nearly all the way up to where his shorts start. Hairs grow out of his ears and nose. He always scratches himself, mostly near his bum. Dad says he has something called piles.

He looks out over the class and says, 'The work has been largely well done, boys, with a couple of exceptions, of course.' Then he looks at me and says, 'Let me just read you a sentence from Eastwood, who writes about a gentleman who was, and I quote, shot down over Dover after he was killed in the Battle of Britain, end quote. How, Mr Eastwood, did your pilot succeed in flying an aeroplane after he had already been killed?'

The class laughs. Everyone looks at me. I want to wee.

* * *

At night Dad sits in his chair reading his pink paper. He drinks his gin and tonic and puffs smoke into the air through his nose. I say, 'Dad? Mrs Davies gave us a question to answer for homework. She said Zimbabwe is something called a democratic socialist country. She said we have to write down what that means. I'm stuck.'

Dad puts his paper down like he's cross. He says, 'I have no idea. The Rhodesians managed their economy centrally with different bodies: the Grain Marketing Board, the Dairy Marketing Board, the Cotton Marketing Board, all designed to set prices in a closed market, kind of like communism. Then the communists get in. What's the first bloody thing they do? They privatise everything. That's the kind of bonkers world we live in!'

I look at my empty question paper. 'Mrs Davies said something different to that.'

Dad says, 'Of course she did. Your teachers are all halfwits. They haven't the faintest clue what's going on around them.'

I say, 'I think I'll leave that question blank.'

Then Mum comes into the sitting room and says, 'Rupert and Doris are here.'

Dad says, 'Ah! Boys, it's the lady who tells great stories!'

A cross-looking granny walks into the room. Then Dad's friend Rupert walks in behind her. The granny sits down next to Rupert on the couch. I go to Mum and whisper, 'When's Doris coming?'

Mum says, 'She's there, sitting next to Rupert!'

I look at the cross granny sitting on the couch. Then I say, 'Her? I thought she was going to be like Mary Poppins!'

The cross granny drinks her tea. I wait for her to tell a story. But then she just talks about grown-up things. Dan whispers, 'Let's go play chess.'

Then I say, 'Yeah, let's go. I bet her stories aren't even funny.'

Chapter 4

Sometimes I wish my big stepsister from South Africa would come up and live with us. She says MacGyver's amazing. I wish I could write a letter to MacGyver and ask him to be my sister's boyfriend. Dad says her grandad's someone important called Bram Fischer.

Adrian's dad drives his white car up our driveway. Adrian gets out in his green shorts and sports shoes and we run to swing on the tyre at the bottom of the garden. But then Dan comes outside and stands near us and watches us play. I shout, 'Dan, go away, Adrian is *my* friend. Why don't you go and find your own friends today? Why do you always have to follow me everywhere? We want to do stuff by ourselves now, more grown-up stuff.'

Dan goes away for a bit and then comes back again.

'Don't be such a dick, man,' I say.

Dan stays around so I punch him in the back and he cries and goes away. And then I think maybe I should have let him stay.

Sometimes when I've been horrible to Dan I wonder what the A-Team would think of me. I hate bullies at school, but I sometimes bully Dan. What would I do if Dan telephoned the A-Team and told them to come and beat me up for beating him up?

Hannibal would say, 'Hey, BA, I've just got a call from Blair Road, Harare, Zimbabwe, to deal with this scumball called Hayden!'

And then BA would say, 'But Hannibal, that's the same fool who asked us to take out Kuklinski!'

Maybe if BA was about to hit me and Hannibal was just about to light his cigar and say, 'I love it when a plan comes together,' I would interrupt him and say, 'Wait, Hannibal . . . wait, you don't understand! Do you have any idea how irritating my brother can be? I don't beat him up for nothing, you know! It's only after he's been super irritating for a super long time. You know, sometimes things aren't just black and white. Look how irritating Murdoch can be. My brother's like Murdoch times one hundred.'

And then maybe Hannibal would be quiet for a moment and think about my words. And maybe BA would say, 'You know, Hannibal, the little guy's got a point. Murdoch really is irritating.'

But maybe they would think my excuses were rubbish. Maybe Hannibal would say, 'What are you talking about? We were here just last week to take out Kuklinski, and now we're here on a call to take you out! You know how difficult it is to commandeer an aircraft from LA, dope BA up and fly all the way to Harare, Zimbabwe? You know how difficult customs can be when BA's got that much jewellery? Would you like us to arrive at your school and then get some excuse from Kuklinski about how you deserved being bullied? Should we listen to Kuklinski?'

And then I would say, 'Hannibal, it's not like that, you don't understand. It's different. Those guys don't think about right and wrong. They just beat people up because they can. And I hardly *ever* do that!'

Maybe some things are not always black and white, like left-wing and right-wing.

*   *   *

I have a secret, invisible friend who is half mouse and half human but still as small as a mouse. In the morning I leave him a special place in my bag so he can be safe from my school books squashing him.

Sometimes when I'm sad I talk to him and he talks to me. He tells me not to listen to the teachers. And not to worry about getting beaten by Mr McLaren. I ask him what would happen if I got killed by a car but then my parents had another boy who was exactly the same as me. I wonder if that boy would actually be me even though the real me would be dead. And then, if my parents had two children exactly the same as me, would one me be able to feel what the other me was feeling because we were both exactly the same? The man-mouse doesn't know, so I ask Dan. Dan reckons that those me's would somehow not be me.

Sometimes I ask the man-mouse about left-wing and right-wing. The man-mouse says left-wing is just another word for being nice, and right-wing is just another word for being horrible.

I wish I could put my invisible man-mouse friend inside my model aeroplane and make tiny controls for him so he could fly it all by himself. That way the plane would be free like a bird and not have to be trapped by strings.

At school I wonder how a man-mouse would start my model aeroplane engine because the propeller is really stiff to flick with your fingers. A mouse is really small and would have arms too weak to flick the propeller. Also, when the engine starts it runs at high revs and creates a strong pull. That means that even if my man-mouse could start the engine, the plane would roll away before he could get into the cockpit.

If my man-mouse went on a long mission he would get thirsty. It would be good if he could have a milkshake or a cup of hot cocoa while he was flying. He would need a special flask because a cup would spill everywhere. Sometimes I wonder how I would make a small straw for him. Would milk still be able to flow through a tiny straw? Maybe the skin on milk is like the skin on water. Maybe that skin would be too strong for a tiny man-mouse to break with his tiny lungs.

My man-mouse makes me think that big things and small things are different. Maybe that's why the water boatmen can run on our swimming pool while I can't. Dan and I always talk about why things are the way they are. Dan always says, 'Yeah, Hayde, I think some things in nature are non-linear.'

Sometimes I hate it that big things and small things are different. I wish I could shrink down a real-life jumbo jet to the size of my bed and have it work like a big one. But I know that if I did that it would probably crash for the same reason that water boatmen can walk on water and I can't.

At night Mum and Beebs lie together on the couch and watch *Knight Rider*. Dad walks in with a strange glass jar. He puts it by the drinks table and then sits down in his green chair and lights a cigarette. He says, 'Who's going to pour me two fingers of gin?'

I shout, 'Yes me, Dad!' and quickly go to the drinks table before Beebs or Dan can.

The glass jar sits next to the gin and ice. It looks strange, like one of those jars that people keep mustard in but instead of mustard it has little brown beads. I say, 'What's in that jar, Dad?'

He says, 'Oh, you won't believe it! Joshua Nkomo gave it to me this evening at another bloody government function. It's supposed to be a cure for AIDS. They had a *n'anga* there parcelling this stuff out.'

I say, 'I thought there wasn't a cure for AIDS?'

Dad turns his newspaper page and says, 'Correct.'

So I say, 'What do you mean, Dad?'

Then Dad says, 'They're a bunch of medieval dumb clucks. Honestly, the whole lot of those buggers are going to be dead in a few years' time.'

I look at the brown beads through the clear glass and wonder what the *n'anga* did to them. They look smelly and they look like they'd leave horrible sticky brown stuff on my fingers if I touched them.

I want to ask Dad lots of questions about why Joshua Nkomo thinks there's a cure for AIDS when really there isn't. But Dad just reads his newspaper.

1990

Chapter 5

Dan sits at the kitchen table in his school clothes eating lunch. Emily washes dishes at the sink.

Mum walks in wearing her dark glasses and her special dress, the one where I always say, '*Come-on-man*, please don't wear that one to school, man-please!' She says, 'Come on, you boys, I'm taking you to Jack the Ripper.'

'Ah, *jeez-like*, Mum, do we have to go?' I ask.

'Yes. Don't you lot think you've gotten into enough trouble for your hair this term?'

'Yeah, Mum, but I hate Jack. He always makes me look stupid.'

'Come on, you two. I have to get Beebs to ballet, and then do grocery shopping for the staff, and then cover your wretched school books, and then the Callinicoses are coming over for dinner. And the house is still an absolute bloody pigsty! In fact, when you get back you're going to have to tidy your rooms . . . Into the car you go, come on!'

Dan slowly gets off his stool. He seems cross. 'I hate Jack,' he says.

'Mum, why do you always have to wear dresses like that?' I say.

We get into the car. Beebs is already inside wearing her ballet stockings and leotard. She checks her face in her small hand mirror and then combs her hair. Dan snatches the mirror from her. 'Ay, give me back my mirror!' shouts Beebs.

'No,' says Dan.

'It's my mirror!'

'It's not your mirror. We're a communist family. It's the family mirror,' says Dan.

Mum opens the driver's door. 'Quiet, you lot!'

'Mum, Dan's taken my mirror!'

'It's not Beebs's mirror, it's the family mirror!'

'Oy, give Beebs back the mirror or there's going to be trouble!'

Dan gives the mirror to Beebs. 'Mum,' I say. 'Is Dad one of the best lawyers?'

'What?' says Mum.

'I said, is Dad one of the best lawyers?'

'Yes,' says Mum. 'He's probably the best lawyer in the country. Everybody goes to him. Even people like Cohen.'

She slams her door and starts the engine. 'Who's Cohen?' I ask.

'Owns Cone Textiles.'

'What does Dad do for Cone?'

She stays quiet and speeds down the roads and past the jacaranda trees.

'Mum . . . I said, what does Dad do for Cone?'

'What did you say?'

'I *said*, what does Dad do for Cone?'

'Oh, um, nothing much . . . They're clothes manufacturers. They're going bankrupt. Your father's saving them a fortune from the banks.'

She carries on driving and looking into the distance.

'Here we are. Out you get, you two! And hurry, I'm late to drop Beebs! Hayde, here's ten dollars for Jack the Hack. I'll be back in thirty minutes.'

We walk into the small shop with plastic kitchen tiles on the floor. Jack stands there with his white shirt and black trousers and his big tummy. 'Yes, yes, good afternoon, gentlemen!' he says in his funny accent. 'Who first?'

I climb into the big chair and look at my hair in the mirror. He puts his fingers on my head and ruffles my hair. 'Okay, I make nice for ladies!'

*   *   *

I sometimes wonder about exchange rates. Dad talks about how one currency can be changed into another one, but I always wonder how people decide how much one kind of money should be worth when it becomes another kind. Like, how come it takes three Zimbabwean dollars to buy one pound but not two or four? Sometimes I wonder if lots of experts sit in a room and calculate the rate by looking at all the different kinds of things you can buy in one country compared to another country. Dad says that one day a coke will cost twenty dollars in Zimbabwe and that one day a pound will be like ten dollars or something.

Dad also says that light speed is always the same. But if someone in a car shines his lights while he's driving, how come the light coming out of his car isn't faster than someone who's shining his lights while he's sitting still in his car?

I forgot that I'm supposed to be doing Social Studies. Mr Robins looks at me like Mr Mavis looks at me, which is the same as how our dogs look at our chickens. 'What did I tell you about leaning on your chair!' he shouts.

'Sorry, sir. I didn't mean to, sir.'

'What have I just been talking about?'

'When? Now, sir?'

'No, last month! Of course now!'

I try to remember what he was talking about, but I can't. 'Take your chair and stand outside Mr McLaren's window where he can see you.'

'Yes, sir.' I stand up and take my chair outside. My tummy feels like an eel is turning in it. I walk along the corridor towards Mr McLaren's office.

I see Dan is already standing in the corridor. 'Hayde, what are you doing with that chair?' he asks.

'I was leaning on it so Mr Robins told me to go and stand outside Mr McLaren's office with it. And what are you doing here?'

'I couldn't find my history book so I did my homework in my geography book. Then the teacher made me hand in my geography book last lesson. So then Mrs Davies got cross when I didn't have my work and chucked me out.'

I put my chair down. Dan leans on the wall with his hand, like he's bored.

I say, 'Should we try flying when we get back home? I think maybe the glue on the nosewheel is dry.'

'Yeah,' says Dan. 'Let's go after I finish cricket.'

* * *

I unpack the aeroplane things from my bag and put them on the cricket pitch. 'Dan, where the hell are the batteries?' Tell me you packed the batteries! You were in charge of that!'

'What?' he says. 'No fucking way! That was supposed to be you!'

'I can't believe you're saying that,' I shout. 'I remember telling you to do it. I *promise* you!'

'Whaaat? You're such a dick! I can't believe it!'

'*Me*, a dick? No, you're a dick!'

We argue until he gets on his bicycle and rides home to get the batteries. When he gets back his eyes are full of tears.

After a while the engine runs and Dan launches the plane. It climbs too quickly. I get scared and point its nose down. The plane smashes into the ground. Dad says war is ninety-nine percent tedium and one percent terror. I think maybe aeroplanes are the same.

I shout, 'How come you launched the plane facing up like that?'

'Whaaat? *Me?* You're the one who over-corrected it into the ground!'

'Yeah, but that's because it was already going way too high into the air when you launched it. You should have launched it straight!'

'I can't believe you're saying that. I did launch it straight!'

We pick up the broken pieces and put them in the bag.

* * *

Beebs and Dan sit on the floor playing cards. The dogs lie next to Dan. I read *George's Marvellous Medicine*.

Beebs shouts, 'Snap!'

'Ay, I put my card down first!' shouts Dan.

'No, you didn't!' says Beebs.

Dad walks in wearing his swimming costume. 'Come on, you lot, stop making a racket. We have a new guest from Canada. And Dave Kitson will be coming by shortly. Come and say hi, we're sitting out by the pool.'

We follow Dad outside. Emily puts the drinks tray on the small table. A man with a large stomach and curly brown hair sits opposite Dad and sips a drink. Dad says, 'Here are my two boys, Hayden and Daniel.'

'Hullo there,' the man says. 'My name's Patrick.' He gets up and shakes our hands.

'Hi, Patrick,' I say.

'Look at you guys! You've got such lovely freckles.'

'I wish I didn't have freckles,' I say.

'Me too,' says Dan.

Dad says, 'Patrick will be staying with us for a few weeks while he finds a place to stay. He's going to sort out our computer issues at the office. He's one of those American computer whizzes. Top lawyer too!'

'Well, Anthony, you're the expert in these parts, not me!'

Dave and Norma Kitson stand on the veranda and wave. 'Hullo there!' says Dad. 'Come on over!'

Dave and Norma shake hands with Patrick. 'Dave has recently moved to Zimbabwe after a long spell in jail,' says Dad. 'We're grateful to have him with us.'

'Nineteen years and five months, to be precise,' says Dave with a smile.

'That is some time to be put away,' says Patrick.

Dad says, 'Apparently he used to miss Mars Bars the most!'

'That's true,' says Dave. 'When I got out of jail a journalist asked me what I'd missed most and I jokingly said Mars Bars. Although, of course, ever since then I've received a steady stream of them through the post. So that's something!'

Emily comes to the table with her grandchildren, Chipo and Tsitsi. Dad smiles, 'Hullo there!'

Chipo and Tsitsi stand with their hands behind their backs and look at the ground.

'You've come to learn to swim, have you?' asks Dad.

They nod.

'Great! Dad puts his gin and tonic down and walks to the pool. He jumps in with a splash and swims to the steps. Tsitsi and Chipo watch him.

'Come on, you can come in, don't be scared!'

Chipo walks to the side of the pool. Dad holds his arms out. 'It's okay, nothing bad's going to happen!'

Chipo looks at me and then looks at Dad. She jumps in and Dad catches her. 'There, you see, that wasn't so bad, was it?'

Chipo smiles and holds onto his arm and kicks in the water.

'Come on, you boys, aren't you coming to swim?'

'Yeah, Dad!' we shout.

*   *   *

Moths and insects buzz around the candle near the chessboard. Dan moves his knight. I shout, 'Muuuuuum, when's food coming? I'm hungry!'

Dan shouts, 'Muuuuuuum, I'm hungry too!'

Beebs shouts, 'Muuuuuuuum!'

Mum's torch shines onto the veranda. Mum says, 'Okay, I'm done waiting for your father. It's already nine o'clock and he's nowhere to be seen. And this fucking curry's been almost impossible to cook on that paraffin cooker.'

'Why don't we get a gas stove?' I ask.

'We'll probably have to if we keep getting power cuts like this.'

Mum puts the food on the table outside. 'What are we eating tonight, Mum?' I ask.

'First course is fruit salad. Then there's chicken curry. And if you eat all your fruit salad, there's chocolate mousse.'

'Yay!' shouts Beebs. 'I love chocolate mousse!'

Dan says, 'Mum, how come we get power cuts these days but we never used to?'

'Because the government didn't want the old Rhodie around who used to run the power grid. So now he's got a job in Switzerland. And it goes without saying that the new guy they've replaced him with is bloody useless.'

Dan says, 'Mum how come the *affies* always break everything?'

'Daniel! We don't use words like that in this house!'

'Why not, Mum? Rory's dad always calls them that. And he says that they'll turn Zimbabwe into Zambia.'

'First of all, we're not like Rory's family. In this family, we don't use words like that. That family is very Rhodie. And second of all, Zambia is much, much worse than Zimbabwe, and if we're going to end up like them, we still have a long way to go.'

'So is Rory's dad right or wrong? Are we actually going to be like Zambia or not?' I ask.

Mum eats her food. I say, 'Muuuuum. Is Rory's dad right or wrong?'

She sighs. 'I don't know . . . I actually don't know . . .'

Dan giggles. 'So is it okay if we call them *affies* then?'

'No, it's not! What would Emily think if she heard you talking like that? Don't you think you'd hurt her feelings?'

'But Mum,' I say. 'Emily told me that she's sick and tired of

Mugabe. And she said Ian Smith was better because at least there were jobs. And she said next time there's a war it's going to be blacks versus blacks and she's going to fight.'

'Well, Emily had a difficult time from both sides during the war. First the Rhodesians shot her cattle. And then Mugabe's guys shot her cattle. So she ended up with absolutely nothing, twice.'

Dan says, 'Mum, what's a Rhodie? How is Rory's family Rhodie?'

'Well, for starters because they're always on Kariba fishing. And they almost only eat steak and chips and takeaway pizza. That's why Rory never wants to stay for dinner. His palate is base. That's Rhodie.'

'But Mum,' says Dan. 'I like steak and chips too.'

'Yes, but you also like other things, don't you?'

'And Mum, Rory's dad said that Nelson Mandela's wife burns people with tyres and petrol, and rapes children and things.'

'Yawn,' says Mum. 'That's also typical of Rhodies.'

The dogs get up and bark and wag their tails. Dad walks through the door in his smart black suit. He smiles. 'Hullo, everyone!'

'Hi, Dad!' we shout.

Dad puts his leather briefcase on the table and sits down next to Dan. 'Who's going to pour me a drink?' he asks.

Beebs jumps to her feet. 'Me, Dad!'

'Anthony, your food is in the oven,' says Mum. 'But we've got no power, so it's going to be cold. Fruit salad. Chicken curry for main course. Chocolate mousse for dessert.'

The candlelight flickers on Dad's face. He seems to be thinking to himself.

'I'm not sure I'm in the mood for something substantial this evening. I think I fancy something light, like a boiled egg and some toast, or something.'

Mum pauses. 'Well, we don't have any power so I can't do you toast in the toaster,' she says. 'But I suppose I could heat the pan up and do the toast that way.'

'Yes, if you wouldn't mind,' says Dad. 'You're so good at that sort of thing.'

Mum stands and walks back inside the house.

'Dad,' I say. 'Can you tell me about Dave Kitson? How come he spent so long in jail?'

Beebs brings Dad his gin and tonic. Dad lights a cigarette and sucks on it so that the end glows red in the dark.

'Because he's a leftie. And because he used to be in the high command of Umkhonto we Sizwe, the military wing of the ANC. He was really hung out to dry by people in the ANC, you know. Others like Joe Slovo went into exile, but not Dave. He stayed and paid a heavy price. And I mean a heavy one. Very tough on Norma and the rest of the family.'

'But why did they arrest him, Dad? What did he do that was so wrong?'

'Well, he believed in the wrong things. He believed that blacks had a right to political representation. At that time expressing an idea like that was considered outrageous, you know. The sort of thing that could get you beaten up in a restaurant.'

'So just because he thought the wrong things?'

'Well, the apartheid state wouldn't compromise. So in the end he had no choice but to target that state and its machinery. But you must understand, Dave wasn't trying to harm the ordinary man on the street. He was attacking the state. And the state was attacking him.'

Mum puts Dad's boiled eggs down in front of him. 'Thanks, Annette,' he says. Then he takes a spoon and bashes the top off one.

'You know,' he says. 'Dave is a very mild-mannered fellow. And very un-bitter about his time in prison.'

Mum sits down. 'Anthony, it's time the children went to bed. It's after ten o'clock.'

'Annette, the children know when they're tired. Don't you kids?'

'Yeah,' I answer.

'Me too,' says Dan.

Mum gets to her feet. 'Well, I'm tired. I'm certainly going to bed. Goodnight everyone.'

Chapter 6

Dan stands on the veranda. 'Who's going to be on?' he asks.

'I'll be on!' shouts Max.

'Wait a minute,' I say, 'I just want to put on my camouflage shirt.' I run inside. When I return, Max and Franz are shouting at each other. *'Franz! Die stimpt ge fellen raus sheun ge plunk!'* yells Max.

Franz yells back, *'Max, halt die klapper! Gangen stauf bist ashloch!'*

Dan and I stand and watch them. 'Come on, you guys,' says Dan. 'Why don't we just play?'

'I'm not playing with Max, he's such a fucking dick!' shouts Franz.

'Come on, little Franzy!' says Max.

'Fuck off, Max, *zehn maller traugumt!*' shouts Franz.

'Die lange velden baum shtauf!'

Franz's face goes red. He chases Max round the garden with a stick. Max laughs. 'Come on, Franzy, run a little faster!'

Dan shakes his head. 'Sheesh, these guys are crazy.'

'Totally crazy,' I say.

In the distance by the gate a black Mercedes turns into our driveway. *Who is that?* I wonder. 'Wait here, guys,' I say. 'I'll be back in a second.'

The Mercedes stops by the front door. A man steps out of it wearing a black suit and dark glasses. He waves at me and smiles. Dad hurries out of the house in his blue suit carrying his old leather briefcase. His hair is wet and black and combed sideways like his pictures from boarding school. The man opens the car door for him. 'Dad, where are you going?' I ask.

Dad pats me on the head. 'I'm just going to monitor elections in Bulawayo. See you next week. Be a good chappie!'

The Mercedes drives down the driveway under the drooping branches and then out of sight. I wish Dad was staying so I could ask him about aeroplanes.

*   *   *

The teacher sits at his desk marking books while the choir sings in the distance. I wish William Golding was wrong about boys. I already know which boys would be murdered if we were stuck on an island. They sit to my left and right doing their homework in neat handwriting. Sometimes I wonder if I would be one of the boys killed. At least Dad's around to protect us from the fly-lords. If I was powerful like Dad I'd be able to stand up to right-wing fly-people.

Dad thinks evil happens because of the system. He says that the system we have now is better than it was four hundred years ago, which is why we don't hang women for being witches, and stuff. He thinks that one day the system will be so good that people won't commit crime.

Sometimes it seems that Dad must be right. But sometimes when I watch boys on the playground I think that some people are just born evil. Sometimes it seems that the best system in the world wouldn't make Kuklinski and Mahenya into nice people.

And sometimes I wonder what Dad even means by a system.

*   *   *

Mum says that when she was small, duiker would eat the roses in their garden. But now those duiker are dead. Mum says that when we grow up our children will only see animals in the zoo because all the wild animals will be gone by then.

If I were the leader of Zimbabwe, I would arrest the guys at school who hunt birds with their pellet guns just for fun. And I would have put Courtney Selous in jail.

Mum says that when she was young she saw Rhodesian soldiers shoot animals with machine guns out of the train windows. I hate whites like that.

Dad puffs smoke into the air and opens his pink newspaper. The TV news plays in the background. Beebs shouts, 'Dad, look, you're on TV!'

I watch Dad on the TV in his dark suit, chopping the air with his hands. He says, 'Yes, the elections have gone well. They've been free and fair. In many ways the system here is more democratic than many countries that we think of as democratic. More democratic than the USA, for example.'

Dad looks up and laughs. 'Look at that, they actually thought to put that clip in!'

'Dad,' I say, 'Please can you tell me more about the olden days in Zimbabwe, when you were in trouble?'

He puts his newspaper down and starts to tell me about the times he used to visit Mr Mugabe in prison. 'People don't understand what kind of courage it took for him to do what he did. Everyone's quick to point out what a hard man he is, but he's endured tremendous things, you know. He has huge strength of character and tremendous drive. And he's been bloody good to the whites in this country. What have the whites ever done for him?'

'So, are you friends with him?' I ask.

'Well, no, not quite,' he replies. 'But I tell you what: if I ever asked him for a favour, he would help me, you know.'

'What happened when you used to visit him, Dad?'

'He was very well spoken, very impressive. At one stage Ndabaningi Sithole told all the men in detention that I was doing a terrible job of representing them. Mugabe was the one who said, "No, we need Anthony." Of course, half the problem was that the differences between Sithole and Mugabe were huge. There was a lot of violence between the two camps: they even ordered hits on each other.'

*　*　*

Dan wears a red Father Christmas hat on his head. He shouts, 'Hey, Hayde, can you bowl the ball to me!'

I take the new, shiny red cricket ball out of my pocket. Dan holds his brand-new bat. I shout, 'Okay, Dan, here it comes!'

Dan swings and hits the ball towards the pool.

Dad and Patrick and some other people sit on the veranda. 'Hey, guys,' shouts Patrick. 'Have you ever tried baseball? You know the rules?'

'Who, us?'

'Yeah, you guys!'

'Um, sort of . . .' I say.

Patrick gets up from his chair and runs onto the lawn. His big tummy bounces up and down. Patrick picks Dan up and holds him upside down and then chases after me. I sprint away but Patrick manages to catch me too. He holds me in one arm and Dan in the other one and pins us to the ground and tickles us. Dan shouts, 'Stop! Stop! *Argh!*'

Mum stands at the dining room door. 'Come on, guys, grub's up!'

Dad tells Patrick, 'Now, you probably won't know this, but Dave used to be in the high command of Umkhonto we Sizwe. And he won't admit to it, being a modest fellow, but he was a bloody good engineer in his day, part of the team that designed the Comet, you know.'

Dave Kitson sits next to me with his grandad-white hair. His skin looks like it would break and bleed if I touched it. Dave laughs. 'I always point out, when people bring up the Comet, that it wasn't my bit that used to blow up!'

Mum carries a big turkey on a plate. 'Happy Christmas everyone!' she announces. Emily follows behind her with the roast potatoes and carrots. We pull the crackers together and put the colourful paper hats on.

Dad says, '. . . back then, when I was married to Ruth, the Rhodesian authorities were shocked that I said I didn't mind what colour the child was. They said, "What? You want to adopt a black?" and I said I just didn't care, that we'd be delighted either way. They just couldn't believe it, they were simply outraged.'

Patrick says, 'Wow, Anthony, that's amazing! Whoever would have thought people ever behaved like that here.'

'Oh, you wouldn't believe how whites behaved here, Patrick, you simply wouldn't believe it! And the names! Countless degrading names. Sometimes you'd just think to yourself, are you buggers actually trying to get yourselves killed!'

Dan sits next to me pushing a crayon into his nose. Dad snaps at him. 'Daniel! Remember what happened the last time you put a crayon in your nose?'

'Huh?' says Dan, like he is thinking about lots of other things instead of paying attention to Christmas. 'Oh, I was just seeing how far up it would go.'

'Dan, be careful. The doctor told you not to do that!' I say.

Dan puts the crayon back on the table. Mum puts a big plate of food down in front of me. I pick up a Christmas card from the table. It has a picture of Mr Mugabe standing to attention next to a Zimbabwean flag. I open the card. 'Dear Anthony, Season's Greetings from State House.' Below a squiggly signature it says, 'His Excellency, Comrade RG Mugabe.'

I put the card down. '. . . to be honest,' says Dad, 'I don't believe in prisons anyway. They're terribly cruel. People go into them and attend quote, Crime University, unquote. They form networks. They come out far more hardened and savvy than when they were put in. And the cost? If they spent that money on education, or health, or welfare, we'd probably have far fewer criminals anyway.'

'Surely you're not suggesting,' says Patrick, 'that we shouldn't apply the rule of law to criminals?'

'I'm just saying, weighing up everything, that it's a waste of money to put them in prison. We need another form of justice. Mindless retribution doesn't work. Prisons should be abolished. They're an outrage. In fact, crime is highest where there are the most prisons. Prisons *cause* crime.'

1992

Chapter 7

The teachers on stage stare down at us. Some of them smile and whisper to one another. Prefects stand at the sides of the hall with their short hair and thick necks. The headmaster walks onto the stage with his black gown swooping behind him.

'Let us sing hymn number eleven: "Jubilate". Everybody!'

The music teacher punches chords into the piano. The hall fills with the deep singing of the seniors. I get goose bumps on my arms. We bow our heads and say the Lord's Prayer.

'Gentlemen, please sit down,' says Mr Kyle. He rifles through some papers on his podium. He looks like the old photos of the last Rhodesian prime minister with his slender bones and white hair and side parting. He reads out a list of boys to see him.

He releases us. We walk past the creepers that cover the walls and the brilliant yellow flowers surrounding the buildings. A tall tree casts speckled shade on the red bricks.

An old man with thick-rimmed glasses walks to the entrance of the classroom. He resembles a priest from another century. 'You may enter,' he says.

Our metal-legged chairs scrape on the wooden floors. The teacher stands perfectly still at the blackboard. 'Morning, gentlemen,' he says, 'I'm Mr Lamonde, your registration master and French teacher. Please be seated.'

He glances at the book in front of him. 'Ackhurst,' he calls.

'Yes, sir.'

'Burt.'

'Yes, sir.'

'Chiriga.'

'Yes, sir.'

'Chiwandire . . .'

After the final name, he puts his pen down and brushes his hair back with both hands. 'Now, about the registration process. First, if you're absent for a day you must bring a note from your parents. Any longer than a single day and you must bring a doctor's note in addition to your parents' one. Do you understand?'

'Yes, sir.'

'And if you don't bring a note, then woe betide! My son downstairs will see you. Have you seen my son?'

Nobody answers him.

'He's the fellow with the big brown beard. Big boy, six foot seven. We fed him *sadza* as a kid, you know.'

A cough breaks the silence.

'When I call your name,' continues Mr Lamonde, 'come and collect your timetable. Compulsory sporting and cultural events are marked in bold.'

* * *

Prefects stand on stage with thick meaty legs and tight shorts. We stand to attention. 'Okay, you guys,' says one of them. 'You're probably feeling quite hard-core, just come out of places where you were at the top of the pile, where you were kings.'

He pauses and looks at us. 'Here, guys, you're nothing. Absolutely nothing. Dog shit.'

'Yes, sir,' we reply.

'I didn't hear you!' he shouts.

'Yes, sir!'

'I can't hear you!'

'Yes, sir!'

'If a senior, even someone only one year above you, tells you to do something, you do it. No questions. If he tells you to do press-ups, you do them. If he sends you to the tuck shop, you go. And you don't just plod, you run!'

'Yes, sir!'

'Each prefect is to be addressed by his surname, followed by "sir".'

'Yes, sir!'

'Okay, split into groups of four. One of the prefects will show you around the school and explain to you how things work. In two weeks' time you're getting a *squack* test. You'd better know the name of every single prefect, the name of every field, every founding father, every teacher, every *word* of the school anthem, and the licence plate digits of the headmaster's car.'

The head boy interrupts him. 'A practical point before we go further,' he says. 'Who of you will be riding to school?'

I put my hand up together with some other boys. 'Okay,' he continues. 'The bike area gets locked at twenty past seven every morning. On the dot. If your bike isn't in the enclosure by then, tough luck. If we find it locked outside, it'll be removed by the groundsmen. Every bike must be locked to the rails in the bike shed by twenty past seven. Okay?'

'Yes, sir.'

'And one more thing,' he says, holding up a small padlock for us to see. 'I don't want you guys using some *chipile* Chinese item like this. Use a proper lock. If I see any cheap items I'll break them off myself. Bikes we find unlocked, or with *chipile* locks, will be taken to the prefects' study. When you get them back, you'll be put on manual labour. And believe me, you don't want to go on manual. None of us likes getting out of bed at half past six on a Saturday morning to take it. I guarantee you will like it even less.'

* * *

My legs burn. The sun bakes my arms. I sense a bead of sweat trickling down my neck. I put my bike down at the front door and take my tie off. I make myself a glass of milk and Milo.

Dan lies on the couch in his school uniform with his own glass of milk and Milo. The three dogs lie curled up at Dan's feet. *Fawlty Towers* plays on the TV screen. I watch the old general on the fishbowl screen look up at Basil Fawlty. 'Fawlty!' he cries.

'Yes?' says Basil Fawlty.

'Here, here . . . I thought you ought to know . . .'

'What?'

'There's a psychiatrist in the building!'

Dan breaks into a smile.

'Dan?' I interrupt.

'Yeah, Hayde?'

'Do you think that Basil Fawlty is mad or sane?'

'Is that a serious question?' asks Dan.

'Um, yeah.'

'He's quite mad.'

'Oh . . . okay.'

'Why do you ask?'

'No reason, really,' I say, worrying that I'm exactly like Basil Fawlty.

'What happened at school today?' he asks.

I chuck my bag on the floor. 'Jesus. I'm on manual labour tomorrow morning. There goes my Saturday. Last time I was on labour they made us run around the rugby field carrying bricks. Some guys puked.'

'I can't believe I'm nearly eleven and going there next year.'

'Well, at least you'll have me to protect you when you come.'

'Yeah, but I'll also have a reputation because of you. I won't arrive with a clean slate. I'll be an Eastwood.'

I search for some words to dampen his truth, but I can't find any. 'Yeah, sorry for that. Where's Mum?'

Beebs answers, 'I don't know but she's taking me to ballet just now. Probably painting in her room.'

* * *

Boys sit and eat their sandwiches. They look like wildlife, like antelope grazing on an open plain. I hear a noise and look up. The other boys stop eating for a moment. They glance over their shoulders. It's a false alarm. I peel an orange.

Then I notice that the others have drifted away, and I see why.

A prefect walks towards me in tight shorts, like his muscles are so big it was difficult to find a pair of shorts that would fit him. I want to escape, but where would I go on the open field?

'Excuse me there,' he says. 'Would you mind just writing your name down on this piece of paper?'

'Yes, sir, Strijdom, sir.'

He looks at what I've written for a moment. 'Thanks. That's all.'

The bell sounds. Feet shuffle along the polished wooden floor. I stand next to my friend Geoff. 'Ay, Foxy, your mother's a whore!' calls another boy.

Geoff looks at the boy. 'Graham, stop causing,' he replies.

'Geoff, I said your mother's a whore!'

'Graham, get lost!'

Graham kicks Geoff in the shins. Geoff faces Graham with tears in his eyes.

'Yeah, you see Geoff!'

'What's your problem, Graham?'

'Nothing's my problem, Geoff, nothing. Have you got a problem?'

Mr Lamonde Junior strides onto the stage. The hall's muttering voices instantly mute. Next to his enormous body the podium is comical, like an ungainly midget-stand. His ape-hands clutch it and adjust it, almost consuming it. We say the Lord's Prayer. 'You may sit . . . Cricket this weekend versus Churchill. All boys to be at Churchill an hour before your game.'

My attention drifts off. I hate people like Graham. Society doesn't need people like him. I really hope someone gives him a hiding someday soon.

'. . . T Bester . . . H Eastwood . . .'

My heart jolts. *What? H Eastwood? What did I do?*

I try to keep calm but my body doesn't listen to my brain. My stomach turns.

Mr Lamonde shuffles his papers in his hand. 'Gentlemen, the best of luck to you for the sporting fixtures this weekend. Do yourselves and your school proud.'

He bounds out with his vast gait. The staff trail behind him. I move my reluctant body out of the hallway and across the corridors and paths. The trees glow splendid greens in the mid-morning light.

Some metres away a line of boys wraps its way around the administration offices and immaculate flower beds.

'What's your crime?' asks the guy in front of me.

'No idea,' I reply. 'Someone took my name down while I was standing around, but I don't know what for. What about you?'

'I have no idea. Could be any number of things. I'm guessing hair but it could be hymn book or garters.'

'Does Lamonde beat hard?'

'Nah, he's a pussy. Kyle is the one to watch out for.'

The queue shortens. The smell of paper and carpet fills my nostrils. I want to wee.

The gunshots of the cane echo through the passageway. Boys leave Mr Lamonde's office holding their bums. They run past us, their faces seemingly half contorted with pain and half breaking into relieved smiles.

A teacher walks past us and grins with her big teeth. 'Oh, I do hope Mr Lamonde is feeling strong today!' she says.

The boy behind me retorts, '*Jeez*, thanks ma'am. I know we can always count on your unwavering support!'

She smiles back at him and then dances into the staff room like she's filled with joy, like she's just won the most-beautiful-teacher-in-the-world competition.

A muffled voice calls out. 'Next.'

I open Mr Lamonde's door. He sits at his desk with a pen in his hand.

'Name?' he says.

'Eastwood, sir.'

'Form?'

'One, sir.'

He scribbles and looks up. 'Are you aware of the school regulations about hair?'

'Yes, sir.'

'So, you tell me, is your hair acceptable?'

'No, sir.'

'When are you going to cut it?'

'Today, sir.'

'Good. Close the door behind you. Place your hands on the desk in front of you.'

He gets to his feet. I think he will stop rising, but he just carries on going until his head is just below the ceiling. Through the corner of my eye I see him lift a cane from behind the curtain.

I watch my hands as they rest on his desk. I smell wood and carpet. The first crack rings out. I want to clutch my burning backside. I wait for some moments. Maybe it's over. A second crack rings out. The momentum of the cane seems to shift my body a little. The urge to clutch my stinging bum is almost overwhelming.

The door opens.

'Thank you, sir,' I say.

Mr Lamonde walks back to his chair. 'Next . . .'

*　*　*

Mum calls us to the dining room. 'I've got something to tell you guys.'

'What Mum?' I ask.

She takes a deep breath and stands with her arms crossed. And then she goes quiet.

'What?' asks Dan.

'I'm pregnant.'

I laugh. 'Oh really, Mum? You should have asked me for a condom!'

I wait for her to say that she's joking. I wait longer. She says nothing.

'Really?' I ask.

'Yes. Eight weeks.'

Shock rises up my throat and bursts out my eyes.

Dan blurts out, 'Mum, you can't. It's not fair!' Tears stream down his cheeks.

Mum stands there silently, looking at us like she's wondering what to do.

'Mum, you have to have an abortion!' shouts Dan.

'I've already thought about it long and hard,' says Mum. 'I'm going to have the baby. That's why I'm telling you.'

'What does Dad say?' I ask.

'He didn't want me to keep it. But I was listening to Miles Davis and I just thought, fuck it, I'm going to have it.'

Dan walks to the veranda and I follow him.

He sits on the chair with his face buried in his hands and he weeps like he's never wept before. Now and again he seems to gulp for air and then continue.

I want to take his tears away but nothing seems to stop them. His face contorts into awful shapes.

'Dan, it'll be okay,' I say. 'Lots of things will still be the same.'

Dan puts his face in his arms. He doesn't say anything.

Beebs sits next to me. 'Why aren't you crying, Beebs?' I ask.

'I was going to bed lots of nights wishing Mum would have a baby. And now she is.'

Dan gets up and walks off. And then the garden is strangely silent, except for the sound of birds and insects.

* * *

The senior boys stand in front of us. Behind them the distant trees stand crisp and vivid against the sky and clouds. A stocky senior moves towards me. He rests his hand on my neck. 'How much do you weigh?' he asks.

'Forty-six kilograms, sir.'

'Lucky for you. Hands up anyone under forty kilograms.'

Some hands go up. He points to a lightie. 'Yeah, you.'

'Wait,' chuckles another senior. 'Got a nice one here. Gavin, you be umpire.'

Gavin walks some steps onto the grass. 'When you're ready!'

Two seniors grab a runt by his arms and legs. They swing him to and fro. 'One . . . two . . . three . . .'

And then the lightie is Superman, his arms stretched out in front of him, his body perfectly parallel to the ground. He flies through the air like he'll save a woman from a burning bus. But then he's a stone.

Bumpf.

Gavin marks a groove in the soil with the heel of his perfectly black shoe. 'Not bad, hey?'

The competing group call out, 'Our oke will do better.' They take their lightie. 'One . . . two . . . three . . .'

And then their lightie is like Superman too. He flies through the air to save the screaming woman from the burning bus.

Bumpf.

Two seniors explode with laughter.

'Record, china!'

One by one the boys fly past me. And as they fly I wish I were the president of Zimbabwe so I could send all the horrible people of this world somewhere terrible.

Like Lagos, for example.

And then they'd all live there and tear each other to pieces. I'd build a wall around them to keep them in.

That way they could just terrorise each other and leave decent people alone.

And then, if one of them came to me and said, 'What the hell? There's no rule of law and all these thugs keep robbing me at knife point and beating me up,' I would just say, 'Pardon me? What's that? I can't hear you! Please speak up, for heaven's sake.

* * *

Dan lifts the wings of our crashed aeroplane and points to a greasy fracture. 'I reckon if we just glue it here it'll still be aerodynamic and not too heavy,' he says.

Dad's shouts interrupt us. 'Hurry up, you buggers! We're going to be late for lunch!'

'But Dad, we're still gluing!'

'Come on, you can do that stuff later.'

'Okay, I'm coming,' I moan. 'But I thought you said we didn't have to come if we didn't want to.'

Mum and Beebs wait at the car. 'Hurry up, you boys!'

'Yeah, you guys, hurry up!' grins Beebs.

Mum puts her feet up on the dashboard as Dad drives.

'Dad,' I say. 'What does your friend Rupert do?'

'He's a professor of English literature at the university. He did his doctorate on Dickens, who I personally loathe. But these days he's a fundi on African literature. And of course, very good friends with Doris Lessing and Christopher Hitchens. And a poof.'

'Really? He's a poofter?'

'How do you know?' asks Dan.

Dad laughs. 'Well, he was in love with me once, you know! It was after I started doing this air force fitness course. It was the only time in my life that I had any real muscle. And of course, Rupert turned round and decided he loved me. He once waited for me for hours at the airport, just to catch a glimpse of me before I got on another flight. Or so he confessed to me, many years later.'

We drive up Cousin Tina's long driveway and through the bamboo and thickets until we reach the house at the end of the gravel. Cousin Tina comes out of the house. 'Hullo! Lovely to see you all!'

A bougainvillea absorbs the house slowly between its beautiful tentacles. In the shade of a towering tree, a group of old people sit on cane chairs. They puff on cigarettes and sip at cocktails. An old man gets to his feet and greets us with whisky breath. 'Anthony, Annette, lovely to see you again!'

Cousin Christopher throws a piece of fillet onto the braai. 'That was a fantastic effort with the art competition, Annette. Where did you come in the end?'

'First, actually!' says Mum. 'I thought it was going to be impossible this year with all the entrants. And I thought it unlikely they'd choose me a second time, so I'm really very chuffed!'

'Jolly good effort!' says Christopher.

'You know,' says Dad. 'I hadn't the faintest clue when I bought her that little paint set all those years ago she'd just teach herself to paint like this.' He puts his hand on Mum's arm. 'She's really rather a talent.'

Mum smiles and sips some more wine.

By the steps near the veranda a cat chews on a half-dead mouse. The mouse's intestines lie unravelled from its stomach, sprawled on the grass like bleeding spaghetti. The cat sets the mouse free and then slams its claws into the dying creature's entrails.

Over and over the cat plays its game, like a child lost in the fascination of a toy. I want to stop the wicked game, but for some reason I just leave the cat to do what it likes.

How many humans are like cats? Would a good system ever make cat-people kinder? Could a cat ever 'feel' what it does to a mouse?

*   *   *

The history teacher stands at the board in his smart trousers and rolled-up sleeves. He scratches his reddening submarine-captain's beard and scribbles on the board. '. . . and it was then that they started sending criminals to Australia,' he tells us. 'It was, in fact, a penal colony in its first conception.'

We all laugh like he just said 'penis colony'.

I put my hand up. 'Sir, was it necessarily a bad thing to send criminals there?'

'Well, Hayden, it was rather cruel and excessive, don't you think?'

I want to say, 'No, sir. I don't think it was excessive at all. In fact, I think it's one of the finest ideas ever conceived. Maybe Lagos would be a better choice these days, that's all. Australia seems like too nice a place for the scum of the earth.'

The teacher looks at me like he's expecting me to agree with him.

'Yes, sir,' I say.

Maybe Dad's right. Maybe people do bad things because the system makes them do those things. Maybe our perception that we have choice is an illusion. Maybe we're just the universe's billiard balls.

The bell goes. Set Three queues up at the door of the classroom. Graham stands there and smiles. 'Eastwood,' he says. 'What are you looking at?'

'Nothing, Graham.'

'Your mother's a whore!' he says.

I smile back. 'She sends her best regards.'

Miss Tingle comes to the classroom door. Graham stands to angelic attention.

'Morning, Set Three,' says Miss Tingle. 'You may enter.'

Chapter 8

Nightjars call in the darkness. A small distance away, the curtains of the house glow a moon yellow. Dan shuffles in his sleeping bag. 'How come Max couldn't come tonight?'

'*Ach*, he didn't want to interrupt his saxophone practising schedule,' says Franz.

'Typical Max,' I say.

The sleeping bags are already wet with dew. Dan props himself up on one elbow. 'Guys, let's make up a story.'

'Okay,' says Franz. 'Who are the characters?'

Dan gazes at the stars above him. 'How about someone called Stagwoft?' he says.

Franz and I laugh. 'What's his surname then?'

We argue over some suggestions. 'Mugwop,' offers Dan.

'Okay, who else?'

'How about Gunbit,' laughs Dan with his engine-revving giggle. 'Gunbit Wallhouse!'

'Right,' says Franz. 'I think we just need to clarify the pronunciation. Should Stagwoft be pronounced "Stagwáft" or "Stagwöft"?'

I roll onto my back. Dan and Franz continue to chatter and giggle. I try to stop my mind from filling with Dad's words. Are our lives really as meaningless as he says? The silent stars above make me think about how I'm nothing compared to the never-ending universe. And then Dad seems right. But when I smell the jasmine that Mum planted and I hear the bats flutter over my head, Dad seems wrong. The chatter fades away.

I open my eyes to see the darkness breaking into greys and yellows. Franz stands barefoot in the distance pissing onto the frosty lawn.

I search the freezing grass for firewood. Dan lies in his sleeping bag.

'Hayde, we've got no milk for tea,' says Franz.

'Oh, no problem, I'll get some.' I run to the house across the freezing lawn.

On the table by the stove sits a note from Mum to Dad. It says, 'Your din-din is in the tin-tin.' Next to it lies the sawn-off foot of a chicken with one of its claws pointing to a tin of baked beans. I grab the milk.

Dan and Franz huddle by a small fire holding their hands close to the flames.

'Are you guys ready for Germany?' asks Dan.

'Yeah,' says Franz. 'We'll be going end of next month. The date's finally in stone.'

Dan goes silent for a moment. 'I wish you guys weren't leaving,' he eventually says. 'I really wish you weren't leaving.'

* * *

I study the book in my hands. The cover picture shows a guy with a gun slung over his shoulder. He seems like a proper man: someone who could walk through the bush for days and survive on biltong and dirty water.

If only I'd lived a hundred years ago when Zimbabwe was still wild and empty; when there was still something magical and unexplored; when nature seemed so infinite that it could never be conquered; when killing animals didn't matter because there were just so many of them. Sometimes I wonder what it would have been like to be my ancestor, Leander Starr Jameson. Or to have shaken hands with Lobengula. I was born in the wrong era.

Mr Chiremba stands at the change rooms twirling a black cord in his fingers. 'Come on hurry, hurry!' he shouts. 'I'm going to bring out black beauty just now!'

'Yes, sir.'

'Line up in three pairs of six.'

He waits with his hands on his hips. 'Ay, Chanetsa! What did I say? I said three pairs of six!'

'Sir, I don't know what you mean!'

'Ay, are you being cheeky, *mupfana*?' He pulls out black beauty and whips Chanetsa on the backs of his legs.

Chanetsa winces in pain. 'Sir, three *pairs* of six?'

The class laughs.

'Ay, you keep quiet!' he says pointing a finger into the crowd. 'Do you want me to unleash black beauty on you too?'

'No, sir,' says the boy, trying to stop himself from laughing.

Mr Chiremba points to the newly formed lines. 'Is that straight?'

'Yes, sir!'

'Ah-ah, straight like a crooked arrow!' he shouts. 'Now come on, do your rugby drill. You know the one! And if you drop that ball . . . ah-ah, *mupfana*, fifty press-ups!'

He inspects us as we pop the ball to one another, all the time fidgeting black beauty to and fro in his fingers. 'Alright,' he interrupts. 'You guys carry on. I have to do some important other-things.'

He walks under the rugby posts and across the field towards the school buildings. The moment he is gone, Graham bumps his shoulder into a new boy. The new boy stops in his tracks and raises a finger at Graham's face. 'Watch it.'

'Are you causing with me?' asks Graham. 'Are you causing?'

'No, I'm not causing,' replies the boy. 'I'm just saying don't bump me like that again.'

We restart the drill. Moments later Graham barges the boy again. 'Ay, Graham, what's your problem?'

'Nothing's my problem! Nothing's my problem!'

The new boy raises his index finger at Graham again. 'I said watch it!'

'Or what? Or what?'

'Graham, don't scheme you're hard.'

'Ah, what if I'm hard? What if I'm hard?'

Knuckles smack onto flesh. Graham steadies himself from a clean punch. He swings back, but the new boy steps out of the way and lands another clean hit. 'Fight! Fight! Fight!'

Graham's head bounces from side to side like a punching bag. It is over within seconds. Graham sits down and spits some gooey blood onto the grass.

'Couldn't have happened to a nicer guy!' laughs Geoff.

The new boy stands teary-eyed some metres away. I approach him cautiously, like he's a wounded animal that might just gore me. 'Are you okay?' I ask him.

He stares into the distance with his glassy eyes. 'I'm fine,' he eventually replies.

'Where did you learn to fight like that?' I ask.

'I got used to fighting when I lived in South Africa. Those boers used to give me shit. But I don't take shit anymore.'

'Well, you can certainly fight. What's your name?'

We shake hands. 'Royce,' he says.

I like Royce. He's fair. Graham isn't fair. Graham isn't anything. He's just like one of those unicellular organisms from my science book that respond to stimuli, like some kind of amoeba. Except he's more unpredictable than an amoeba. Graham is like a mad amoeba, like an amoeba on drugs.

The bell sounds. Mr Chiremba returns unexpectedly. 'You can go,' he tells us. 'But don't be lazy! Shower! If I find you with dry hair . . . ahhhhh, *mupfana*, I'm going to give you something special.'

We break into a trot for the change rooms.

When I'm dictator of Zimbabwe I'll make Royce the Minister of Justice. Then he can oversee sending people like Graham to Lagos. And then the country will be mostly peaceful. Some people will steal because they're starving. But that'll be easy to fix because I could feed them with all the money saved from prisons and police stations.

One day I'll do the calculations. I'll find out the GDP of Zimbabwe and the amount of money Zimbabwe spends on prisons and policemen. And then I'll estimate how much stuff people like Graham break and steal. And then I'll find out how much it'll cost to chain Graham to a donkey and send him to Lagos. And then I'll see how much money is left over to feed the poor. Maybe it'll be enough. But even if it isn't, it'll be a good start.

Sometimes democracy seems like a stupid idea. Who in their right mind would let people like Graham vote? If enough Grahams voted they'd ruin the whole country.

When I'm the leader of Zimbabwe I'm going to make a voting exam to test whether people understand what they're voting about and whether they're compassionate enough. The only trouble with testing for a good heart is that people like Graham would just pretend to have one. So maybe I'd have to have spies to tell me who were the Grahams among us.

And I'd have to be careful and handpick the spies myself to make sure those spies weren't Grahams themselves. Because I bet Grahams would love to become spies. And I bet they'd all pretend to be nice to get spy jobs. And then they'd run the country behind my back and recruit other Grahams.

The problem of choosing spies worries me. Because I reckon that once people like Graham make up a certain percentage of the people running the place, then it's like Mr Lamonde always says: 'Woe betide.'

Sometimes I wonder how democracy exists at all.

*   *   *

The drums roll. A guitar clangs. The fishbowl TV screen fills with explosives and men in combat uniform. The Rolling Stones blare out 'Paint It, Black'.

Dad stubs out a cigarette. 'What is this claptrap?' he asks.

'It's a TV series. *Tour of Duty.*'

'Fucking Americans and their bloody Vietnam propaganda. Why do people watch this junk?'

'Dad, it's just a TV show!'

'It's not just a TV show. This is how they brainwash their nation with their right-wing agenda. The US was absolutely humiliated in that war. Humiliated! They had to rescue the last of their troops off their embassy roof with helicopters. And they dropped more bombs on Vietnam than were dropped by all sides combined during the Second World War. That's quite something. Is there any mention of any of this? Any mention of the My Lai massacre?'

'The My Lai massacre? What was that?'

'The Americans went in and massacred an entire village of civilians. They'd allegedly been tipped off that the Viet Cong were there. But with their usual blundering, they arrived there long after the Viet Cong had left and then raped and murdered almost everyone. Hundreds, if not thousands, of people. Nobody would have known about it either, had it not been for a single helicopter pilot who reported the event. These shows like *Tour of Duty* just sanitise this savagery, make it look like the US was noble and courageous. Their involvement was cowardly. They were barbaric.'

Dad's words sink into me. *Tour of Duty* seems suddenly sinister, suddenly right-wing.

He continues with his argument. He seems so often to talk about the world as though it's full of men who sit in rooms and plot evil. He sees them wherever he looks. And he talks about Mr Kyle as though he's in cahoots with shadowy right-wing leaders. But when I see Mr Kyle walk about the school, I just see an old-fashioned man who believes in discipline and God.

The closing credits roll down the screen. Mum and Beebs sleep on the couch next to each other. The dogs splay their legs out across the floor. Dan sits on the carpet with some tweezers in his hand and picks at his foot. 'What are you doing, Dan?' I ask.

He seems almost tearful. 'Mum always puts thorns in our hiding places. It's impossible to play Ghostbusters without getting your feet spiked. It's so stupid, why do we even bother having a garden if we can't run and hide in it?'

'I know,' I say. 'I got a thorn last week too. And the chickens just root between them anyway.'

'I've had it! I'm starting a communist revolution. Tomorrow.'

'What do you mean? Like what?'

'I don't know . . . Something . . .'

* * *

Mrs Ramsay stands at the blackboard scribbling maths. *I hate the way Americans say 'math' instead of 'maths'*, I think. *And how they pronounce 'aluminium' and 'adult'. Why can't they just speak English properly?*

The bell rings. 'Okay, boys, remember your homework is due on Friday. Go when you're ready.'

The criminals queue outside in a line. 'Graham! How are you, *shamwaz?*'

He scowls. His body language seems different now. His eyes seem to be missing their usual sparkle. 'Eastwood. *Hokoyo!*'

'See you later,' I say. 'Just going to hang with that new guy, Royce. You guys have met, hey?'

He spits at my feet and then puts his bag over his shoulder and walks into the classroom.

* * *

I sit on the veranda reading Agatha Christie's *Hickory Dickory Dock*.

Dan walks past me bare-chested and disappears somewhere into the garden. I glance up to see him dragging pieces of thorn tree across the lawn and under the long shadows cast by the late afternoon sun. He puts them in a pile and returns with more. 'Dan, what are you doing?'

'Oh, just a revolution,' he calls back.

I giggle and then he echoes my giggle.

I put my book down and go to him. He empties a bottle of methylated spirits onto the pile. The thorns burst into blue flames. We hold our hands up to the roaring furnace. 'There,' says Dan. 'That solves that!'

*   *   *

Dad sits in his green chair and smokes. Moths flutter through the smoke and bump into the lamp above him. He waves his hands about like he's speaking to a theatre of people instead of just Dan and me.

'Mercedes designs cars for intelligent and wealthy middle-class professionals,' he says. 'They invest in simple technology that works and not in, quote, gewgaws, unquote.' He pauses. 'Do you know what I mean by a gewgaw?'

'No,' I say, wondering what other people would think if they saw his hands thrusting through the air like he'd just drunk ten cups of coffee.

'A gewgaw is essentially a futile icon. The Hyundai, you'll notice, has electric windows. They may look fancy, but I tell you right now, they'll be broken within two years. That's what I mean by a gewgaw: a functionless artefact. The Merc has wind-up windows that you'll see will last us twenty years. The extras are purposefully kept simple because they know people with brains aren't after gewgaws, they're after quality. I tell you, every time I get in that car I think, Jesus Christ, those Germans designed this properly. Just look at the painstaking workmanship on it. Hats off to those buggers, I tell you. It's a bloody miracle they built that country up so quickly after it was bombed to smithereens. Could teach the people here a thing or two, you know.'

I make my excuses and leave Dan to listen to Dad. In my room I stand naked in front of the mirror. Pubic hair grows from what was once smooth skin. Pimples of different sizes and shades of red pockmark my cheeks and neck. My bony chest seems to be filling with muscle. Even my jaw and brow seem to be changing. And I smell different. I sense I'm watching a puppy grow into an ungainly dog. I'm watching innocent, big, watery puppy eyes turn into those small, dead adult-dog eyes.

I flex my arms in the mirror. They're getting stronger. Haven't I always wanted to be stronger? But I would rather time were going backwards. I would rather not grow old and die.

Dad talks about life as if it means nothing. Because if we're just atoms mingling together, then we're also just arbitrary. Sometimes Dad's view of the world seems so empty. Sometimes I wish I was more like the Christians. At least they believe in something.

Sometimes naked girls crowd out my thoughts. What would those girls think if they knew what really went on in my mind? I'm definitely supposed to like girls. Liking boys is a sin. But liking girls too much is also a sin. We must like girls enough to give them flowers and poetry. But we mustn't like them enough to actually mate with them. Because that's wrong. But not as wrong as liking boys.

Sometimes I wonder how men manage to convince women to have sex with them. Sometimes I wonder how there are six billion people on this planet. How would anyone even begin to convince a girl to get naked?

I hear a knock at the door. 'Hayde, can I come in?' asks Dan.

I quickly cover my body. 'Yeah.'

Dan walks in and sits down on my bed. He seems upset. I wait for him to say something but he sits silently. 'What, Dan?' I eventually ask.

He twiddles the hair on his head with his fingers. 'Mum got the gardeners to replace all the thorns in the garden.'

A flush of irritation sweeps through me. 'I'm sorry,' I say. 'Why don't we just burn the whole bunch again?'

He doesn't respond. 'Dan,' I repeat. 'We could just burn them.'

His eyes wander into the distance. 'Nah. Mum never listens. She'll just replace them. She always wins.'

*　*　*

Mr Lamonde Junior stoops his head out of his office and comes to stand in the hallway. 'All six of you come in,' he says.

He towers over us with his bushy beard and gorilla eyes. 'Gentlemen, I understand that you were sent to me and beaten two weeks ago for failing to attend manual labour. Do I have that right?'

'Yes, sir.'

'It has since been brought to my attention that the attendance list for that day was not, in fact, handed to me as it should have been, so the lot of you will have, in fact, been accidentally beaten. Did all of you attend that manual labour?'

'Yes, sir.'

'Gentlemen, this is a school error for which I apologise. Each of you, in light of this error, will receive a credit beating.'

He sits down and opens up a jotter-book. 'However, let me make this clear,' he continues, 'this is not – and I repeat, not – a free licence to flout school rules. This waiver is discretionary, not some automatic get-out-of-jail-free card.'

My racing heart slows.

'Now, announce your names from left to right . . .'

The door closes behind us. We walk silently down the hall. 'Good afternoon, ma'am' we say to a teacher in the hallway. Our feet step onto the outside brick. 'Fuck yeah!' Boys dance about high-fiving each other and laughing. A guy pretends to be doing it doggy-style with an invisible girl.

I walk past the flowerbeds and under the trees and to the playing field. Adrian and Geoff stand together on the field eating their food in the morning sun. 'So what happened?'

I grin. 'Get-out-of-jail-free card!'

*　*　*

The headlights of Max and Franz's car shine up our driveway and illuminate the shrubs and trees. Their father gets out. 'So Hayde, Danny, are you ready to go?' he asks in his German accent.

Max and Franz sit next to each other in the back of the car. The passing streetlights reflect flashes of yellow and white into the window. Tears force themselves out of my eyes.

Max and Franz's dad opens the boot and lifts out some suitcases. 'Okay, you guys, get together now, I want to take a picture.'

The four of us link arms. 'Come on!' says their dad. 'You have to smile, ja! Don't worry, they will be back to visit!'

Max and Franz disappear behind the wooden panels of the departure gates. Dan sits down and plants his head in his hands and cries. I put my hand on his back. 'Dan, are you okay?' I ask.

He says nothing. His face remains buried between his arms.

Eventually he looks up, red faced, eyes blood-shot.

'Come on, Dan, our lift's here, we need to go.'

He gets to his feet without saying anything. He wipes the tears from his eyes. 'I'm ready,' he says. 'Let's go.'

* * *

Mum stands over me. 'Come on, darling, it's time to get up. Here's a cup of coffee. We've got to be on the road in ten minutes.'

Dad rushes boxes over to the Mercedes. 'Come on, you bloody kids! Get a move on!' he shouts.

We pack into the car. Mum sits in the front seat with her stretched-pregnant stomach. I sometimes wonder if there's actually a baby in there.

The telephone lines pass by the windows. I wake to the sound of everyone laughing. 'Daniel, you're too much!' says Dad, wheezing with his smoker's laugh.

I rub my eyes. 'What are you guys laughing about?'

'We've been thinking of names for the baby,' says Beebs.

'Dan, tell Hayde your suggestion!' says Mum.

'Truck-driver.'

I burst into laughter. 'I think that wins it. I'm for Truck-driver!'

Barren communal lands pass by the window. Uncountable goats turn grassland into desert. An emaciated peasant sits on a cart and beats an equally emaciated donkey. 'Dad,' says Beebs. 'How come we're allowed into South Africa now?'

'Well, it's only in the past few months. Change is in the air. They've removed the ban on the ANC. They can't be bothered to keep track of people like me anymore.'

'So does that mean we can go on holiday to South Africa lots?' asks Beebs.

'Yes, from now on we can go whenever we like!'

'Dad. When did you decide to fight apartheid?' I ask.

'You know,' he says. 'I was at boarding school. I must have been thirteen or fourteen. I heard a fracas in the distance and saw a bunch of schoolboys gathering. A young coloured fellow was being savagely beaten by two Afrikaner policemen. It turned out he was just a petty thief. Slightly built chap. And by Jesus these two big beefy Afrikaner policemen laid into him, beating him with truncheons in front of everyone. The chap pleaded with them, but they wouldn't stop. In the end he was just lying there, a bleeding mess.'

Dad goes quiet for a moment. 'That was the day.'

His words penetrate me. My father. My hero.

Louis Trichardt sits like an intricate and shiny Legoland, its colours fresh and distinct. Vivid yellow flowers huddle together at each roundabout above immaculate black-and-white chequered curb stones. The highway is pothole-free, blemishless, sliced perfectly in half by a fresh white line. 'I can't believe it, Dad!' I say. 'Look how nice everything is!'

Dad laughs. 'Rhodesia was better managed, you know! Not a curb stone out of place. We looked down on the South Africans for being backward and inefficient.'

'Dad,' says Dan. 'How come it always happens like that? How

come whenever a place gets independence, they always break it? Like Mozambique and Zambia, and now kind of like Zimbabwe?'

'Well,' says Dad. 'Look at your own history. Your ancestors were colonised by the Romans. Many of the European tribes were just as technologically behind as the African ones here. When their empire fell, we spent a thousand years before we had a sewage system again. It takes a long time to rebuild systems.'

'But then, Dad, why did you support them coming into power if you knew they'd just break it?'

Dad pauses for some moments. 'Because, morality aside, it was inevitable that the game was up. Giving away power sooner is better in the long run. The whites here just didn't stand a chance because there were just never enough of them to cling on, and never would be. And you must remember that things here happened differently to America and Australia. When they colonised those places, they just wiped the locals out. When whites colonised southern Africa, the reverse happened: modern medicine, food security, the rule of law. Life expectancy went up, child mortality plunged like a stone, all factors that produced an explosion in the African population. When I was a boy, the population of Rhodesia was less than two million. What's it now? At least ten million.'

Dad stops to light a cigarette. 'You know, at least the Afrikaners have had the humility to recognise their position. The generals came out and said to the leadership, "Listen, no matter which way you look at this, no matter what you do, you're going to lose. Go and negotiate now while you still can." The Rhodies? Not a chance! Arrogant, deluded. Thought a small bunch of them could just dig their heels in forever and take on the world. Nincompoops.'

We sail past giant green-and-white road signs for Pretoria. Dad's answers only raise more questions.

Dad points into the distance. 'Your old ancestor, Leander Starr Jameson, Prime Minister of the Cape, and first governor of Mashonaland, would have come somewhere round here with his horsemen for the Jameson Raid. It failed miserably, of course. The Uitlanders were never going to revolt as planned. Another bloody halfwit, that Jameson. Your mother's side, luckily.'

'Dad,' asks Dan. 'How did you end up back in Zimbabwe?'

Dad coughs out more smoke. 'Well,' he says. 'My problems of course started long before I returned here. In the sixties, I was still in South Africa. I was active in the communist party. The apartheid government's response at that time to any opposition, no matter how small, was furious and rabid. I was married to Ruth at the time. Her father, Bram Fischer, advised me to get out before I ended up in prison. And I found myself back in Salisbury.

'Unfortunately, ties between the two countries were strong, and the South Africans warned the authorities here. Before long, the Rhodesian secret police were following me around. There was this one dumb cluck who made it quite obvious that he was following me. I'd drive out the house and see the same old brown car in my rear-view mirror. One day I was hiding a journalist in the boot under some clothes and papers. The agent's car followed us. We were bloody worried we'd get stopped and searched, so at a traffic light I got out of my car and went over to the agent's window and crapped all over him. I told him he was doing a useless bloody job and that I'd report him to his superiors.'

He pauses and puffs on his cigarette.

'And then what, Dad?' I ask.

'And then the bloke just drove off. Of course the next day the same car was there with someone else, but luckily by then the journalist was long gone!'

* * *

Dan and Beebs stand next to each other on a boulder. I watch them from below, treading icy Cape water. 'Come on, you guys, jump!'

Dad and Mum sit on the beach close by. Dad sits covered up in towels and a hat.

'Mum, watch this!' shouts Dan.

Mum looks up. 'I'm watching! Jump!'

Dan hesitates for a moment. Water splashes into my face. Then his head pokes up next to mine. Beebs jumps in after him.

'Come in for an ice-cream!' shouts Mum.

1994

Chapter 9

Prefects throw a rugby ball among themselves. The entire school is tightly packed onto the benches and lawn. 'Form Ones!' shouts a prefect.

'Yes, sir!' they screech prebuscently, causing their seniors to burst into resonating laughter.

'Are your nuts ever going to drop?'

The Form Ones stand rigid and silent.

'I said, are your nuts ever going to drop?'

'Yes, sir,' they mumble.

'I can't hear you!'

'Yes, sir!' they scream shrilly, making everyone erupt into laughter again.

The head boy paces in front of us.

'Guys,' he says. 'Give this practice some heart please. Do these next few war cries properly and you'll get time to eat some food. Okay?'

I search for Dan in the crowd. He stands behind the rows of Form Ones with some of his classmates. He is still small.

The full animal kingdom surrounds me. On the rugby field the silverbacks grunt and mingle with each other. In the stands sit the orangutans, chimpanzees and gibbons. And on the floor perch the vervet monkeys. I want to protect Dan from the silverbacks and the chimpanzees. But how can I when I'm just an entry-level baboon?

Three prefects huddle together on the pitch in front of us and lock arms with one another. *'Mamatotoya!'* they scream.

'Eeya!' we echo.

'Mamatotoya!'

'Eeya!'

'Mama . . . Mama . . .'

'Eeya . . . Eeya . . . Eeya . . . Eeya!'

The school cheer and clap. The prefects unlock their arms and stand tall, their faces red from the strain of their cries.

'Again!' shouts the head boy. 'Louder!'

* * *

Miley moves around the edge of the coffee table like he's trying to break everything he can reach. Beebs gives him an action man. Miley grabs it and then bashes the plastic man's head on the table.

Dad's chair sits empty. The TV drones on in the background. Dan sits on the sofa reading *The Remains of the Day*. I read *Surely You're Joking, Mr Feynman!*

Dan puts his book down. 'What's that smell?' He lifts himself off the sofa and checks Miles's nappy. 'Argh, Miles has crapped! And it's all green!'

Mum inspects Miles. 'He sure has!'

'Nings!' I shout.

'Nings!' shouts Dan.

'I'm not dealing with this tonight,' says Mum. 'I'm calling in the dog squad.'

'No, Mum, don't! It's disgusting!' I shout.

'Zesa, Honkie, Stompie . . . Come here, doggies!'

Pattering paws grow louder and louder. The door bangs open and the dog squad skid their way over the parquet floor with wagging tails. Mum takes Miles's nappy and puts it on the floor behind the sofa where no one can see it. We hear licking and slurping sounds.

'Jesus!' I yell, covering my ears. 'Does anyone else in the whole of Zimbabwe feed baby poo to their dogs? I mean, for God's sake, can't we just be normal for once?'

'Take a chill pill, Hayde,' laughs Mum. 'It's just a way of relocating it to the garden. It's fine, although I agree it doesn't sound fantastic.' She covers her ears and grimaces.

The dogs finish their poo salad and wag their tails triumphantly. Fresh from the excitement of the moment, they run up to me and lick my leg.

'Ah, fuck! Now look, Mum!'

I shoo the dogs from the sitting room and close the door. What would girls think if they saw my family? What would happen if they knew we were the kind of Neanderthals who fed our own dogs our own shit in our own sitting room? Would I ever be able to convince any of them that I was worth kissing? Our family should be more like a normal family. Mum should dress more like normal Northern Suburbs madams. And our dogs shouldn't be the kind of dogs that eat our roast beef off the table when we're not looking.

Dan gets to his feet and walks out. He leaves *The Remains of the Day* behind on the couch.

*   *   *

Dan sits at my desk. He pins some balsawood pieces to a square of chipboard. The radio burbles in the background. 'Hayde, can you pass the glue?'

I sand cavities into struts and blow wood dust into the air. The particles hover and swirl in the light. Dan breaks the monotony of the background radio.

'Mrs Boyd-Clarke had me beaten today.'

'How come?' I ask.

'For being irritating.'

'Irritating?'

He snorts a laugh. 'Yeah, I got bored in maths. So I just started pretending not to understand what she was talking about and kept asking her to explain stuff again and again. Then other guys started doing the same, and she ended up spending like thirty minutes explaining something so basic that it was impossible for her to simplify further.'

'So what happened?'

'Eventually she just snapped and said, "Daniel, enough! I'm sending you for a beating!" And I said, "How come, ma'am?" and she said, "Well, because . . . well, um, you're irritating me!"'

'Was it bad?'

'No, I just got one. And it was super soft. Mr Desai just read the note from her and rolled his eyes and planted his face in his hand. He must have thought she was crazy or something.'

'I wonder what she must have written. "Daniel has been pretending for some time not to understand anything and it's finally driven me completely bonkers. Please thrash his botty."'

Dan giggles. 'Yeah, I wonder!'

I hand him the sanded balsa struts and he pins them to the board. He takes the crossbeam and presses it into the cavities I've carved.

'More glue please, Hayde.'

The lights flicker and the room goes pitch black. 'Fucking hell!' shouts Dan. 'Every time I try to do something useful the power goes off.'

A dim yellow illuminates the doorway. Mum holds Miles in one arm and a candle in the other. 'Hi, you guys. Here's a candle. Come and get dinner.'

'Coming, Mum. What's on the menu?'

'It's a slightly experimental Austrian dish for mains and profiteroles for dessert. Needless to say, your father's not home, so we'll just start without him.'

* * *

Heads and bodies bob up and down in front of me. I stand next to Geoff. Adrian dances with a girl under the shifting lights. Dr Alban sings 'It's my life'.

Boys like Adrian just stand where they are and girls come to them. When guys like me stand still, girls stay far away, like they're trying to minimise electrostatic repulsion.

I wonder why I'm even here. I should have stayed at home with Dan. Why didn't I just play chess with him when he asked? A picture of him at home alone with the dogs enters my mind. We might have finished the wing this evening and been able to fly aeroplanes tomorrow.

A dancing girl catches my eye.

In a moment it's as if a bolt of lightning from her hair has struck my heart and stomach and cast a spell on me. I watch her long blonde hair bounce on her shoulders. I watch her long legs; her delicate wrists; her collarbones, thin and elegant but somehow strong.

She moves like something wild, like a horse nobody could ever tame.

I wonder if Dan would be ashamed of me. I wonder if he would think me weak for being so transfixed by this girl. Would he think I was letting him down? Yes, because I am. Because Dan and I had promised each other long ago that we'd be like Peter Pan. We'd promised each other that we'd never be older than nine, and that we'd play hide and seek and build forts forever. Maybe that's why I used to cry when I watched the *Jungle Book*. Maybe that's why I would want to shout out, 'Mowgli, go back to the jungle! Don't follow that girl!'

It's sad to think that it's like Dad says, that we're just programmed to like girls so we can pass on our genes, that I'm nothing more than a temporary vehicle of no value.

Sometimes I tell myself that I'll show this Evolution character what I think of him. I tell myself that I'll never chase a girl and never have children. I tell Mr Evolution that my willpower will override him.

But this girl in front of me grips me with her magic and draws me in with her hair. If Mr Evolution was here, I would say, 'Sir, you can have my soul and you can have my meaning . . . if I can just have her.' Because if I had her, then she'd be all the meaning I ever needed.

The song changes. 'A la la la la long' booms out across the night sky and moonlit trees. The girl walks from the dance floor towards us.

Geoff holds out his hand and she takes it.

* * *

The dogs lie at my feet. *Blackadder* plays on the TV. Dan appears at the door in his school uniform. 'What happened to your knees?' I ask.

He hobbles to a space on the couch and sits down with his glass of milk and Milo. He lets out a sigh. 'A prefect made me crawl round the side lines on my hands and knees for about an hour.'

His knees and elbows look like they've been sandpapered raw. 'What did you do?'

'I accidentally walked onto the first team rugby pitch.'

My face flushes with anger. 'I hate those pricks!'

Dan seems startled by my fury.

I expect him to be angry about the malice and futility of what's happened to him. But his face holds nothing. I want revenge. I want to torture those savages. I want to beat them. I wait for him to say something. *Anything.*

The anger drains out of me to leave a sense of helplessness. What kind of brother am I if I can't protect him?

Dan puts down his empty glass and wipes away his milky-brown moustache.

'Mr Gordon said there was this prefect at his school in the seventies. A year later the headmaster read this prefect's name out on the list of people killed in the Bush War. He said his friends just erupted

— 90 —

into cheers and clapping and whistling. Apparently, they all went out for beers that evening and danced.'

'I wish I had Mr Gordon as my biology teacher.'

Dan picks at his wounds and then changes the subject. 'How was your day?'

'I hate the English language. That's all I can say.'

'How come?'

'Mrs Jack was talking about not using clichés for similes. And I thought about it. And she's just wrong. I've decided clichés are fine for most similes, most of the time.'

'Man, I was just thinking that the other day!'

'Thank goodness it's not just me! Original things that genuinely stand out don't necessarily make good similes.'

'Yes . . . she stood out like . . . a T-Rex in a no-pets-allowed restaurant . . . gives the impression that she stands out, but not in the right way.'

I blurt out a laugh. 'Exactly! She gave the example of "standing out like a sore thumb" as being terrible. And I thought, Why, what's wrong with that? It allows you to get the point that the whatever-it-is, stands out. If you said, "He stood out like a person with a head in a whole room full of decapitated people, who were packed like sardines next to him, and propped up by artificial means, for comparison's sake," then it just wouldn't flow well.

Dan giggles. 'What about, "She stood out like the last loo roll on a ship afflicted with salmonella poisoning, owing to poor refrigeration practices by the chef, and then subsequent poor stock calculation practices by management!"'

I snort my Milo out my nose. Tears of laughter roll down our faces. 'Wait, I've got another one!' I say. 'He was as shocked as an astronaut who'd just arrived on the moon to find a cow walking about and chewing on moon-dust, which of course would be deeply surprising on the grounds that, first of all, there's no atmosphere on the moon to support respiration and, second of all, the moon's surface oscillates between absolute freezing in the shade, and hundreds of degrees Celsius in the sun, meaning that any cow should either be frozen stiff or burned to a crisp, depending on whether or not the sun was shining!'

Dan looks at me. 'Uh . . . yeah, Hayde.'

'Not so good?'

'Uh, no, it was totally fine, Hayde. Totally fine. Just that there would be no oxygen for the cow to burn in.'

'Fair point. What would happen if you heated a cow up to five hundred degrees without any reactive chemicals about?'

'Well I suppose the proteins would denature and then moisture would get driven off into space . . . hang on, I thought of another one! How about, "He was as quiet as Naas Botha at a Quantum Electrodynamics conference?"'

I snort my Milo out my nose a second time. Dan giggles uncontrollably. 'That, Dan, would be very, very quiet!'

*   *   *

Dan and his friend Toubab practise pole vaulting in the garden with an aluminium pipe. The two of them take turns to pivot through the air and land on an old mattress. Dan hovers for a moment in perfect stillness and then falls to the mat. 'Yes! I did it!' he cries.

Toubab speaks in his strange half-American accent. 'Hey Hayde, have you seen my new Judo rolls?'

Toubab climbs up a branch of a nearby msasa tree. 'That is crazy high! Don't jump, you'll hurt yourself!' I shout.

Toubab leaps off the branch and hits the ground. In a split second he rolls onto his feet. 'Ta da!'

'How did you do that? How did you not break an arm?' I ask.

He laughs. 'Physics. I just transferred the downward motion into sideways motion.'

Dan clambers onto the same branch. 'Hey, Hayde, check this other trick that Toubab showed me. It goes something like this . . .'

He throws himself into the air and catches onto a branch below him. His body swings to a horizontal position. For a moment he hangs in the air perfectly still and horizontal to the ground. Then he falls like a plank and hits the grit. He gets to his feet and looks around like he's wondering what's going on.

'Shit, Dan! Are you okay?' I yell.

Dan clutches his arm and shouts, 'Oh my God!'

'What's wrong? What's wrong?'

'My arm!'

'What's wrong? Is it broken?'

He holds his wrist up. 'Is that broken enough for you?' he screams. It looks as if someone's fitted a second elbow to his forearm.

'Oh my God!'

Dan lets out penetrating shrieks. 'Mum!' I shout. 'Dan's broken his arm!'

* * *

A gaggle of girls stand by the swimming pool in front of me. They hold hands with each other and giggle as they jump into the water. A splash hits my legs. I throw meat onto the sizzling braai.

'Beastwood, can I get you a drink?' asks Geoff.

The girl from the party walks towards us in her bikini. Her wet blonde hair hugs her head and drapes onto her shoulders.

'Hi, we haven't met,' she says to me. 'I'm Sarah.'

I want to look into her grey-green eyes. But I sense that if I do her eye-lasers will melt me. I look into the distance instead. 'Hi, I'm Hayden.'

She walks over to Geoff and punches him on the arm. 'Come, Geoff, come and swim, man!'

'I've just been in,' he says. 'How about when I've finished eating?'

She grabs him by the arm and pulls. 'Come on, just come for a bit!'

Geoff stays on his feet, rigid as a tree. She laughs. 'Come on you guys, come and help me get him in!'

The gaggle of girls drag him by his arms and pull at his legs. Geoff laughs, 'No, you guys, I've just been in!'

Geoff wrestles them for a moment from the edge of the pool. He grabs two of the girls and takes them in with him. Sarah swims a length of butterfly. She moves effortlessly, like a dolphin, like she was made in the sea.

Sarah . . . that's a simple name, a beautiful name, I think.

* * *

Dad sits in his green chair. 'Won't you pour me a gin and tonic? Two fingers of gin.'

He lights his cigarette and puts his feet on the coffee table. 'You know,' he says. 'I was just thinking about the Cuban Revolution on my way home from work. When I was a young man, that Castro fellow was such a hero to me, you know. Imagine the courage it takes to go and invade a country like that and topple its dictatorship. The first time he failed. But that didn't stop him. Up he got, gathered another crew of men, and then tried again. The second time he was successful, of course. And the first thing he did was give the mafia twenty-four hours to get off the island. *Dup, dup, dup* . . . No more organised crime in Cuba!

'How come the Mafia were scared of him?'

'Well, he just said, "If you don't leave, I'll shoot you!" And so they packed up and left right there and then. And as things stand, Cuba now has more teachers per capita than any other country in the world, and that despite the fact that they're one of the poorest. And why are they so poor? Well, the bloody Yanks have had a blockade against them for years, tried to kill Castro several times. There was even a plot by the CIA to put a chemical in his food that would remove his beard, the theory being that his whole image and gravitas depends on it, and that without it, he would be significantly weakened.'

Dad laughs and coughs. 'Bloody Yanks! You really can't write this stuff!'

'Why don't the Americans like him?' I ask.

'Well, because he's a man of the people. Because he's a leftie. Because he challenges American business interests. Have you seen the size of Cuba? Tiny island, poor, hardly armed, and the paranoid bloody Americans are up in arms about it. Castro has survived every attempt to get rid of him, and boy does that piss the Americans off.'

I get to my feet. 'Thanks, that's interesting. I need to go to bed now, got homework to do in the morning. Maybe if you want to talk about interesting things like this you should come home before eleven o'clock.'

'And another thing,' Dad continues. 'Cuba also has the highest per capita number of doctors in the world. Higher than Britain, higher than America, higher even than Germany. Honestly. And the bloody Americans are paranoid that something like that could spread. Imagine, healthcare spreading to their country. What a horror!'

*　*　*

Dan and I knock the table tennis ball to each other. 'Fifteen–twelve!' shouts Dan. He serves again. We rally furiously. I hit the ball into the net. 'Yes! Sixteen–twelve!'

The gate bell rings in the distance. Emily appears in her apron. 'Haydie, there's somebody at the gate for you!'

'Who is it? I'm playing table tennis.'

She grins and breaks into a laugh. 'You must answer it. It's someone special!'

'Dan, sorry, let me take this.'

I pick up the gate phone. 'Hullo?'

'Hi, Hayden? This is Sarah from the braai.'

I gather myself. 'Oh, hi.'

'Geoff told me you live here. I live down the road from you. He mentioned you'd be able to deliver a letter. Is that okay?'

'Sure, come in.'

I rush to the veranda. Dan waits in his underpants next to the table. He swings his bat about. 'Come on, Hayde, let's play, let's play!'

'Shit, shit, where have I put my frickin' clothes?' I groan.

'Hayde, who's here?'

'It doesn't matter, just someone I know. I need to find my clothes!'

'Your shirt's under the tree over there.'

'What about my fucking shorts?'

I find them under the table. 'Argh, damn! So unstylish!'

I hear a knock at the front door. Sarah stands in front of me. She hugs me. My stomach fills with butterflies. 'Thank you so much for doing this!' she says.

'No problem,' I say. 'I'd be happy to.'

She presses the note into my hands. 'Nice house you have. Do you want to show me around?'

Through the window Dan stands in his underpants holding his bat. He notices us and then vanishes.

Sarah sits at the piano. 'Who plays this?' she asks.

'My mum. She plays a lot. She once trained as a concert pianist in Vienna, actually.'

'She must be incredible.'

'Yeah, she is.'

Sarah plays 'Für Elise'. Her long fingers glide across the keys.

'Where did you learn to play?' I ask.

She stands and closes the lid. 'I used to go to lessons . . . Did your mum decorate this place?'

'Yeah. Those are *New Yorker* covers she's decoupaged the doors with.'

'Wow! And are these your mum's paintings?'

'Yes,' I say. 'She loves painting.'

'She's clearly very talented.'

I open the door to my room. 'So, how much do you think Geoffrey likes me?' she asks.

'Oh, I'm sure he likes you a lot,' I say.

'Do you want to see my aeroplane?' I ask.

'Um, sure,' she says.

I carefully remove it from the hook on the wall. 'Here's the receiver,' I explain. 'And over here are the little engines that move the elevator, ailerons, rudder and throttle. They're called servos. You have to put them above the wing like this otherwise they tend to mess with the centre of gravity.' I flick the propeller. 'This is the engine. It's got a quarter horsepower and a pretty amazing power-to-weight ratio. To put it into perspective, a lawnmower's engine has about one horsepower. My engine's about four times less powerful than that but hundreds of times lighter, so the power-to-weight ratio is actually quite staggering, maybe even as much as an ant's.'

Her eyes fidget. 'Cool, Hayde. Who are those pictures of on your wall?'

'Oh, that's Max and Franz. My German friends.'

I want to tell her that the right frequency of electromagnetic radiation has to be beamed to the aeroplane and then absorbed by the receiver. I want to tell her how the signal is converted into a current that travels along the cables to the electric motors. I want to explain how clever it is that radio signals can be used in this way to direct a flying object through the air. I want to tell her that the wings have to have the right shape to generate lift and then explain what that shape is. And then tell her that the working explanation of why lift happens doesn't really make sense. I want to tell her that fat wings create more lift but also more drag. And then I want to explain that my plane is almost like an organism because so many things have to work together at the same time to keep it alive. I want to tell her that the plane is just like a mouse or a bird or a bacterium in that its processes must be perfectly coordinated for it to work.

And I want to tell her that a model aeroplane is civilised, that there are five thousand years of maths and science in it. I want to tell her that if a caveman could see a piece of wood flying through the air like a bird, he'd think it was magic. But it isn't magic; it's just civilised people thinking and working together. I want to tell her that it's important to do civilised things like make aeroplanes, because without things like that, the Grahams of this world would probably turn the whole place into Lagos.

Then I want to explain that my aeroplane is interesting because it's modern but looks like it's old at the same time, like it was sent here in a time machine from the First World War. I want to say that I like the way ancient things sometimes seem simpler and gentler than modern things. I want to say, 'That's a bit of a contradiction, don't you think?'

She walks to my desk and studies the photos of Max and Franz on the wall. 'Wow, they're gorgeous,' she says. 'So did you hear that Kim Bloomfield and Adam Randall broke up?'

'No,' I say.

I cast my eyes to the letter in my hands. It smells of perfume. It's covered in neat handwriting with little red hearts surrounding the big word 'Geoff'.

* * *

Miles sleeps on my chest. Dan sits next to me reading *Moby-Dick*.

Our president comes on the TV screen. He waves his hands in the air. Dan says, 'He looks like he's being puppet-controlled by aliens.' And for a moment the president's hands seem perfectly controlled by invisible strings. I giggle. Mum and Beebs snort with laughter. Dad coughs up phlegm and cackles.

Sarah's grey-green eyes sit in my mind and stare at me. Someday I want to sit at the piano and play something brilliant for her. Maybe if I do she'll notice me. 'Mum? Would you teach me that tune you sometimes play on the piano?' I ask.

'Which one?'

'You know, the one that goes *da-da-duh-da-duh-da-duh-da*.'

'Oh, you mean "The Entertainer" by Scott Joplin?'

'Yes, that one.'

'Why don't you learn how to read music and then you'll be able to teach yourself?'

'That sounds like hard work. Can't you just show me?'

Mum gets to her feet. 'Dan,' I say. 'Would you take Miley for a moment?'

He lifts Miley's floppy body from my arms with his plaster-cast arm. 'Sure. Come here, little Truck-driver!'

I sit at the piano. Mum stands over me. 'Okay, here're the first few notes.'

My sausage-fingers move clumsily across the black and white keys. She sighs. 'I just wish you kids had learned to read music when you were younger. But no, your father had to sabotage it and convince you it was a waste of your time.'

'For God's sake!' shouts Dad. 'Would you please not play the piano at night? It's an infernal bloody racket!'

'Dad, calm down! It's not loud!' I yell back.

'Hayden! It's late now. That thing should be played before I get home, for Christ's sake! Antisocial bloody instrument!'

The room goes black. 'Well! That puts an end to that dispute,' says Mum. 'I'll get some candles.'

'Jesus!' shouts Dad. 'What's going on in this bloody country?'

Chapter 10

Mr Kyle walks onto the stage with his Count Dracula cloak dragging behind him. He stands at the podium. 'Gentlemen, please sing "Amazing Grace".'

He stands with his hands by his side and looks into the distance as if in deep thought. He straightens the papers in his hands. 'Gentlemen, today we'll be saying a prayer for the victims of the Rwandan genocide, and then we'll immediately observe a minute's silence. There are . . . bad things happening on that side of the world.'

Thousands of kilometres away, hundreds of thousands of people hack each other to death with blunt pangas. The quiet hall makes it seem like the genocide might not really be happening, like it might just be a misunderstanding in what someone heard and then told someone else. But I feel that it's real. I see the genocidaires among us, the lizards camouflaged as humans. I see them.

Mr Kyle reads the cricket results. 'Thank you, gentlemen,' he says, gathering his papers. He leaves an empty stage. A prefect fills it. The hall is instantly quiet again.

'Bradley McGowan, get up here!'

Somewhere in the crowd a skinny runt gets to his feet and nervously tucks his shirt into his shorts. He shuffles his way to the stage, clumsy like a newborn antelope. The runt stands before the silverback and the silverback glowers at him. 'I don't know what to do with you . . . What should I do with him?' he asks the crowd.

'Hit him, sir! Hit him!' shout the orangutans and bonobos.

The runt stands there silently. 'Dance!' shouts the prefect. 'Dance like Michael Jackson!'

The runt moves like a faulty robot without oil, like some twitching avian creature, like Mr Bean before being executed. The crowd laughs.

To my left and right I see them, the genocidaires, waiting for their moment to kill, waiting for their moment of invisibility. I must watch out for *them*.

* * *

The maths teacher scrawls her symbols on the board. Geoff leans over to me. 'Hayde,' he says. 'I think I'm going to break up with Sarah.'

'How come?' I ask.

'I like Shadia more. Sarah and I . . . I don't think we're right.'

'Those two girls know each other. I think it's going to cause some politics.'

'Yeah, it's going to be complicated.'

Back at home, Sarah comes to visit me again. She sits at my desk, her long blonde hair falling onto the table surface. She flips through my photos of Max and Franz. 'They're both so gorgeous,' she says. I look over her shoulder at them. She's right. They're blond and golden and handsome.

'So,' she says. 'Geoff is coming over to my place this weekend, I'm so excited! Did he give you a letter for me?'

'Not this time,' I say.

'Why are boys so frustrating?'

* * *

The late morning sun shines in through the big dining room window and onto my bowl of cornflakes. Dad appears at the doorway. 'Hayden, I need to get some things from the shops. Be a good lad and keep me company.'

The car radio voices drone on hypnotically with Sunday Christian messages. Through the window, the flowers are reds and whites and purples and the sky is a perfect blue with fluffy white clouds.

'So, what's the latest with the Cone Textiles case?' I ask.

He pauses for a moment, as if he's wondering whether he has the energy to tell me. 'They're really in the shit at the moment. I think they're going to go under, you know.'

'How come they're in so much difficulty?'

'It's a combination of factors, really, the biggest of which is the cheap clothing imports being dumped on the local market. The local textiles industry can't compete in that environment. The second is that some machinery imports got delayed. They're sitting in Durban, accruing costs but staying idle and producing no turnover. Quite soon, Zimbabwe will just be another raw cotton exporter, no different to any of these other half-wit countries.'

The car jolts.

'Ah! Bloody potholes!' shouts Dad. 'Fucking hell, look at the state of these roads! This never happened when your grandfather was Minister of Transport.'

He stops the car outside the shops and wanders into the entrance with his pale, skinny legs and loose blue shorts and jet-black hair. He opens the car door again holding a carton of Madison Red and a bottle of gin.

'Victor Cohen is a good chap, you know. Bloody furious with the government for how they've handled the situation. And quite right, too. At the last meeting, Cohen stood up at the table, pulled his pants down in front of the government and bank people and said, "You've fucked me up the bum! That's what you've done, fucked me up the bum!"'

The Christian messages drone on. Noreen Welch reads the news. Dad drives in silence, as if the radio is suddenly his only company. Sarah's face fills my mind. Butterflies fill my stomach. We turn into our driveway.

'So,' Dad says. 'Do you think Danny's beating his meat yet?' Sarah's beautiful face vanishes.

'I don't know, Dad. How should I know?'

He turns the engine off. 'I started beating my meat when I was nine,' he says. 'I think Danny's beating his meat.'

* * *

Dad warms the backs of his legs by the crackling fireplace.

'Dad,' I say. 'A boer rugby team from some place called Naboom-spruit is coming on tour to our school next week.'

'Ah, yes, the boers will be wondering what a black country looks like. They'll be wondering what's in store for them.' He puffs on his cigarette and laughs. 'Hopefully they won't panic when they see the state of our roads!'

'Or our electricity,' I add.

'When I was a young man, the apartheid regime seemed so invincible. We had no idea that things would ever change. It's remarkable. And you know, Nelson Mandela wouldn't be where he is now if it weren't for Bram Fischer. Hell, if Bram were here now he'd be so chuffed. It's really quite tragic that he didn't get to see what he died for. He knew bloody well at that time that he had to save Mandela's life at any cost, that one day the Nats would need someone they could negotiate with. It's happened just like he said it would.'

'Dad,' I say, 'are you, like, friends with Nelson Mandela and all the ANC people because of your time in the SACP?'

'I know a number of the ANC people very well. I once gave Thabo Mbeki a car.'

'Who's he?'

'One of the ANC people. He's quite high up.'

'So, what would Nelson Mandela do if you asked him for a farm?'

'He'd give me one, you know. He'd give me one! Of course, I would never ask, but he would help me out if I did.'

'So are you still a member of the communist party there?'

'Of course! I joined in the sixties and I've never relinquished my membership, although I'm not active anymore.

'You know, when I eventually returned home in the seventies, none of the law firms in Harare would touch me because of my links to the SACP. I only discovered this, actually, when a secretary who'd worked for me tried to get employment with another firm. She couldn't find work. Not with them, not with anyone.

'The secret service had informed her new employers that she was some kind of security risk because of her connection to me. When I heard about it I went to the Rhodesian authorities and I said, "Why have you created problems for this young woman? If you have an issue with me, come and speak to me." The man there didn't know how to respond; he seemed almost scared. I realised in that moment that I was seen as this very smart leftie, a bit danger-ous. I was a bit like Bram, you see.' He stops and looks at me. 'I've told you about Bram's history, haven't I?'

'Yes, of course you have,' I reply.

'Because Bram was a radical leftie, but he was also Afrikaner aristocracy. He was one of the Afrikaners' own; a contradiction. It was the same with me, really. My family was Rhodie-Rhodie. Ian Smith visited my house when I was a young man. My mother was always fond of him. And my father won his constituency hands-down every year he stood for election in Bulawayo. He was very wealthy, was Minister for Transport for a while, a pillar of the Rho-desian community. So I came from this well-to-do Rhodie family, which Rhodies knew and respected as part of their establishment. And yet I was this intimidatingly clever radical in their eyes. They half feared and despised me, and half revered me.'

His hands jut and thrust as he speaks. 'And what I find hilarious is that the coloureds are going to vote for the Nats. They've turned around and said, "Actually, we also hate the bloody kaffirs! We're one of you! We're Afrikaners too!" Bloody stupid Nats, they should have got the coloured vote when they could. It might have changed the game for them. Political suicide. Oh well, learn the hard way, boys.'

*　*　*

Sarah sits on the floor next to a pile of *Just Seventeen* magazines. Tears fill her grey-green eyes. Her Rapunzel-like hair drapes across her shoulders.

I picture Dan where I left him, holding the balsa wood in his hand, asking if I'd help him fix the engine mount again. I told him I'd be back soon but I know I won't be. He'll be sitting at my desk, sanding the mount by himself. He'll probably wait for me for some time and then go to his room and read.

Sarah rises. 'Thanks for coming over,' she says. She puts her head on my shoulder, 'I can't believe this has happened; I can't believe Geoff broke up with me,' she says.

I want to say something, but my mind is empty.

'Thanks Hayde, I really appreciate you coming down here.'

*　*　*

Dan stands barefoot in the garden. He holds a rugby ball in his hands.

'Hayde, sketch this!' He drop-kicks the ball perfectly through the centre of the forked msasa branches. 'I've been practising,' he says.

'You should try out for fly half.'

'Nah,' he says. 'I think I'm better suited to fullback.'

I grubber the ball to him across the brown-and-yellow winter grass.

Muffled music unexpectedly interrupts the sounds of the evening. A beige VW Golf turns into the driveway. 'Hold on Dan, I'll be back in a moment,' I say.

'What Is Love?' thumps out of the car's open windows.

Sarah jumps out and leaves her sister in the car. She seems excited.

She seems as though she hasn't just broken up with Geoff. 'Hayde, come, we're going on a trip!'

'What?'

'Just get in the car, Hayde. We're going on an adventure!'

'Hang on a second . . .'

I run to the forked msasa tree. Dan stands some yards from it with the ball under his arm. 'Hayde, are you coming to kick with me?' he asks.

'Sarah's just got here with her sister. She wants me to go somewhere with her.'

Dan seems startled.

I wait for him to speak, but he says nothing. He sets up the ball on the ground for a place kick.

I want to say sorry. I want to tell him that we can play another time. I want to say, 'I'm sorry I broke our promise about girls. I'm sorry we're older than nine; I wish we weren't.'

He kicks the ball perfectly through the trees again. 'Bye, Dan,' I say. 'See you later.'

'Bye, Hayde,' he says.

Sarah leans on the car. 'Come on, we're waiting!'

'What do I need to bring?'

'Just jump in!'

'What, like this? With shorts and no shoes on?'

She opens the door. 'Yes, quickly!'

Her sister turns up the volume on the stereo.

'What the hell does "calling Mr Raider, calling Mr Wrong, calling Mr Fame" mean?' I ask. 'Who the hell is Mr Fame? These lyrics are so pointless.'

The sisters shriek with laughter. 'Hayde, it's Mr Vain, dumb-ass!'

Sarah reaches into a bag and pulls out some clothes. 'Hayde, I've got some special things for you. We're dressing up today!' She holds up some silver spangled tights.

'I can't wear those!' I say.

'Oh yes you can!'

'Where are we going?' I ask.

'We're going to surprise Emma at the airport!'

Oh my God, how embarrassing! I think. *What if there's a school pre-fect there? Then he'll see me dressing up in this crazy dress and think I'm a 'moffie', and then I'll be in trouble.*

* * *

The South African rugby team stands in front of us with their hands on their hearts. They sing 'Die Stem'. Their hair is short and their bodies are dense with muscle. *Are they really just fifteen?* I wonder.

The referee puts his arm into the air and blows his whistle. I break from the scrum and throw myself at their scrum half. He brushes me off. *'Fok jou ma!'* he shouts.

I watch him from the ground for a moment. My teammates try to hold him, but he writhes against them like an angry fish. The ball falls to the ground. The South Africans surround it like a pack of dogs in some feeding frenzy.

The final whistle goes. The scoreboard is embarrassing.

We stand at the edge of the field and shake the South Africans' hands. Their captain smiles and speaks with his thick boer accent. 'You-guys-played-really-well-except-for-your-kaffirs.' He clamps my hand with his. His arm is dark. Next to his, mine looks like raw chicken.

You really shouldn't speak about your cousins like that, I think.

The South African coach clutches a beer in his giant paws. It seems like a Lego-beer. 'How tall is your coach?' I ask the fly half who said *'Fok jou ma'*.

'Ag,' he says, trying to find the English. 'I think six foot ten inches. He is big, but his heart is tiny. You know, in Afrikaans we say that people who have a small heart are kind.'

'He's even bigger than Mr Lamonde!'

'Yes, he is big, but there are many big people in South Africa.'

'Are you guys farmers?'

'Yes.'

'You know, when I was small my dad told me that if I drank cow piss I would become strong,' he says, rolling his r's. 'So one day I went to the barn and stood behind a cow and waited for it to piss. I took a whole big mouthful and swallowed. Then I went to my father and told him. I thought he was going to be really proud of me, but then he just laughed and laughed.'

His teammates stand by and listen with their grass-burned faces and short hair. They bellow big, deep laughs. Their frames are large. Their hands are rough like sandpaper. Their jaws are the jaws of men. They seem like hard people. Maybe one day they'll be the only whites left, because Africa is no place for sissies.

* * *

'Mrs Temlet,' I say. 'I really don't understand why you think Shakespeare is so great. *Macbeth* is so unrealistic. Doesn't Shakespeare know that people can be born evil, as well as become evil?'

'Oh, don't be silly, there's no such thing as evil,' she laughs. 'People are more complicated than that.'

'Ma'am, that's what all my English teachers always say. But some people really are just evil. You can see it if you look hard enough. Just watch the playground at breaktime. Some people are like evil amoebas. They just like being evil for its own sake, as though evil is a goal in and of itself. Some people are as indifferent to suffering as cats are.'

She seems to ignore me.

'And ma'am,' I go on. 'What's the point of studying something so old fashioned? I don't understand any of the English Shakespeare writes. Why can't we study Agatha Christie? She has interesting things to say about people too.'

'Oh, for goodness' sake! Like what?'

'Well, for example, all the bad guys are invisible. They hide in plain sight. They're camouflaged as normal people but they're actually monsters inside. And it's scary because not all of us have Poirot's secret powers. Most of us are just toyed with by people who see us as mice. Isn't that an important thing to think about?'

She walks off. I want to say, 'Ma'am, *The Merchant of Venice* has a crap plot. It's so lame to hinge a story on someone being unable to accurately weigh a pound of flesh.'

I want to write a paragraph into *The Merchant of Venice*. Hercule Poirot will sit with Hastings in the courtroom watching Shylock's case unfold.

He will turn to Hastings. 'This is the most ridiculous case I have ever seen, Hastings. *Sacré bleu*, this judge is a fool! Nothing in life is accurate or certain: a pound of flesh can be taken to three significant figures with a triple beam balance. He is a man most stupid, Hastings. What more does he want? Are three significant figures not sufficient? If we are to pursue certainty, like this man suggests, then we will only swing from one barbarism to another. When you go to a café, Hastings, and ask for a cake, does the manager come to you and say, "Excuse me, monsieur, I regret to inform you that we cannot provide it to you because we are unable to weigh the recipe's flour to an infinite number of decimal places"? Is that the madness this judge wants in life?'

And then Hastings will turn to Poirot and say, 'Yes, I say, Poirot, that's a good point! And blimey, can you understand a single word of what's being said in this trial? It's like they're all speaking in some kind of pidgin Teutonic dialect. It's impossible to decipher. And to think we're in Venice where one would've thought the locals would be speaking in Italian. Most peculiar.'

And then Poirot will say, 'Yes, Hastings, the fault is not with you but with these imbeciles. They are just bluffing, trying to make it seem like there are hidden depths to their words. But they do not fool me, Hastings; they do not fool the little grey cells.'

I wish I had a time machine. Because if I did, I'd transport

Shakespeare to Lagos. And then he'd be able to read *The Merchant of Venice* to all the Grahams. *That would be genius!* I think to myself, *Because it would punish the savages for being savages, and punish Shakespeare for being Shakespeare!* I would just sit Shakespeare down on a chair among the savages and say, 'Savages, today we are going to have a reading by Mr Shakespeare. He will be telling you a very long story called *The Merchant of Venice.*' Then I'd hand Shakespeare a manuscript and say, 'Here, you can read from this . . . edited version. I've taken the liberty of introducing one H Poirot to perform the cross-examination, and the court is now presided over by one Chief Justice E Blackadder.'

And then I'd turn to the savages and say, 'And don't let me catch any of you talking because, you see that man, up there on that tower with his Uzi? He'll drop you dead before you can think, "What the hell is Dolph Lundgren doing in Lagos?"'

Mrs Temlet walks over to my desk and throws an almost-empty paper onto it. 'Hayden,' she says, 'this is the lowest mark I have ever given anyone.'

I smile. 'Thank you, ma'am. That means a lot.'

* * *

The smell of the old black leather seats in Steve's dad's car reminds me of church when I was seven years old. In the window, I can almost see the Christian-happy people giving me tea and biscuits on the lawn of that old church, as if that moment in time is hovering in the dancing reflections, as if Steve had never left for Britain.

I wonder if someday Sarah will fancy me. Maybe when I'm older and manlier and handsome. But maybe I'll never be handsome; maybe I'll be like this forever. But if I did become handsome, then I'd marry her.

And I wish I was closer to Dan.

I wish he could still cry in front of me like he used to.

He must think I'm weak that this girl comes round to the house and gets me to fix her bicycle. But if he only knew how magical I felt about her, he'd forgive me.

We turn onto the winding road that takes us down into the valley. The hills are yellows and browns in the fading light. We glide over the slopes and through the mopane trees. Now and then, yellow-billed hornbills glide through the warm air with their peculiar centre of gravity.

The lake glimmers like crude oil and silver in the distance. A guide with sun-battered skin greets us at the water's edge wearing veldskoen and khaki shorts. 'Let me take those bags,' he says to us.

The speedboat whooshes across the water. The wind seems almost oily as it flaps my hair about. In the distance, a line of hazy mountains rises up from the green-and-grey water. Beige dots shimmer on the horizon. Slowly they grow into an island and reveal a veranda nestled among trees. We climb out of the boat. A lady at reception shows us to a pair of thatched huts. Across the water a speedboat pulls a water skier behind it.

The air fills with the smell of roasting potato and leaves and dust. In the falling darkness, we make our way to the open-air dining room.

A guide comes to our table. Insects flutter above his head. 'So, what activities do you guys want to do tomorrow? We've got Drew doing the early morning game walk and a fishing trip going out after breakfast.'

'I like the sound of the early game walk,' says Steve's dad, Phil.

'Great guns. I'll put you down for that. Our guy will come and wake you at quarter to five. Get a good night's rest if you can.'

'Well, we're off to bed now. We'll be fresh and ready tomorrow.'

The guide walks off. 'Was that you water skiing on the lake this evening?' I call after him.

He stops. 'Yeah, it was beautiful. Like glass out there, hey.'

'But weren't you scared of getting eaten by a croc? What if you'd come off close to shore where they wait? I saw three huge ones there this afternoon.'

He laughs as he moves off to the next table. 'The trick is not to come off, hey!'

Insects screech in the night as our knives squeak on our plates. 'Alright, time for bed,' says Phil. He rises to his feet and walks into the darkness with Steve and me trailing behind him. 'Steve, it's barely nine o'clock!' I whisper.

Steve puts his finger to his lips. 'Just come with me for now. Don't make my dad angry!'

We follow Phil to his room and say our goodnights. 'Come on, let's go to the bar for a bit,' I say. 'I can't sleep this early.'

Before long we find ourselves at the small thatched bar. The area is empty except for two tall men with overflowing stomachs and tiny shorts. We sit down on some stools near to them. Insects fly about in the light and bash themselves into the light bulb directly above us.

'What's it like being at school in the UK?' I ask Steve.

'It's horrible. I hate it. I wish I could leave.'

'But they don't beat you and stuff, and you don't have to wear a uniform! Surely it's amazing?'

'I thought it was going to be amazing, but the feeling lasted about three days. Now I go to bed at night wishing that they had the cane there. The way those guys treat teachers . . . you just wouldn't believe it, hey, no respect. It's like the students run the school instead of the teachers, like a prison being run by criminals.'

It hits me: how could I be so stupid as to believe that if a school stopped being horrible to its students, the students themselves would stop being horrible to one other?

It's as though the British Government thinks that all children are good and that they only do bad things because of the system. And then, by that logic, if they remove discipline and bad teachers . . . voila, all children will be good! It's as though the British have learned about evil from Mrs Temlet.

One of the men interrupts us. 'Hey, you boys, isn't it past your bed time?'

We laugh shyly, as if to say, 'Yes, Mr Big Scary Rhodie, you're right, we're not supposed to be here.'

He turns to the guy behind the bar. 'Barman,' he says. 'Get these two boys a drink or ten.'

We glug down the first round. The Big Scary Rhodie seems impressed. 'Barman!' he says. 'Get these guys another round of drinks. Something stronger this time, Jack Daniels and . . .'

'I know . . . cream soda!' shouts his friend.

Steve downs the dark-green goo and then looks momentarily ill. 'Barman, more Jack Daniels and cream soda!' cries the Big Scary Rhodie.

The world tilts back and forth. The Big Scary Rhodie downs a shot. 'Eish,' he groans. 'My mouth feels like the inside of a Greek bus driver's glove.'

His friend erupts with laughter. I snort the Jack Daniels out of my nose. '*Shamwari*,' the Big Scary Rhodie shouts to the barman, 'some tequila and Drambuie!' Then to us, 'Do you guys know how to play match stick?'

The world in front of me blurs and turns. 'Steve, I'm going to vomit.'

Steve holds his watch up to my eyeball. 'We should get to bed now. We have to be up in three hours.'

We stumble through the darkness back to our beds. I lay my head down on the pillow. It seems like I've only blinked when a sharp knocking at the door wakes me. 'I don't want to go on this walk,' I say to Steve. 'I'm going to puke.'

'No, Hayde, we've got to go!'

I try to sit up but flop back down. 'Steve, why do you always have to be a goodie-goodie?'

He pulls at my arm. 'Get up!' he says.

The guide wears tight khaki shorts and veldskoen. Phil inspects our sleepy faces and furry eyeballs. 'You guys are looking worse for wear. Not used to early starts, hey!'

The guide walks ahead of us with his gun and rustles through the buffalo grass. I wonder if I'll vomit on my shoes. The blackness of the night begins to melt away. I want to lie down and curl up in a bush. *I'll just look at my feet until this is over*, I think.

I gag, but nothing comes up from my poisoned stomach.

Steve comes over to me. 'Hayde, what are you doing!' he whispers angrily.

'I can't help it, Steve, it's a frickin' reflex!' I shout-whisper back.

'Well, hold it in until we get back.'

The guide's veldskoen move one foot in front of the other. *Maybe his veldskoen will hypnotise me*, I think. *Maybe I can just watch them until I find myself at home again.*

'Look here,' the guide says, pointing to the dust. 'Fresh lion spoor. Follow me as quietly as you can.'

He creeps ahead some metres. He points. 'The pride's under that tree,' he says. The cats get to their feet and drift into the distance.

Please don't vomit! Please don't vomit! I think.

A rustling sound to my left startles me. My gaze flicks to a lion crouching in a nearby thicket. Its paws are huge. Its yellow eyes fix themselves on me.

'Don't run!' yells the guide.

I want to run, but I'm frozen, like someone cut the wire connecting my brain to my legs.

For a moment it remains there. Then the thuggish body springs from its crouch. I wait for it to thump me into the dust. But then it's gone. Gone like it was never there, gone without so much as a swaying branch.

The guide's gun remains fixed at the thicket.

'You have *no idea* how lucky you've all just been,' he says. 'Someone's morning nap got cut short and he isn't happy about it.'

The lion roars from somewhere in the dense bush. Its guttural vibrations penetrate my bones.

The guide breaks into a smile. 'That retreat upset his pride a bit! These predators are all ego, hey.'

My hangover is gone. *Result!* I think.

The guide lowers his gun and seems to relax. 'We were just on the edge of its attack radius, you know, which is why it hesitated before making a decision. It would have killed someone if we'd been half a metre closer.'

'But wouldn't you have just shot it?' I ask.

'Easier said than done at that range. And remember, they don't come at you straight; they come in a circular path. Your chances of hitting a target like that after a sudden fright are poor. And from that distance you've got no more than two seconds to raise your gun, aim and fire.'

'So we were lucky?' I say.

'Put it this way,' he says. 'When I get back, I'm going to be having a stiff Scotch with my porridge.'

We plod along in the growing heat. *He's right*, I think. *Predators are all ego.*

What if I had been killed? Mum would have got a call saying, 'Hullo, Mrs Eastwood, your son has unfortunately been eaten by a lion.'

But would the lion have actually dared to eat my Jack-Daniels-and-cream-soda-poisoned stomach? And if it had eaten me and torn my stomach open, Phil would probably have come and seen exactly what was in my stomach and realised I'd bunked out last night. And that would have been embarrassing. But then what would the embarrassment matter if I was dead?

And if I had died, who would have missed me the most? Would it have been my family? Or would it have been Sarah?

*   *   *

I put *The ABC Murders* down and glimpse the bright afternoon sun through the window baking the sandpit outside. Over and over, Poirot's words run through my mind. A fly settles on your fore-head, maddening you with its tickling until you kill it, because it's just that: a fly.

— 115 —

Over and over, Poirot tortures me with his observations.

Is everyone capable of that evil? Is there a filter in our brains? One that allows us to love our own but hate the *other*? And if there is such a filter, does it mean that even the most moral and righteous of us can pass someone through that filter and turn a human into a fly?

It worries me that we're all potential killers, and that I too am just a killer in waiting.

'Hayde, how about a game of table tennis?' asks Dan.

The msasa trees cast speckled shade onto the table. 'Dan, have you ever read any Poirot books?'

'Yes. They're quite good, I suppose.'

'Do you think Agatha Christie understands how people work? Or do you think her stories are shallow?'

'Agatha Christie's too female for my tastes. Sherlock Holmes uses the power of reason, logic and evidence. But Poirot isn't realistic; he thinks like a woman, always focusing on psychology. A guy would never think like that.'

'I just wonder sometimes about Agatha Christie's idea of evil. Reading *Macbeth*, you'd think there was no such thing.'

'Yeah, but what about King Lear? He's basically evil.'

'*King Lear?* That book's not even on the set list! Why are you reading *that*?'

'I just picked it up in the library the other day.'

'So, you mean, basically, that whenever I ask my teachers about this stuff, and they say, "Nobody's born evil, blah, blah", they just haven't really read Shakespeare properly? Because the only answers they ever give me are about *Macbeth*.'

'Yeah, Hayde, basically. Now on to serious matters: throw for serve!'

Beebs appears. 'Hayde, Sarah's on the phone for you.'

'Okay, thanks Beebs. Dan, hold on, I'll be back in a moment.' I plonk my bat down on the table and trot away.

'Hi, Hayde,' says Sarah. 'How are you?'

'I'm good. Can I call you back later when the sun's set?'

'Ah, come on, Hayde! It's practically dark outside already.'

'I wanted to finish my game with Dan while there's still light.'

'Come on, Hayde! How was your day?'

Guilt engulfs me, but I try to wish it away. 'It was good. Didn't get into any trouble. You?'

'I came first in English Literature! I love Miss George so much. She's so inspiring.'

'Well done, Sare, that's great! I really can't remember the last time I did well in English.'

'How come?'

'I don't know. I always feel like people just make stuff up that isn't even there. And then when I do the same and make stuff up, everyone thinks I'm talking rubbish.'

'Hayde, you probably are talking rubbish . . . Hey, can you do me a favour?'

'Yeah, of course.'

'My bike's got a flat tyre. Do you think you could fix it?'

'Yeah, sure, when would work for you?'

When I finally return outside the garden is silent and dark. Nightjars are already calling. Dan is gone.

1996

Chapter 11

Mr Lamonde Senior seems like he's trying to speak us to death. The heat of the day turns my bones into lead. 'Eastwood, what's wrong with you, man!' he yells.

I sit up bolt straight. 'Sorry, sir. I'm paying attention now.'

'Well, just stop staring off into the distance like that. Anyone would think you're in love!'

A muffled snigger comes from the class. I want to say, 'Yes, sir, I am in love. In love with someone who doesn't love me.'

Adrian turns to me. 'Beastflow, what's going on with you, man? You're not all there.'

I want to tell him the truth. I want to shout, 'Adrian, I just can't stop thinking about her every day, all day, all the time. And I don't even know why anymore. I don't even know what's happening in my brain. It's like my whole life would be perfect if only she'd like me back. And I'm so ashamed that everything feels so empty without her.'

Adrian looks at me like he's looking into me and through me, like he's waiting for me to tell him why I've become this zombie-creature. I sense I ought to say something. 'Hayde,' he says. 'It's been two years now. It's too much.'

I want to say something, anything, but I'm too ashamed to.

* * *

Miles giggles and runs about the sitting room floor. He kicks a rubber ball and chases after it. 'I'm going to get you, Truck-driver!' I shout. He squeals and his pocket-wrestler legs scamper behind Dad's chair.

Dad puts out his cigarette and lights another one. 'Please keep it down, Hayde.'

'Hayde,' calls Mum. 'Won't you go and get Dan and Beebs? Grub's up in the dining room.'

Dad looks up from his paper. 'I got a call from Roman the other day. His daughter needs a place to stay next month. You'll enjoy meeting her, I'm sure.'

'Who's Roman?' I ask.

'Old friend from university in South Africa. Lives in London now. Horribly tortured by the apartheid police in the seventies. His mother smuggled him out of the Warsaw ghetto in a sack of oranges when he was just a toddler. Tough bugger . . . Sophie, his daughter, has just finished studying French and journalism.'

'When's she coming?'

'I must check with Roman. End of the month, I think.'

Mum appears at the door again. 'Are you guys coming for dinner or aren't you?'

'Annette, for God's sake, can't you see I'm in the middle of speaking!'

'Fine,' she says. 'Eat when you're ready.'

'Where was I before your mother interrupted me?'

'Argh!' I hear echoing down the hallway. One of the dogs yelps. I hear scuttling paws. 'You fucking animals!'

Mum comes to the door again.

'What?' I ask.

'Stompie's just jumped up on the table and eaten the fucking roast beef. That's what. And now my toe's sore because I kicked him. And of course he's completely bloody fine!'

'For Christ's sake, Annette!' shouts Dad. 'Why don't you pay attention? You know what the dogs are like!'

'Anthony, I've asked you to come through twice now. You want me to just sit at the table by myself, do you?'

'Why not? What's it matter if we're there with you? We'll come through when we're ready. Honestly, I don't know what's wrong with you sometimes.'

Dan appears at the door with Beebs. 'Mum, where's supper?' he asks.

Mum limps off. 'In Stompie,' she says.

*   *   *

Mum's piano plays in the distance. Dan walks in to my room doing his tie. 'Hayde, I don't suppose you have a spare geography project lying around, do you?'

'Unlikely. When does it need to be in by?'

'Forty-five minutes' time.'

'And how far have you got?'

'I wrote down the title when I woke up. But I haven't had time to do the rest.'

I shake my head. 'I did a project last year on something touristy. Maybe we can just find that on the computer and print it out?'

We go to Dad's study and turn on his computer. Dan manically taps at the keys. All we find are Dad's naked women. Dan's eyes well up. 'Now what am I going to do?'

We return to my room. I reach above my cupboard and bring down a box of old school notes. We scatter the papers on the floor and scrabble through them frantically.

'Got it!' Dan shouts.

'What?'

He flips through the dog-eared pages of something I did a year ago. I inspect the pages over his shoulder.

'Dan, they're full of teacher's comments.'

He bunches them together. 'Ah, don't worry about that!'

'And what about the last page? It says "by Hayden Eastwood".'

'Details, Hayde, details.'

He stuffs the papers into his rucksack and hurries out of the room.

*   *   *

Light shines through the window and illuminates the dust floating in the air. The radio whines its weekend Christian messages. Tiny particles float and swirl in the light with random motion. And yet the drifting isn't random. Nothing is random. Everything in the universe is cause and effect.

I hold the tailplane up and inspect its edges. I sand it some more.

My stomach fills with a sense of dread. Sarah will never want to be with me. Sometimes I wonder if my life is worth anything at all without her.

Dan steps in. 'Hayde, can you help me with something?'

I follow him to his room. 'Would you hold this bar straight while I mark it for drilling?'

'What are you doing?'

'I'm making a pull-up bar. I need to get stronger for pole vault. Just hold the bar over here.'

He marks the wall with a grey pencil. 'Drill, please,' he says.

A penetrating whine fills the room. I block my ears. A brilliant blood-red dust sprinkles to the floor. Dan fiddles with the iron bar and its mounting brackets. I hand him a screwdriver. He presses it into a screw and puts his weight into it. He jumps onto his new bar and does some pull-ups.

'Tell me, what did you do about the red marks on "your" assignment?' I ask.

He drops down with an involuntary snigger. 'I just cut them out with scissors.'

'And what about the bit that said "by Hayden Eastwood"?'

'I just cut out "Hayden" so it read "by _____ Eastwood".'

I snort a laugh. 'And you think she'll accept that?'

'You know these teachers, Hayde, they're so stupid. You can get away with so much.'

* * *

I peel off my rugby jersey and walk to the kitchen and open the fridge. Dan sits at the counter barefoot in his rugby shorts.

'Any news on the project?' I ask.

'No, but I did get an interesting result for biology. I handed in nothing all term, so I got zero for my overall coursework result and was pretty worried about what the Divisional Head would say about it. But I came first, with one hundred percent, in the exams, so my score averages to a C. Mr Guildford just looked at me and shook his head and said, "I don't know what to do with you."'

'Hayden,' Mum calls in the distance, 'Phone for you. It's Sarah.'

'Sorry Dan, give me a moment.'

I pick up the phone. 'Sarah?'

'Hayde, can I ask your advice?' she says.

'Go on . . .'

'I've just had the biggest fight with my mum. She said I've already been out too much this month, and that I can't go to Christine's party on Friday.'

'Sorry to hear that.'

'I was just like, "Hayden doesn't have any stupid rules about having to be home all the time." And Mum was like, "Well, we don't run our house like that! We actually have rules here! Blah, blah, blah . . .".'

'Yeah,' I respond. 'My folks are definitely quite different about rules.'

'I know. It just gets me down sometimes. I just feel like my mum's always trying to control me. I wish she could just be more like your mum sometimes.'

Dan stands next to me unexpectedly. He holds a bat in his hand and taps it against his leg.

I cover the receiver with my hand. 'Dan, I'm on the phone, I'll come and find you in a second . . .'

He walks off. A sinking feeling fills my stomach.

* * *

Dan sits under a nearby tree, quiet and stony-faced. The school egrets peck at the perfect grass behind him.

'Why are you looking so bleak?' I ask.

'I just had geography. Mrs Bardwell crapped all over me for my project.'

'What did she say?'

'Ag, she just went off on some tangent about Judgment Day.'

'What was your punishment?'

'Not that much actually. She gave me a double detention and demoted me to Set Two. But the crazy thing is that she thought it was my work. Rory got in far worse trouble than I did.'

'Why, what had he done?'

'He hadn't done his project either, so he did an internet search and printed the first page he landed on. He gave the printout to Mrs Bardwell without even reading it. The work was signed by the original author. Mrs Bardwell was screaming, "At least Daniel has handed in his own work!"'

I chortle. 'That's kind of like a victory!'

Dan's glum face breaks into a partial smile. He wipes a tear away. 'Yeah, I suppose so.'

* * *

Mr Desai stands in front of us speaking Bulawayan-Indian. 'Okay, guys, before I get on to other issues,' he says, 'I need to raise a very important issue.'

The wall of boys watch him in silence.

'A lot of guys have been sent to me for cheating in tests this week. Guys, that's not good enough! It's very disappointing! I don't want to hear stories like that!' He points. 'You can ask Matsinde what happened when I saw him last week. Ha! He will tell you, in fact, that I was quite harsh with him.'

He says the word 'harsh' like he's breathing fire with it: 'haaaaaarrrshhhhhh!'

I think, *Eastwood, note to self: don't cheat, otherwise Mr Desai will be fire-breathingly harsh with your backside.*

We shuffle out of the echoing room and hurry to French. Mr Lamonde Senior sits at his table poring over his papers. '*Asseyez vous,*' he says. 'I have your test results with me. I see very few of you made any effort to learn the material. Most of these papers are a disgrace.'

He stands perfectly straight, his oiled-down white hair, immaculate. 'And what's more, some of you have failed despite the fact that you clearly cheated. Ewing! Rawling! Why do you have the same mistakes as Eastwood?'

'Um, I copied from Ewing, sir,' Adrian finally says.

'And I copied from Eastwood, sir,' adds Ewing.

'This is outrageous!' blares Mr Lamonde.

'Sorry, sir,' they say, hanging their heads low. 'Sorry.'

'And Eastwood!' shouts Mr Lamonde again, 'why were you allowing someone to copy you? Talk about the blind leading the blind! I've had enough of this!'

He scribbles a note on some paper. 'Here. Go to Mr Desai and give this to him, the three of you.'

The three of us!

'Sir, I didn't cheat!' I protest.

'Eastwood, cheating is a two-way process. If you allowed them to copy, you cheated!'

Our feet clip-clop down the cold cement corridors. We knock at Mr Desai's door.

'Yes, guys, what can I do for you?'

'Sir . . . um, we've come to get beaten.'

'Oh really, what for?'

'Um . . . for cheating, sir.'

Mr Desai places his hand over his face. 'Ahh, guys, I've just spoken to you about that twenty minutes ago.'

'Yes, sir.'

'I mean really, guys, you don't want to take me seriously, ha? You know I'm going to be harsh with you, ha?'

'Nings first,' I say.

Adrian closes the door behind him. Mr Desai breathes fire onto his backside.

I turn to Adam. 'That sounds haaarrrssshhhhh!' I say.

I try to think of the minutes ahead when it'll be over, when all that'll matter is that I have a good story to tell Sarah. And if she laughs, then it'll have been worth it.

*　*　*

Mr Kyle stands on the stage in his long Dracula robe. 'Would the following boys please see me after assembly: H Eastwood, G Featherstone.' I wait for more names, but today he calls only ours.

We wait outside Mr Kyle's office. The corridor smells of tobacco and carpets. The secretaries' typewriters cluck in the background.

'Come in,' says a voice.

Mr Kyle's withered face peers at us. He lights his pipe and blows purple-grey smoke into the air. 'I've had reports from some staff that neither of you have been raising your hats to greet teachers in the corridors of late. Why not?'

I wait for Geoff to say something, but he stays quiet. 'Um, sir,' I say. 'I think that maybe the problem is that I just didn't notice those teachers, sir, because if I had I would definitely have greeted them thoroughly, sir.'

'So why didn't you notice them?'

'I don't know, sir. Sometimes I just think about things and don't really notice what's happening around me, sir.'

'Like what kind of things?'

'I don't know, sir. Like important things to do with school, sir. Like . . . *The Merchant of Venice*, sir . . . sometimes I think about the nature of evil.'

The corner of his mouth rises, like he's trying to hide the slightest of smiles. 'The nature of evil? That's what the Bible is there to teach you. Read more of it.'

'Yes, sir.'

'And don't you think you ought to pay more attention to what's happening around you in life?'

'Yes, sir. From now on, I'll pay much more attention, sir.'

'And you?' he says, penetrating Geoff with his translucent gaze.

'Yes, sir, me too, sir, like Eastwood, sir.'

'Alright, don't let me have to speak to you about this again. Off you go.'

*   *   *

Dan places the rugby ball on the grass in front of him. Behind him, the trees tower their lightning-bolt branches into the darkening sky. He takes some paces back, runs at the ball and strikes it through the air in a graceful parabola. It bisects the fork in the msasa tree.

'Nice one, Dan!' I shout. 'You struck that well.'

'It's easy. Make sure you keep your head down in the run-up. Don't take your eye off the patch of ground under the ball. Not even after you strike.'

Dan kneels on the ground and balances the ball once more on the yellowing grass.

'Hi, guys!' I hear to my left. Sarah jogs towards us across the lawn. 'I was close by and thought I'd say hi!'

She walks up to Dan. 'Hi, Dan. How are you?'

Dan looks at her like he's startled, like he's just seen the only woman in the universe climb out of a space ship.

He shakes her hand. 'Hi,' he says. 'Fine thanks.'

'So are you guys going to kick your ball around or make me tea?'

Dan boots the ball away. 'I'll make some tea.'

I balance the ball on its tip and try to kick it like Dan showed me. It swerves into the bushes. Sarah laughs, 'Nice one, Hayde. Super accurate, hey!'

* * *

Dan and his friend Rory sit on the carpet in his room. They move plastic goblin-like creatures about on a board. 'Dan, what game are you playing?' I ask.

'*Dungeons and Dragons.* Do you want to play?'

'Ah thanks, I'd like to but I'm going for a walk.'

'Really? Who with?'

I pause for a moment. 'Sarah.'

He looks at me like he might say something. The gate bell rings. 'I'll get that,' I say. 'Probably my lift.'

A car I've never seen before idles outside. A guy I don't recognise sits in the driver's seat. With his ape jaw and his stylish cap he seems like the handsome kind who would kill me in a fight in three seconds.

Sarah rolls down a window. 'Hayde, are you ready to go?'

I want to shout, 'What the hell is this? And who the hell is this Neanderthal? I mean, I know he looks as if he plays rugby for New Zealand and everything, but really, what am I going to talk to him about?'

The boy gets out of his car. He smiles and grips my hand. 'Howzit, I'm Mark,' he says.

* * *

I pop a pimple on my chest and smear pus on the mirror in front of me. Sometimes I imagine myself dead. And I imagine how she'd react, or what she'd think if she saw my dead body. I tell myself that she'd be devastated, that seeing my lifeless face would make her see that she'd been in love with me all this time. She would see the beauty of what she'd lost in me, and she'd mourn me for some time.

I imagine her finding me sitting in the car, dead. I imagine the soundtrack to it: The Beatles, 'Let It Be'. I would dress well to look as good as possible in death. It might help her realise what she'd lost.

Stop. You're going mad! I think. *If you were dead you wouldn't be there to see all that. Idiot!*

I face my wardrobe. I punch the back of it. The bang echoes through the room. My knuckles sting. The sting infuriates me. I punch again but harder this time. The wood splinters. Blood-prints of my knuckles force themselves into the jagged cracks. I study the flaps of torn skin. I curl into a ball on my bed and cry uncontrollably. I feel as though my mind has lost control of my body. My body convulses and heaves like it's someone else's. That body, the one I was connected to earlier in the day, seems to tingle and burn. But it tingles and burns like it's not mine, like I only borrowed it from someone.

Someone knocks at the door. 'Hayde,' calls Mum. 'What have you been hammering at this time of night?'

'I'm just fixing my bicycle, Mum.'

'Well, when you have a moment can you come and do some Miles-time? I've got to sew Beebs's ballet costumes, and Miles wants to play.'

'Coming, Mum. Just give me a few minutes.'

I pick myself off my bed. *Something has to change*, I think. *Something has to change.*

* * *

The washing machine's metallic whir reverberates into my bedroom. A spider moves across the white ceiling above me. I watch it edge towards the wall. The old eel slithers and slides in my stomach. I wish it was there because of school. Then I'd be able to get rid of it by getting beaten, or doing manual labour, or going to detention, or just doing the work I was supposed to do. But this eel is different. It seems colder and bigger. It seems like it's there all the time and like it might just be there forever. This eel is poisonous.

I open *Moby-Dick* and read a paragraph. I stop. What was it that I read? *Eastwood, tell yourself what you've just read.* I remember nothing of it. *You mean to tell me you haven't absorbed a single scrap of information from that whole paragraph?*

I read the paragraph again. Someone knocks at the door. 'Yeah, what is it?' I call.

'Hayde, I want you to come and say hullo to Sophie.'

I unlock my door. Mum stands next to a young woman. Her face seems to transmit a peaceful happiness. She smiles. 'Hullo!' she says in a husky English voice. 'You must be Hayde!'

I extend my hand to her, but she brushes it aside and hugs me.

'Hayde,' says Mum. 'Emily's bringing some tea to the veranda in a mo'. Why don't you join us?'

The eel metamorphoses into a worm. Mum sits on a bamboo chair and pours a cup of tea. Sophie gestures to my shorts. 'So, what's going on with those? They're hilarious!'

'Oh, these?' I say. 'They're school shorts.'

'You're kidding me! You wear grey shorts as part of your uniform?'

'Yes. And long grey socks up to my knees.'

She laughs but it seems like she's trying not to. 'Oh God, that's just so funny. Please show me.'

'How long are you here for?' I ask.

'Oh, two weeks or so. I've just finished university and thought I'd take off some time to figure out what to do with myself.'

'Well, you'll definitely see me in a full outfit then.'

'I hope so,' she says. 'What kind of a school makes you wear clothes like that?'

'Let's just say it's an old-fashioned school.'

'Is it mostly white guys?'

'Yeah, mostly. Maybe sixty percent. The rest are ministers' kids, Indians, mixed-race guys.'

* * *

I ride up the driveway and put my bike at the kitchen door. Emily washes dishes. 'Hi, Haydie,' she calls.

'Hi, Emily,' I answer.

I open the fridge and get the milk out. Sophie bursts into laughter. 'Oh my God, I can't believe your uniform!'

'I know, it's arb,' I agree.

'Arb? What does that mean?'

'Don't you use that word in England?'

'No,' she says. 'Never heard it before.'

'It's short for "arbitrary". If you describe someone as "arb", it means they're, you know, little better than a beast.'

'Arb! That's so funny. Need to remember that one . . . And you use phrases like "little better than a beast"! What on earth are you smoking, man?'

'Oh, I got that sentence from my friend Adrian. I think he stole it from *The Merchant of Venice*. He uses sentences like that when he's talking to teachers about people like me.'

'Do you often quote Shakespeare?'

'Good God, no! I hate Shakespeare! He's basically ruined my life.'

She giggles. 'Oh my God, you're too much!'

Her mood is infectious. I feel unexpectedly pleased that she laughs at my humour.

'Do you have a girlfriend?' she asks.

'No,' I say. 'It's complicated. There's this girl I like, but she doesn't like me back.'

'So why don't you bin her then? Seriously, man, life's too short. Get another one. One who appreciates you.'

'Easier said than done.'

'No, it's not! It's easy! Don't be ridiculous!'

*   *   *

Peculiar grunting sounds come from behind Dan's bedroom door. I knock.

'Come in,' Dan says.

His arms are spread on his pull-up bar and his body heaves up and down. Sweat trickles down his back. The outside light casts shadows across his glistening body. Man's hair grows from his legs. His frame is thickening. The muscles on his back flex and striate as he extends and contracts his arms. At fifteen he's becoming a man.

'Dan, do you want to come and kick the rugby ball with me?'

He continues with his pull-ups. 'Thanks, Hayde. I'm heading off to Rory's in a second to play *Wolfenstein 3D*. Maybe when I get back.'

My stomach reacts to his words. 'Oh, okay, see you later.'

Sophie comes in behind me. 'Two things: Hayde, there's a phone call for you. And do either of you guys want to come and talk to me on the veranda while I have some coffee?'

I trundle down the passageway and lift the receiver. 'Hayde,' says Sarah, 'Can you do me a big favour? The chain's got really loose on my bike and keeps coming off. Do you think you could have a look at it today?'

'Sorry, today's not good,' I say. 'Perhaps another day.'

'What about tomorrow?'

'Well, I promised Sophie we'd go to the botanical gardens. Sorry. Can't someone else help?'

Sophie raises a cup of coffee to my face. She whispers, 'Don't take any shit!'

*   *   *

The phone rings. It's Sarah.

'Hayde, you won't believe it but Mark and I broke up today.'

'I'm so, so sorry. What on earth happened? I thought you guys were going well?'

'I'll explain it all when I see you. What are you doing now? I'd really appreciate a visit if you wouldn't mind coming over. I need some company.'

'I'll come in an hour or two. I promised Sophie I'd help her with a job application.'

'Hayde, please. I really need you now.'

I go to her house and find her sitting on the floor in her room.

'What happened?' I ask.

'We just weren't right for each other. We had nothing to talk about. It was getting me down being with someone I could hardly talk to.'

'You don't seem that upset.'

'No, not really.'

'Oh, okay. So positive outcome. Did I really need to come down here?'

'Hayde, do you think we'll ever be more than friends?'

'What? You're the one who's always talking about being friends. And I agree with you. We should be. We're probably not right for each other.'

She walks over to me. Her Rapunzel hair drapes across her shoulders. Our gazes lock. I expect her to look away, but she looks straight back at me. I move my head closer to hers. She reaches forward slightly. Without thinking, I kiss her on the lips.

Chapter 12

Bob Marley plays on Sarah's stereo. She puts down her copy of *Vogue*. 'Hayde, let's have a skinny dip!'

'Are you sure there's nobody else here?'

'Yes, of course I'm sure. They're all playing golf.'

I walk about naked at the water's edge. The trees seem to sway lethargically in the wind. Sarah slips her hand into mine. 'Come on, Hayde, let's jump in together.'

'Okay, one . . . two . . .'

A loud scream pierces the air. Sarah's mother runs out of the house waving her hands in the air and shrieking.

I grab my underpants from the water's edge and run behind the house where nobody can see me.

'What the bloody hell do you think you're doing?!' screams her mum. 'We just can't trust you to do anything on your own, can we?'

A door clangs shut. Sarah and her mother shout at each other. I catch my breath and gather my thoughts. Should I come out and explain myself standing in my underpants?

No.

I scramble over the wall and drop down onto the road. Toddlers tug on their mothers' dresses and point at me. Men stare.

I pretend that I'm normal, that there's nothing wrong with a naked white boy running through suburbia with nothing to guard his dignity but a pair of frayed old Y-fronts.

* * *

Adrian and I stop outside the maths classroom. Adrian turns to me. 'So Hayde, what's going on? How long have you been seeing her?'

'I'm not sure, a couple of months, officially.'

The new teacher motions for us to enter. He stands a head taller than us. His bones are large and his forearms long and wide. The top part of his back is straight, but the bottom part hinges so that he stoops over like a baboon. His jaw is unusually square. He looks as if he's been sewn together from the parts of several men, one of whom is seven feet tall to account for his overly large head. With his short hair he looks like Frankenstein's monster. The only thing he needs is a giant bolt through his neck.

On the board he chalks four big Cs, one beneath the other. He turns to us as if he'll say something but then turns back to the board and finishes his words.

'Christianity.'

'Cold showers.'

'Corporal punishment.'

'Cricket.'

'I am Mr Pollard,' he says. 'These are the four Cs I live my life by. The same four Cs that we will do mathematics with.'

We laugh awkwardly.

Mr Pollard paces up and down like someone trapped in a haunted castle. Beads of sweat form on his face and neck. 'Know this,' he says. 'When I was teaching in the bush, before Independence, I got seven As from my A-level class.'

He steps forward to block a make-believe cricket ball with a make-believe bat. 'That's seven As! *Seven As!*' he shouts. He goes quiet again, as if his own bellowing voice frightened him.

'The inspector didn't believe it,' he says. 'He hot-tailed it out there to see for himself. Those seven As were with *me*! So we can do it again together! But you have to work with me. You have to say, "You're not going to get me out!"' He strides forward and hits another make-believe cricket ball with his make-believe bat. 'You're not going to get me out!'

Dad says that he and Mr Pollard were at boarding school together in Cape Town; that every morning they got up at sunrise and had a cold shower; that every morning they went to chapel; that twice a week they did cadets; that every day they did sport. He says Mr Pollard won a Rhodes Scholarship to Oxford University. And he did that at a time when sport counted as much as schoolwork for a scholarship.

Mr Pollard puts his chalk to the board and scribbles. His bones are still those of a sportsman. Some people say that he had a nervous breakdown at university. Dad says, 'Never recovered. Bonkers, you know. Absolutely bonkers.'

*　　*　　*

I put my vodka and coke down. 'Pass me the chutney, Dan.'

I scoop a dollop onto my plate. 'This rabbit is pretty mediocre,' I say.

'Sis, Hayde, how could you eat that poor rabbit!' says Sarah.

Dan stops the waiter. 'Excuse me, could I have another beer, please?'

'Make that two!' adds Sarah.

'Unlike you to drink beer, Dan.'

'Yeah, I thought I should give it a try tonight,' he laughs. 'I'm quite liking it; I think I might just have lots!'

Sarah holds her beer up in the candlelight. 'Hayde, cheers to you finishing your last exam!'

'Cheers, Hayde,' says Beebs.

Dan shouts, 'Speech! Speech!'

I rise. 'Ladies, gentlemen, esteemed patrons of the establishment. I'd like to thank all the people who made my exams possible, most notably Mr Desai for flaying my botty so regularly . . .'

'Waiter,' says Dan. 'Could I have a whisky, please?'

'Me too,' adds Sarah.

'Dan, Hayde, let me take a picture of the two of you!' says Sarah.

The camera flashes.

Sarah shifts over and puts her arm on Dan's shoulder. 'Dan you're not stable!' she says.

Dan puts his arm on her back. They fall over together onto the restaurant floor and burst into laughter. Diners at a neighbouring table look on with disapproving glares. The waiter shuffles awkwardly by, as if he's trying not to notice, as if he's not quite sure what to do with two teenagers giggling uncontrollably on the floor.

'Dan,' laughs Sarah. 'You're so hilarious!'

Dan mumbles something incoherent and then, together, they roar with laughter.

*   *   *

Mr Pollard scribbles nonsense on the board. He mumbles, 'Don't forget to joob-joob; never forget to joob-joob.'

Adrian leans back on his chair. 'Hayde. All I can say is that women are a crap design.'

'What do you mean?'

'If I bought a video recorder and every month it went crazy and stopped working properly, I would take it back to the store and get my money back. You would never tolerate that kind of thing in a household appliance. But chicks. Every month, bru, every month.'

'What's going on with you two now?'

'Last week she starts shitting on me, saying I never listen to her, that I never take her seriously, blah, blah, blah. This week? She's shitting on me for having gotten bleak after her tirade last week. Suddenly she's not complaining that I don't listen to her but that I *do* listen to her. Last night she's like, "Why did you go and take all that stuff I was saying so seriously! You should have known that I'm always irrational and crazy when I'm having my period." What the fuck, bru? Bad design, that's all I can say.'

'Sorry to hear that, guy.'

'Anyway, water under the bridge. What happened with you this weekend?'

'Oh, dude, it was so embarrassing, I don't know if I should discuss it.'

He leans closer. 'Go on, Bitchflap!'

'Well, last night I tried to pay a visit to Sarah's house, at, like, three am. I climb over the gate, no problem. But then, dude, the dogs came up to me. I'm like, "Here doggies, good doggies, nice doggies!" but they're suddenly in night-time mode or something, and they start barking furiously at me like they've never seen me before.'

Adrian winces. 'Bitchflap, Bitchflap, wherefore art thou Bitchflap . . .'

'And have you seen those hounds? *Shamwaz*, they are huge! I'm going, "Shh! Doggies, shut the hell up you stupid mutts!" No use. They bark furiously. The next thing, the lights go on in the house and Mrs Hamley is shining a torch out the window and shouting, "Who's there?" I was busted by the spotlight as I climbed over the wall.'

'So what did she do?'

'She was shrieking all kinds of things: "What do you think you're doing coming here in the dead of night? Wah, wah, wah." It was horrible, I thought she was going to pull out a shotgun!'

'And the old man?'

'Ag, he's pretty passive, hey. He just stood there while Mrs H tongue-lashed me.'

Mr Pollard turns to us. 'Eastwood, Rawling! Please be quiet. I'm asking you nicely.'

Geoff says, 'Ah, sir, I think you should rough them up, sir. Distracting the class, sir.'

Mr Pollard shrugs his shoulders slightly. His apey arms hang down in front of him. 'No, Geoffrey. Please, boys. I'm asking you nicely.'

*   *   *

Dan sits in the computer room tapping away at the keyboard next to Dad's temple of cigarette butts. The printer whines next to him. 'What are you doing?' I ask.

'I've just been working on code that generates 3D images that pop out at you from the page. Just printing a test.'

'Seriously? You managed to work out how to do that?'

'It's not that complicated really. You just need a vector image that you replicate with slight differences. It's the differences that fool the eye into thinking it's 3D.'

'Incredible that you worked that out!'

'Well, I cheated. There was an article I read about the principles of 3D.'

'Even so! And what did you code it in?'

'Just BASIC, which is a bit messy but it works nonetheless. Wish I could get my hands on C.'

The printer spits out the giant digits of 3D text. Together they spell 'S A R A H'.

*　　*　　*

Angus steps out of his rickety red Beetle. He looks different since he was expelled from our school. His short hair has grown long. His swarthy complexion and locks of dark hair evoke a Navajo warrior from an old Western. 'Are you coming flying?' he asks.

'I'm keen. Let me ask Dan.'

I knock at the computer room door. 'Yeah?' says Dan.

'Angus is here. Do you want to fly his new Mitelstick?'

Dan taps at the keyboard. Computer code fills the screen in front of him. 'Not today, Hayde. Next time.'

Angus waits at the car. 'Is Dan coming?'

'No,' I say. 'For some reason he isn't.'

Angus steps into the driver's seat and puts his dark glasses on. 'Well, no use standing on ceremony. Let's go.'

The old Beetle roars and vibrates as it speeds down Blair Road.

'Why isn't Dan coming?' asks Angus. 'He used to be a regular pilot.'

'I don't know. He's not the same these last few weeks. Hopefully he'll snap out of it sometime.'

Angus eventually pulls the car into a wide-open field. 'So,' I say. 'I hear you guys had a snake club at your old school.'

'Yes. Although there ended up being two in the end, one for us and one for the seniors, mostly because they'd make us identify snakes by their Latin names, and beat us when we got them wrong.'

'Good old-fashioned education, eh?'

'Once, they took a group of us into the sticks and tied a rope around this guy's neck. They made him climb a tree so that if he fell he would hang himself. And while he climbed they threw broken bottles at him. After that day we figured it would be better to form our own club.'

'And did that stop the nonsense from the seniors?'

'No. During one holiday we found a new place for our club in an abandoned water tank at the opposite end of the school. It was fit for purpose once we put a roof on it. One of our members was from a nearby farm.

'His parents found a four-metre-long python in their fields. So we ended up with this incredible creature, the height of a coffee table when it was all coiled up. The seniors broke into our club one night and stole it. So I went with a friend to steal it back again. We snuck up to their clubhouse. I got on my friend's back and reached up to the window. But when I touched the frame I immediately felt this incredible jolt, like I'd been kicked by a horse.

The next thing I knew I was on the ground. The seniors had wired the window frame to the mains power supply. Where I'd touched the metal frame, there were these perfect red stripes on my palms. At roll call in the hostel that night we were made to display our hands for inspection.'

'What happened then?'

'I received . . . some punishment,' Angus replies.

I wait for him to say what happened, but he doesn't. 'And so what happened to your snake club?'

He lifts the wings into his hands, pulls the plane out the car and lays its magnificent wings across the ground. 'Last I heard, one of the seniors had kept the python in his room for some weeks and then killed and skinned it.'

'Our school must have seemed like a playground in comparison.'

He connects a small battery to the plane's engine. 'Yeah, you guys have a summer camp!'

I bolt the wings onto the fuselage. 'How's Sarah?' he asks.

'She's good,' I say.

'Eish,' he says. 'She's amazing. If you weren't going out with her I'd definitely be putting my best foot forward . . . Right, flight tests all done. Bags firsties!'

* * *

Bush spills out onto the water's edge. A boy in the water fumbles with his skis. On the bank, farmworkers' kids with bare feet and scraggly shorts stare at us wide-eyed, like they're mystified by why white men would tow each other behind a boat.

A skier rises from the water. Wind rushes through my hair. In the distance, tractors line up in perfect rows, like a collection of giant pinned insects.

My classmates sit next to me, red-eyed from smoking *mbanje*. I sometimes wonder if they see the beauty in front of them, the magnificent trees and sky and clouds and red earth, the smells of the dust and grass, or if it's all just grey to them, something to be anaesthetised against. I want to belong to these people, and yet somehow it doesn't feel right. They offer me their drugs, but I decline.

I have my fill of skiing and return cold and wet to the shore. I warm my hands on the crackling braai. A girl throws some meat on the grill. She glances at me as I shiver. 'Hi, I'm Kirsty,' she says.

'I know,' I reply. 'We were at nursery school together.'

'Really?' She looks surprised. 'I don't remember you.'

'I actually came to your fifth birthday party. For some reason, I remember the driveway of your home and the place where you kept horses. And for your information, you wore a small white dress that day.'

'How do you remember things like that? I can't remember anything about my life. I just remember being small, and then big.'

'I have no idea. Some things I remember in vivid detail. Other things, like when my homework is due, I tend to forget.'

She flings her long chestnut hair back and reveals a row of perfect teeth. 'Why aren't you with the others on the boat?' she asks.

'I've been in the water too long; I'm freezing. And let's just say that the guys on the boat aren't exactly good conversation; a drunken-stoned driver speeding around with a minor god complex and a crew giggling about things that aren't funny. Not my scene.'

She smiles. 'I take it you're not smoking anything today, then?'

'No.'

'Not even cigarettes?'

'No.'

'That's unusual,' she says. 'Who knew you were such an old man!'

'Lady, you have no idea how old!'

'I must say, smoking has never been for me, either.'

'I have to go now,' she says as she gets a scrap of paper out her bag. 'But here's my number. Give me a call sometime.'

* * *

Cold night air rushes through the open window of Adrian's Toyota. His hair blows around wildly. 'Bru, this last weekend was crazy.'

'How come?'

'I had to get a lift back from Jane's farm with her dad. We sat in total silence for the whole journey back to town. I scheme he knows I'm *poinking* Jane and he's not happy about it.'

'You didn't say a word?'

'Bru, what was I supposed to say? I just sat there stony-faced. I almost wanted to just say, 'Sha, Mr Clark, I'm really sorry, I didn't mean to violate your daughter's *gweel*.'

'Silence was the right option.'

We pull into Rugs's driveway. He pokes his head out the door. 'Okay, boys, the Ruckus Bringer is here!' he shouts as he jumps into the car.

'Flap, have you tuned Rugs about how you were busted by Sarah's boetie. That is the best story ever.'

'Ah, sha, Adrian. I still have trouble sleeping after that moment, still wake up in the dead of night with shivers of embarrassment.'

'Yeah, Bitchflap, I think you should share that story,' laughs Rugs.

'Okay, it goes like this: I'm at Sarah's house and nobody else is there. She's not allowed to have her door closed when male visitors are around. On this particular day everyone is out so I think, Hey, why not go into her room. I suppose it goes without saying that before long we're making out—'

They interrupt me with laughter.

'—and next thing, we hear footsteps and Sarah says, "Hayde, shit, someone's coming! Quick, hide!" I think, hide where?'

'Oh boy,' says Rugs. 'I can see this ending in tears.'

'So I climb under the bed and Sarah jumps between the sheets like she's just been sleeping. Next thing, her eighteen-year-old brother – huge, scary guy – opens the door and has a brief chat with her. Then I hear, "Hayde, how are you today?"'

'Busted!' shouts Rugs as he convulses with laughter. 'What happened then?'

'I call out from underneath the bed, "Hi, Nick. Fine thanks, and yourself?" He just stands there and talks to me for about ten minutes. On the way out he says, "Hayde, it's not a bunk bed".'

'Bitchflap, Bitchflap, how did he know you were there?'

'I don't know . . . I think one of my toes was sticking out from under the bottom of the bed, or something.'

Chapter 13

Heads move up and down in time to the deafening music. My eyes search among the red and green lasers for Sarah. I rest my hands on the bar. 'Could I have a vodka and coke?'

Sarah puts a hand on my arm. 'Hayde, come and dance!'

'In a moment, when I've finished my drink.'

She floats away into the noise and people. I search for Dan among the bobbing heads. In a corner of the hall, his date sits alone biting her nails.

I glimpse Dan in the distance and go to him.

'What are you doing? You can't just leave Ashley there in the corner. She invited you to this dance, man, go and say something to her. Give her some attention or something!'

Dan stands there, like my words are part of the background music, like he can't quite hear what I'm saying, like he's some kind of mule listening to the mad barkings of a human.

Then he wanders into the sea of bobbing heads and through the artificial smoke, still alternating red and green in the beams of light.

Some minutes later I search for him again. I see him in the far corner, bent double with laughter, next to Sarah.

*   *   *

In my room I find Angus unexpectedly stooping over a bottle of model aeroplane fuel. He momentarily stops siphoning my fuel into his bottle. 'Damn it,' he says. 'Now I'm going to have to pay you for what I'm stealing.'

I laugh. 'Don't worry about it. We made lots.'

'We're totally out,' he tells me. 'The chemist seems to be in short supply of methanol; in fact, of everything. Want to come flying with us? Roswald and I are just heading off to the Polo Club.'

I knock on Dan's door. There's no answer. I try the handle, but the door's locked. 'Dan, do you want to come flying? Angus and Roswald are heading out now for a session.'

I wait for an answer, but there isn't one.

'Dan, answer me, I'm asking you a question!'

'No, don't worry about me. I'm going to stay today,' he finally replies.

'Are you sure? That's what you said last time . . .'

He opens the door, out of breath.

'Are you really, really sure?'

'Yeah. I'm going to carry on training.'

He jumps back on his pull-up bar.

'Okay, suit yourself,' I say. 'You're missing out.'

Angus waits for us in his Beetle. The giant wings of a red aero-plane stretch from the windscreen to the bonnet.

'Fellows,' Angus says as we drive off. 'I think we're going to have to change location. We're running out of light and it's a long way to the Polo Club.'

'Where should we go?'

'There's a place close by that we sometimes fly at.'

The wind rushes through the open windows. 'So, Ang, how exactly did you get yourself expelled last year? Is it true that you lit up a cigarette in geography?'

'Yes,' he says, 'It certainly is.'

'What exactly happened?'

'At the time, not much. Mr Chavanduka just looked at me with his wide eyes and said, "Mr Wakeling, I think you have something to show me." I went to his desk and gave him the packet of smokes. Nothing happened at the time, but the next day I was on the list to see Kyle.'

'And then?'

'He was quite civil actually. He asked me what was going on with me. I was pretty belligerent so he lost his patience and said, "Well, I think I need to beat you now." And I said, "Well, I think you don't!" And he said, "But I have to!" And I said, "Well, no . . . I don't think you do!" So, finally he said, "You're no longer welcome at this school."'

'So what did you do?'

'I just walked out of his office. He followed me from a distance to the bike shed. It was locked, so I had to climb over the fence. He just stood there watching me lift my bike over the fence.'

I laugh. 'That's incredible! And did they still let you write your O levels at the school?'

'Yeah, if you can call it writing. On my Shona paper, I just wrote long strings of mooooooo's everywhere.'

If only Dan were here to hear this story. *I'll have to tell him when I get back home*, I think.

We turn off the tarred road and onto a red soil track carved into the dense bush. A soldier stands at a boom with a machine gun in his hands.

'Guys? This place doesn't seem very welcoming!' I say.

'It's a military base,' Angus says. 'But don't worry, we've been here before. They're usually fine about it.'

The Beetle stops at the boom and the soldier walks up to us with his gun. Angus's friend rolls down his window. 'Let me handle this. I can speak Shona.'

'Excusu me,' says Roswald. 'Do you theenk meb we cen fly our *ndege* ova hea?'

The soldier pauses for a moment as though he's searching his internal soldier's manual for the bit that says, 'What to do if some barefoot white boys pitch up at your military base with a strange small aircraft and ask you in an appalling Shona accent if they can fly it.'

'No, you cannot fly,' he eventually says.

'But pleeeez, *shamwari*!' begs Roswald.

'Ah, no,' the soldier says. 'It is forbidden for you to come into this area. Nowadays, things are different.'

'But pleeeez! Last week but one we cem here end thet utha guy, Psychology, sayd we cen fly!'

'Ah, no,' repeats the soldier, breaking into a smile. 'You cannot!'

Angus sighs. 'This isn't working. And it's too dark to fly anywhere else.'

*   *   *

The tentacled trees pass by the open window. My hair flaps and flicks in the wind. Music plays out of the car's tinny speakers. 'Boys who like girls who like boys who like girls . . . oh it must be someone you really like . . .'

Sarah sits next to me wearing her dark glasses. 'I love these days, Hayde, they're so beautiful. I love the light and the colours. And the open spaces.'

'And the smells,' I say. 'Leaves and vlei. We're lucky. How many places in the world are this beautiful?'

She points into the bush. 'Let's pull over there.'

I open the boot to get my backpack out. We climb a hill and find a tall tree with a magnificent canopy. 'How about here?' I say.

I take out a blanket and put it on the damp, speckled leaves. I lay some snacks out.

'Hayde, that's a bit of a basic picnic, don't you think?'

'What's wrong with jam and butter?'

'You could have put just a little more thought into it.'

I look at the jam and butter. They seem suddenly insubstantial. 'Yeah, I suppose so,' I say.

I lie on the blanket and stare at the branches and leaves above me. Sarah rests her head on my chest. The sky pokes its brilliant blue through the swaying leaves. 'Those patterns are amazing,' she says.

'Have you ever wondered why a caterpillar only ever eats a small portion of a leaf and not the whole thing?' I ask her.

'No.'

'It's because leaves, when they're eaten, set off a chemical cascade that culminates in genes for tannins being activated. The leaf quickly gets unpalatable so the caterpillar has to find a new leaf.'

I wait for her to say something. I stare at the intricate patterns of the leaves against the sky. *There's no need for her to say anything*, I think. I put my hand on her neck and move my fingers along it gently. 'Hayde,' she says. 'Have you noticed this gland on my neck?'

'Where?'

She takes my hand and places it under her jaw. I gently press it. 'It feels like a swollen lymph node to me.'

'It's been up for a while.'

'Maybe you're fighting off some kind of low-grade infection.'

'I don't know,' she says. 'It just sometimes worries me. It's always up.'

'Have you been to a doctor?'

'Yes. She said it's nothing to worry about.'

'Have you ever considered the eventuality that you might be dying of cancer?'

She bursts out laughing. 'Yes, I had actually, Hayde!'

I join in her laughter. 'Well, it's almost impossible to get cancer when you're young. I have never even known anyone our age who got it.'

'Yeah, I suppose so,' she replies. 'I don't know anyone either.' She leans over and smears some jam onto a piece of bread. 'What's going on with Dan? He's been funny with me recently.'

'I don't know, I think he fancies you. I think I understand in some way what he's going through. I just don't know what to do about it.'

'I don't know if he does fancy me. I think he sees me as more of a friend.'

'Well, maybe, but otherwise I just don't know how to explain his mood.'

'Maybe he's just going through some changes. Look how mad you were feeling last year.'

'Well, that was definitely because of you!'

'No, some of it was because of me. The other bit was you!'

Her words sink into me. 'Yeah, maybe I haven't really thought about that properly.'

'He really looks up to you, you know.'

'Does he?'

'He said as much to me. He told me that he really admires you, that he wishes he could be more like you.'

'He told you that?'

'Yes.'

'Really? That's nice, I never knew that. What did you tell him?'

'I told him that you felt the same.'

'Thanks for doing that.'

'I don't know what's wrong with you guys. You adore each other and yet it all remains unsaid.'

I look into her grey-green eyes. 'I suppose it does. I suppose it does . . .'

She rests her head on my chest and dozes off.

*　*　*

'Van, what's wrong, are you cross?' I ask.

'No,' he says. 'Why?'

'You just seem cross,' I say.

'No, I'm not cross.'

'Are you sure, Van, because you're looking quite cross.'

'I'm not cross, okay?'

'Sheesh, Van, I was just asking, hey. No need to get cross.'

'I'm not cross!' he shout-whispers back at me.

'Hey! Van! You're sounding a little bit touchy there.'

'Van, I'm shocked and *horrored*,' exclaims Geoff. 'Is there any need to get so touchy when Hayde's just asking if you're cross?'

'I wasn't cross, okay? I was just sitting here doing my maths, and now you guys are telling me I'm cross and it's making me cross. Yeah, so now I'm getting cross.'

'That's what we were asking, Van, whether you were cross, and now you're admitting that you are, which is what we were asking about in the first place,' I say.

'Fuck, you guys are driving me crazy,' says Van.

Geoff and Adrian cackle. 'Come on, Van, lighten up, man. There's no need to get angry,' says Geoff.

Mr Pollard shouts from his desk. 'Quiet!'

We carry on teasing Van. Mr Pollard gets to his feet and paces around the classroom. He closes his eyes and breathes into his clenched fist and strokes his elbow. 'I said quiet!'

He moves between desks. 'Eastwood, Rawling, stop talking!' he shouts.

'Rough them up, sir!' the class shouts.

'Quiet, stop shouting that!' shouts Mr Pollard.

The class giggles.

'Chittenden, I said quiet!'

Chittenden looks at Mr Pollard. 'Sir, I wasn't talking!'

'Chittenden! Why did you speak again? I said quiet!'

He boxes Chittenden in the head. Chittenden's face bashes into the desk. Chittenden covers his head with his hands. Blows rain down on him.

'Rough him up! Rough him up! Rough him up!' we all shout.

Mr Pollard leaves Chittenden and rushes to the next noise-maker. Like a shark surrounded by too much blood he rushes for one boy only to be distracted by another. *Bang, bang, bang!*

He strides to the board with his big steps. He strokes his elbow and breathes silently into his clenched fist. With a giant shrug, he lifts his hands as if to say, 'You have beaten me.'

'Guys, please,' he says softly. 'Please help me here . . . please calm down.'

The bell sounds and he dismisses us. My feet slide over the concrete floor. I had once walked through these corridors with a sense that I was about to be eaten by lions. But now I wonder if those lions were ever really there.

Maybe Dan is seeing monsters where there are none. Maybe, like me, he will step through his madness and puzzle about what it was he was once mad about. Maybe he'll realise that his craziness is only the chemicals of adolescence reacting like sodium in water. He'll see that when the sodium has effervesced and ignited the bubbling hydrogen, and the solution has frothed like a crazy witch's potion, there'll be only sodium hydroxide left, as calm as a pond on a windless day.

I find Dan sitting with his friends under a tree. I sit down beside him and greet him. He is friendly to me, but his eyes look into the distance, as though his pupils have stones behind them. And so often I wonder what lies behind those stones.

* * *

I pin the struts of the wings to the plane and then sand the ribs so that they fit together properly. Dan stands next to me holding balsa. He seems less interested in aeroplanes than he used to be. Maybe he's one of those people who grows up and stops liking them.

Silence hangs in the air. I want to say something to him about the mess between us. But what?

'Dan, what are we going to do about the engine mount? If we put it on the front it'll be way too nose-heavy.'

Dan tilts the plane from side to side. 'I think it'd be best to build a mount and put the engine above the wing,' he says. 'That's the only way we'll get around the balance issue.'

* * *

I flick the propeller and the engine splutters to life. The mount that Dan built seems to be strong enough. He signals to me with his hands above the deafening whine.

'I'm ready,' I shout.

He runs barefoot across the empty field and into the setting sun. The plane rises into the sky.

It's flying!

The initial climb is good but something is wrong. It slides sluggishly out of the sky and touches down onto the grass. *What's wrong with it?* I wonder.

Dan runs over and picks it up. Once more he runs into the fading light and launches it. Again the plane climbs and whines. But once more it loses power and comes down on its belly.

I scream above the whine, 'I think the engine's mounted too high above the centre of gravity. It's tilting the nose downwards!'

Dan shouts back. 'Yeah, let me hold it here while you shift it forward. The bands are in the box.'

We fiddle for a moment. The plane seems ready to fly again. I offer Dan the remote controls. 'Do you want a go?'

'No, it's okay,' he shouts. 'You go.'

'Are you sure?' I ask.

His eyes seem vacant.

'Are you sure?' I repeat.

'Yeah, Hayde, it's okay, you go.'

Without saying more he runs and launches the plane into the sky. It wobbles through the air and loses height. A teetering wing hits the earth. At once the field around us is completely silent.

The engine mount lies in pieces next to a pair of shattered wings. The rudder and elevator lie cracked and splintered some feet from each other.

— 154 —

I expect Dan to be frustrated with me, to shout at me for what has happened, to be angry that his beautiful mount is broken. I wait for him to tell me that it was my fault, to tell me we should have designed the mount differently. But he just stares into the darkening night.

And then it's no longer the broken aeroplane that bothers me, but Dan's penetrating silence and vacant eyes.

* * *

I sit at the piano and fiddle with some chords. 'Imagine there's no heaven,' I sing. 'It's easy if you try . . .'

A banging sound interrupts my notes. Over and over it rings down the passageway. It seems to come from Dan's room. *What's he doing in there?* I wonder. An uneasy feeling fills my stomach.

Kirsty pokes her head through the door. She takes her sunglasses off. 'Hullo!' she says. 'Johanna and I are going to the movies tonight. Would you like to join us?'

'What time?'

'Soon! Why don't you get ready? We'll wait!'

'Sure,' I say. 'Give me a few minutes.'

'What was that I heard you playing?'

'It's a John Lennon song. It's called "Imagine". One of my favourite songs by one of my favourite songwriters.'

I play it for her. 'I've never heard it before, but it's lovely,' she says. 'And you play it so beautifully.'

'Let me get ready,' I say. 'Give me five.'

I pass Dan in the hallway. His eyes seem absent and distracted. I glance at his hands. His knuckles are bruised and scabbing. Flaps of skin seem to have torn themselves off and glued themselves back again with clotted blood.

I want to say something to him. I want to tell him that if it's about Sarah, then I know what he's going through. I want to offer him some kind of solution to it all.

Kirsty waits impatiently at the door. She calls for me. Before I can make eye contact with Dan he vanishes into his bedroom.

Emily calls in the distance. 'Haaaaydieee, teleephoooonnne, Sarah for you!'

I rush down the hallway. 'Sorry, Kirsty, let me just take this call.'

Emily hands me the receiver.

'Hi, Hayde, I'm just wondering if you're still coming round this evening?'

'I'm supposed to be coming round tonight?'

'Yes, you said you were going to.'

'I can't tonight. Why don't I come by tomorrow?'

'Why can't you come today?'

'Kirsty's here with her friend. We're going to movies.'

'What? Really? What's going on between you two?'

'Nothing Sare, seriously, nothing.'

'Don't fuck with me, Hayde!' she shouts. 'Don't tell me you don't have feelings for her. She comes and visits you a lot and you don't spend time with me like you used to.'

'We're going in a moment. Can we talk about this tomorrow?'

'Tomorrow? How about right now!'

'So you want me to miss going out to movies just because you want to talk now. Seriously, Sare, really? Don't you think that's a little selfish?'

'It's like I'm not even a priority in your life anymore.'

'Sare, you are. We just spend so much time together and I wanted to do something different for a change. I don't stop you from hanging out with your guy friends. I don't say anything about you hanging out with Dan.'

'That's different,' she says.

'It's not different,' I say. 'It's totally not different.'

Kirsty stands on the driveway, pointing to her watch. 'I've got to go,' I tell Sarah. 'I'll come by yours after the movies.'

Kirsty puts a tape into the deck of the car stereo and lowers her sunglasses over her eyes. A growing feeling of dirtiness comes over me, as though I've sinned, as though I've already cheated on Sarah, as though I've let Dan down.

And yet I feel free, beautifully free.

* * *

The car hums through the inky night. Only our yellow headlights guide the way. 'Did you remember to order poppadums?' asks Mum.

'Yes, of course,' I reply.

The car hits a pothole. 'Bloody power cuts!' says Mum. 'You can't see any of these wretched craters when the streetlights are out. These past couple of years, the cuts have really started getting out of hand.'

I stop the car outside the restaurant. 'Don't forget to give them the coriander from me.'

I return to the car.

'What do you think is wrong with Dan?' Mum asks. 'Do you think this thing with Sarah is really getting to him? I bumped into Gill Hamley at the shops the other day and I told her that it was no longer clear who Sarah's affections were for. Gill sounded quite taken aback really.'

I peer out into the darkness. 'I don't know what to say to him about it.'

'Well, I'm worried,' Mum says. 'The other day we were in the car and Dan was driving wildly. He had this look in his eyes, slightly crazy. I said, "Daniel, you can't drive like this!" I had to say it a few times before he seemed to come back to earth and snap out of it. It was very unnerving.'

'I don't know what to do about it, Ma. And I don't even know if I've understood what's going on correctly.'

I park the car in the driveway. We go inside with the curry and poppadums. Dad mutters to himself as he reads his paper by candle-light. Beebs sculpts warm candle wax in her hands.

'Where's Dan?' I ask.

'I don't know,' says Dad. 'Won't you call him?'

I walk down the pitch-black passageway. 'Dan,' I call. 'Come for supper!'

There's no reply. I shine a torch into his room. It's empty. I make my way down the passageway and call for him again. The side door from the stoep opens. His dim silhouette emerges. 'Is it dinner?'

'Yeah. Have you just been outside?'

'Yeah,' he says.

'What, just arbitrarily walking around in the dark?'

I wait for him to tell me what he's been doing, but he says nothing. He brushes his way past me and towards the pale orange light flickering at the entrance to the sitting room.

*   *   *

Sarah and I walk in the park. The air is dry and grassy. It reminds me of when Dan and I used to ride our bicycles through it. It reminds me that he used to be happy. I put my arm around her shoulder. 'I worry that you flirt with Dan sometimes,' I tell her. 'That you lead him on. Maybe you should be more careful.'

She seems taken aback. 'He's just a friend. I promise you he knows that. And how do you know it's me he's upset about? Maybe it's other stuff too.'

I think, *Yeah, maybe she's right. Maybe I've got it completely wrong. Maybe there are a hundred other things more upsetting to him that I don't even know about. But maybe all that's happened is that he's in love with her. And if he is, then all that's happening is that he's feeling the same as I did some months ago.*

But Dan isn't me. He doesn't respond to difficulties like I do. The old eel twists in my stomach unexpectedly.

We continue our walk in a strange silence.

'Hayde,' she finally says. 'I just feel it's so difficult to do right by you sometimes.'

'I'm sorry,' I say. 'I just don't know what to make of this situation. Sometimes I really wonder what's real and what isn't.'

I knock on Dan's door when I get home. He doesn't answer.

'Dan, are you there?'

I press on the handle. No one is inside. On his desk sits the disfigured glider next to its broken engine mount.

His school scarf hangs off his pull-up bar.

I pick the engine mount up. Its plywood is still intact, but there is a crack along the glue line and a clean break where it once attached to its mounting stilts. I wedge a screwdriver into the glue line and lever the strips of plywood apart.

I mix some glue on a piece of old cardboard. Then I lift one of the strips of plywood and study its surface. A sinking coldness fills my stomach. A secret is etched into the wood, its author thinking it would be mummified forever: 'I love Sarah'.

Chapter 14

I do press-ups and sit-ups on the grass near the veranda. Dan wanders towards me from the sitting room door. His frame is filling with more muscle. He looks slender but strong. Soon he'll be a man. Maybe someday he'll be stronger than me. 'Do you fancy a game of computer rugby?' he asks.

I catch my breath. 'Yeah sure, of course. I'd love to.'

Dan seems to have unexpectedly emerged from his moping silence. His walk seems more buoyant.

We sit at the computer. Stick-figured men wearing little pairs of pixelated white shorts run onto the fishbowl screen. The whistle blows and the cheers of the crowd roar through the tinny speakers.

My player breaks Dan's defence. Dan's players chase the wrong man. My man dives over the try line. 'Nice one, Hayde,' he says.

I score again. Dan's movements become agitated. I do a set move and then abort it.

'Ah, you fucking cunt!' he shouts at me. 'You shouldn't be allowed to do that move. It's not fair; the algorithm for automated tackling is crap. It doesn't know what to do when you've aborted the move half way through. What kind of idiots designed this algorithm! You shouldn't be allowed to do that! You shouldn't be allowed to abort moves!'

'Come on, man, I got that try fair and square.'

Dan mumbles and returns his focus to the game. He scores in a flurry. The score evens and his temper subsides.

With minutes to go, my man picks up a dropped ball and runs the length of the field. 'Try number three!' I shout.

Dan brushes the disappointment off and steels himself for a final rally.

My fly half kicks the ball. Dan's wing catches it and makes a last attempt for the line. A gap opens. His man runs through it and into an empty patch of field. Pixels from the try line, my men tackle him.

Dan hits pause. 'No ways, that couldn't happen, your fullback just materialised. He just appeared! He couldn't have been there! He came from off the screen to tackle me. The computer's cheating!'

He rattles the desk with his hands. It's like watching him as an eight-year-old again.

'Dan, chill out, man. How could he have just appeared?'

'And fucking hell, my guy went over the line. How come it didn't give me the try?'

'Dan, you know how this thing works. If you get tackled before the line and then roll over the line, it doesn't give it you!'

Dan reaches over and switches off the computer.

'Don't be such a fucking spoilsport!' I shout.

'No, this stupid fucking computer, it's cheating. It's cheating!'

I push him. 'Why did you have to ruin the game?'

He pushes me back. We grab each other. I try to lift his legs from underneath him and drop him to the floor like I used to when we were boys. But he's become strong. His burly legs remain firmly planted on the ground.

He shrugs me off and storms out. 'Fuck you, you fucking wanker! You're such a fucking prick!'

'No, fuck you!' I shout after him.

I lie on my bed and hold my face in my hands. My adrenaline dies away. What's happening to us? It's like we're seven and eight years old again.

But in those days at least we were close.

* * *

Dad stands by the drinks cabinet in his dark work suit. He pours some gin over the ice cubes in a glass. 'I went to see the school today,' he says. 'Dan's maths teacher requested a meeting.'

I look up from my book. 'What happened?'

He puffs smoke into the air above him. 'Well,' he says. 'I explained to her that Dan's always on the computer creating the most baffling graphs and algorithms. I told her I didn't understand any of them. And, of course, when I said that, she knew at once that his mathematical ability was way above hers, and that she couldn't possibly fathom what he did either.'

His hands jut through the air manically. Ash falls from his half-finished cigarette onto the parquet tiles. He lowers himself into his green chair. I wait for him to continue.

But then . . . nothing.

He picks up the *Financial Times* and litters ash onto the floor. The conversation is over.

My stomach goes queasy. I want to translate the mushed-up soup in my head into words, but I'm incapable of translating soup into thought. The phone rings in the passageway. Dull, thudding footsteps grow louder. Then Dan's voice answers, 'Hullo?'

I wait for him to say something else, but the initial greeting is followed by silence. He puts his head through the doorway. 'Hayde, it's for you.'

When I get to the receiver, Dan is gone.

'Hayde,' says Sarah, 'what's going on with Dan? He didn't even greet me. He hasn't spoken to me in days.'

I want to offer a solution. I want to explain it away. I want to say something to her. And I want to say something to Dan. But every time I'm near him, the words seem somehow caught in my throat, like a scream in a silent movie.

Mum calls, 'Dinner's ready, come and dish up in the kitchen!'

Dan drifts into the sitting room. He sits quietly on the sofa, his eyes staring somewhere into the far distance. Mum looks him up and down. 'Come on, Dan, cheer up! What's eating away at you?'

A pulse of anger surges through me. I want to shout, 'You don't do that, Mum! You don't say absolutely nothing to him all day and then suddenly confront him in front of everyone about what's eating him up! You don't do that! What's wrong with you?' I want to explode and yet, if I do, it'll only embarrass Dan further.

I wonder if he'll respond to Mum. I wait some moments. And then, as though Mum hadn't even said anything, Dan picks up Miles and moves to the fireplace.

I study the food on my plate. I no longer feel like eating, but I cut into the steak. And then the only sound in the room is our metal cutlery clinking and scratching on our plates.

* * *

A chemistry textbook rests on my knee. I plonk my coffee down on the little stoep table. Miley stands a few metres from me holding Dan's biplane precariously in two hands.

Dan stands across from Miley, seemingly light-hearted. 'Come on Miley!' he says. 'Throw the plane into the sky!'

I watch Dan as he plays with Miles. His spirits seem to have lifted again. A sparkle of life has returned to his eyes. He seems animated and buoyant.

'Dan,' I say. 'Miley is going to destroy that biplane. The top wings are going to break off.'

'That's okay, Hayde. I don't mind. I'm giving it to him.'

Miley tries to throw the plane. It leaves his hands but falls backwards. The rudder breaks off. Dan picks the biplane up off the floor.

'Do it like this, Miley.'

Dan swhooshes the plane through the air. *'Ga ga ga ga,'* he says, simulating the noise of a four-stroke engine. Miley runs behind Dan, squealing with delight.

I study Dan's limbs as he moves. He'll be a strong and graceful pole vaulter next athletics season. And then he'll be the handsome one as well as the clever one. For a moment I feel sorry for myself, sorry for being the lesser man, sorry for being in the shadow of someone so much better than me.

'Dan,' I call. 'I'm going to put my Number Ones on for the rugby game. Are you coming with me?'

He calls back from the garden. 'Yeah, Hayde. Just give me a few minutes to get my clothes on . . .'

I slip into my grey trousers. The late afternoon sun streams through the window. The game today will be a good one. Dan pokes his head through my doorway. He stands in front of me in his trousers and blazer. Around his neck he wears his deep-green school scarf.

At school he takes his place on the stand among his friends. I watch as he talks to them in an unusually animated way. His hand gestures are wild and jerking. His friends burst into laughter at something he's just said.

A strange weight lifts from me, and it's only now that it's lifted that I realise how heavy it was. This silly period in our adolescence is drawing to an end. We'll grow a new relationship as men. And we'll be close again.

I breathe in the smell of dust and grass. The soft light casts long shadows across the rugby field.

This evening is beautiful, I think. *And I'm grateful for all my blessings, for my privileges, for the gift of life itself.*

The referee holds his hand to the sky and blows his whistle. Men thump into one another at the centre of the pitch. The school bursts into spontaneous shouts and clapping.

The game finishes. I glance over to where Dan sits. He shakes the hands of his friends and makes his goodbyes.

'Dan, are you ready to go?' I ask.

'Yes. Coming now. Is Sarah still coming for dinner?'

'Yes,' I say. 'She'll probably be at ours already.'

At home the dining room table is already set. Sarah carries through a beef casserole and places it on the table. Mum lays some roast potatoes down in front of me. 'How was the rugby, guys?' she asks.

'Really good, thanks, Mum,' says Dan.

'I also enjoyed it,' I say. 'That English side were small, but, sheesh, they were skilled.'

Dad joins us. Dan and Sarah sit next to each other. Now and then Dan makes a joke and Sarah laughs. 'Wow, this is the first time we've had a meal together in a while, guys,' says Mum.

We move to the sitting room. Dan picks Miles up and takes him to the fireplace. He loads his hands with pine cones from the wood-box. 'Miley,' he says. 'Watch this, it's called juggling!' Dan dances the pine cones in the air and Miles watches them, transfixed. Eventually Dan drops one and puts the remaining ones on the table. I turn the page of my book. Dan walks out the door and closes it behind him.

'I'm taking Dan's lead and hitting the hay,' I say. I walk up the passageway past Dan's closed door. I brush my teeth. Sarah hugs me from behind. 'I'm just going to see if Dan's up and have a word with him.'

I climb into bed and lie in the dark. The cold July air drifts through my open window with the smell of grass and dust and wood. I take some moments to appreciate the weight that has left my body. *Life can be so beautiful*, I think.

Sarah climbs into bed next to me. 'I knocked on his door,' she says, 'but he's asleep already. I'm so glad he's speaking to me again.'

I turn out the light. 'Me too,' I say. 'Me too . . .'

Chapter 15

I open my maths textbook and write equations down on a piece of paper. I wonder if I'll pass the exam tomorrow.

The phone rings and then stops. I hear Miles knock on Dan's door and call for him.

Dad shouts, 'Come here, Hayden! Come here right now!'

The tone of his voice irritates me. My patience with his outbursts grows thinner by the month. I can only imagine he can't find the pliers again, or something. And yet, as usual, he's probably the one who lost them.

Dad shouts again.

'Chill out, old man!' I say.

But there's an urgency in his voice that I've never heard before. I hurry towards the banging.

He stands at Dan's door, his eyes wild and scared. 'Quickly, open the door,' he shouts. 'Daniel's killed himself.'

Time slows to a halt. And then it seems to start again in double-time.

I throw myself at the door. My loud bangs produce no answer. Is Dan even in his room?

There's no space in the passageway for a run-up, so I take a single step back and ram the door with my shoulder. It's stubbornly strong. Panic grips me. My own shouts echo off the door in front of me. I throw myself at it over and over again.

Finally the lock buckles. With one more hit, the door swings open. I rush into Dan's room.

He hangs awkwardly, but perfectly still from his pull-up bar by his green school scarf, his bum raised slightly off the ground, his hands clenched at his sides, his scarf taut under the weight of his body. His head rests on his chest to one side in an uncomfortable position. His eyes are closed. His face is milky white.

An intricate web of red, cotton-like fibres runs from his ankles to his thighs. Each strand is distinct. For a moment, I wonder how many capillaries there are in a human body. And then I realise that I'm not looking at Dan but at a corpse. He's been dead for hours. My vision turns white and my face tingles and burns. I scream and wail and bang on the cupboard door with my fists.

I hear Mum coming down the passage. She asks what's going on.

For a moment my world is clear. I want to lie to her. I want to explain how Dan can look like this without him being dead. I search my brain for excuses; for something I can say to stop her from coming in; for some scientific explanation for how his legs can look like that without being full of dead, non-circulating blood.

But at once she's screaming. All I can think to do is leave the room. And I leave without touching him because I'm too scared. He'd only be cold like the wall, something other than what he should be. And I can't bring myself to touch that otherness.

I somehow find myself outside. The white fog clears. Trees tower above me. A hoopoe hops around on the lawn. It's a normal Zimbabwean winter morning with cold dry air and dry brown grass and a clear blue sky.

*   *   *

I sit at my desk trying to remember what happened. My heart thumps and wrenches.

Disconnected snapshots flash through my mind: Dad rabidly searching for the suicide note he would never find; Dan's dark-green school scarf with its white stripes; the web of red engulfing his legs; the awkward angle of his neck, hanging bent like one of the servants' slaughtered chickens; the peaceful look on his face; his clenched fists; Mum clutching him on the bed and wailing as she hugged him, his arms and head dragging like a rag-doll with every attempt she made to lift him. She clutched at him as if she was unable to understand his fate. I've heard that some elephants only leave the corpse of their young when the smell of rotting meat poisons their hope. That's what she made me think of.

But it is worse for her, worse for us.

Humans think they understand death because they imagine they understand biology and physics. But an elephant never asks why or how. It accepts death without needing to understand it. We puzzle over what makes a cell work, and we ask why a stone cannot live and why a door cannot think. Humans are tortured by endless questions. An elephant asks nothing.

Adrian appears at the front door. He hugs me without saying anything and leads me to his car. We drive for some minutes until a water-filled quarry stretches out in front of us. We skim stones across the clear, clean water.

The quarry is grey and blue and empty, like the barbaric dreamscape of a mystical dead planet.

Chapter 16

Mum faints. Dad stands over her waving his hand.

An animal in me seems like it'll spring out and destroy the fur-niture and windows. I place my hand on the wall and stare at my fingers, as though watching them will somehow calm me. I sense I'm lifting out of my own body and watching myself look at my own hand from above. And all the while my heart races like an engine jammed in full throttle.

In the middle of the stage, a microphone sits on a tall stand. Flowerpots and pretty shrubs line the sides of the stage.

People take their seats. Mum sits blank-faced in the front row. Sarah sits next to me.

Rupert Benning-Thwaite reads a poem about a spitfire pilot, and then a poem that Dan wrote when he was thirteen years old. The poem is about animals at a waterhole. Something startles them and they look up anxiously. Eventually their nerves calm. They put their heads down and drink once more. But all the time the vultures are diving and stalling above them. The last line is: 'They're safe, they think!'

The way the vultures dive and stall in Dan's poem reminds me of the aeroplanes we used to make.

Tears run down Sarah's face. She clutches a piece of paper with scribbles on it. She gives it to me. I look at it briefly. I hate what it says. It seems so superficial, so banal, so unlike anything that Dan would ever have wanted. I hand it back to her.

Dad talks about how Dan loved to play rugby and about how Dan was so much smarter than him.

I walk onto the stage and look down at the people in front of me. 'I haven't really prepared anything,' I tell them. 'I just thought I would talk about whatever came into my mind. I don't want to say things that are going to glorify him, or paint him as some saint. I always find funerals like that cheesy . . .'

My mind is blank, like a dead man's encephalogram. I stumble and wait.

'I just think that what happened was terrible, and we should learn from what happened so that something terrible like this doesn't happen again . . .

'I don't know what I'll miss about him the most. He used to do silly things. I remember him trying to kill a mosquito by flicking a coin at it from across the room. He always used to do things like that. I'll miss that . . .'

I sense I've given away too much. It's time for a joke.

'I'll try to look on the bright side,' I say. 'At least I won't have to share the car with him anymore . . .'

My mind empties again. I think more words will come to me, but they don't.

Men bring Dan's coffin onto the stage. Only a thin layer of wood protects my eyes from seeing him. But what is he now? He's no longer a 'he' but an 'it', and it, whatever that is, will somehow resemble Dan but be something else. I sense that I'm watching myself from above, from a distance. I want the men to take it, him, whatever it is, away.

The gardeners eat food at the table and sip on drinks. Vince Weber's jazz blares. For a moment it seems as if Dan is alive and listening to his favourite music, as if the garden has life in it instead of death. And then a man switches off the power and there is absolute silence.

The last flicker of Dan's short life is whisked away to the far reaches of an endless, bleak universe.

*   *   *

The night around me is empty and lonely and cold and dark. I switch the CD player on. A song plays but for some reason it's muffled and garbled.

I press stop and then play again.

Nothing.

I check the cable running from the CD player to the car radio and try again. The sound is still garbled. I take out the CD and clean it.

No difference.

Something dangerous boils in me, something that will burst out and kill me. I want to pick up the CD player and throw it out of the window so that it breaks the gravitational pull of earth. I want to scream my bones out of my mouth.

I pull the car over onto the verge of the road and with shivering hands feel the speakers in the dark and check their connections.

I press play again. This time the music is perfect and crisp. And then for some moments I sit in silence as the terror drains from me, in silence as I contemplate just how close I am to becoming irretrievably mad.

*   *   *

The house sits on Blair Road like a graveyard, and the people who live here have become ghosts that float through it. The evenings are cold and smell of smoke and dust and brown grass and winter. I gaze at the licking fire.

When I was small, I scampered around in the cool, dry night and inhaled the brown grass and the dust, and it made me happy. But that was then. Sometimes I wish myself dead, but then it seems as if I almost am. And I'm surprised it's like this. When I was small,

I cried when the cat died and when the dog died, and I cried when my great-grandmother died. I thought if a person died you became sad like you did over a cat. Maybe just a bit more, because people are more important than cats.

Mum walks into the sitting room with Miles in her arms. They sit down and watch the flickering fire with me. Miles fidgets and gets to his feet. He waddles around with his toy gun saying, *'Pwoo, pwoo!'*

Mum stares into the distance with granite eyes. 'I can't believe your father's gone off to work like nothing has happened,' she says. 'It's bizarre.'

Miles stops his playing and toddles over to Mum. He tugs on her jersey. 'Mum, don't tell Dan, but he's never coming back.'

Dad walks through the door and to the drinks table. He pours himself a gin and tonic.

'How was work, Dad?'

'Ag, so-so.'

He sits down in his green chair. 'Annette, have you got any more Valium?' he asks.

'Yes. The doctor gave me a whole stack.'

Mum gives some pills to Dad. He washes them down with his gin and tonic.

'You know, the more I think about it,' he says, 'the more I think that Danny was just mad. The signs were there, from a young age, that there was something not right with that boy.'

'Dad, I disagree,' I say.

'Why is that?'

'Because Dan wasn't mad. He was saner than me and I'm still here.'

Dad's eyes glaze over. 'No, I think you're wrong, you know. I think you're wrong. That strange detachment, those tantrums as a child; that's not normal, you know.'

'What is normal, Dad?'

Dad raises his eyebrows at me, as though he's butting my challenge away like a goat. Anger rises in me, but I clench my jaw and push it down. And then I'm grateful to feel something.

'You know,' says Mum. 'Danny was just so different to the rest of my children. Out of all of you, he demanded the least affection.'

Dad rises unexpectedly. He seems suddenly possessed. 'Danny!' he calls, 'Come on, Danny, why don't you come down and join the rest of us?'

He walks down the hallway. His calls for Dan reverberate through the house.

'Oh, shut up!' I finally shout.

And then there is total silence.

*   *   *

I wake with a thumping heart and cough furiously. A glob of phlegm fills my mouth. I go to the basin and spit it out. It's thick and clear and sticky, like nothing I've ever seen.

I study myself in the mirror: my eyes are pink and pus-filled. I gulp down hot coffee to scorch away the pain of my sore throat. Mum and Dad lie unconscious in their bed. Next to them are empty bottles of pills.

I walk down the passageway to the kitchen.

'Morning, Haydie,' says Emily. She looks down at her hands, as if the thought of meeting my gaze is unbearable.

*   *   *

The biology teacher stands in front of his board. 'Your mock-exam results are back, and I'd like to go over a few things. First, can someone please tell me what life is, in a biological sense?'

A boy puts his hand up.

'Yes, Changara,' says the teacher.

My jotter-book is empty. Maybe that's all Dan was: an ordered lump of carbon and hydrogen.

'. . . well, you're right,' the teacher says. 'A virus is a bit of a troublesome thing to characterise. Yes, it does have DNA, but it doesn't necessarily pass the "life test", as it were. Then again, viruses are arguably the most successful life form. Just think, they have none of the baggage that we have, no biochemical machinery to worry about.'

Where is the line between life and death? Can a scientist create order out of matter with the twist of his controls, creating ever more until he can finally say, 'Voila! There is now life where before there was none'?

The teacher draws chemical shapes on the board. But instead I see Dan's legs, strangled by that web of red. My heart races again. One day I too shall die and my bones will be dust, and this big universe will swallow me up like I never existed.

* * *

I dream that a cell is just a big machine and that death is what happens when its parts stop moving. I go to a molecular process and shout, 'You over there! Why have you stopped working?'

The molecular process says, 'I've stopped working because my neighbour who turns me has stopped working.'

So I ask his neighbour why he's stopped working. 'Because that process over there has stopped working.'

I follow the chain back to find the one process that has prevented each downstream process from working. *I'll make this one part work again*, I think, *and then the other parts that depend on it will have to work once more.*

I find Dan, lying with his web of red and I jump-start the crucial stopped pathway like a motorcar engine.

I wake up overjoyed because I've brought him back to life. I want to tell Mum. I want to wake Dan and have a splendid breakfast together. But then I realise that he isn't here. He isn't anywhere.

The dream eats at me. I look at the fibres running through a wooden chair and wonder why they can't think. I look into the dog's eyes and wonder what happens in her dog-mind.

Dad walks up to me in the sitting room. 'Don't you think I'm bonkers? You know, properly bonkers? Isn't it me that's mad and not Dan?'

'Dad, don't be silly. It's not your fault. You couldn't have changed what happened. You're not mad,' I tell him.

He holds my gaze briefly with his drunken, watery eyes and then staggers off.

*   *   *

Dan and I play hide-and-seek in the garden. I search for him everywhere. After a while I call to him: 'Dan, come out now, the game's over.'

But he stays hidden in the silent garden.

Then he swings like Tarzan from one of his favourite trees. I approach, but he vanishes.

I find myself in the sitting room and see the backs of his legs disappear through the doorway. He's barefoot and wearing his rugby shorts. I follow him up the hallway. His legs disappear through the next doorway.

I know where he'll be, I think.

I go to his bedroom and open the door. There he is: hanging from his pull-up bar, his legs strangled in the web of red; his face indifferent, pale.

I wake with a jolt.

I've dreamed something terrible, I think. *Thank God he's safely asleep in his room.*

But then I realise that my life is the nightmare and my nightmare is the only place of hope.

Chapter 17

The car radio blares out Rolling Stones songs. *Mick Jagger makes being selfish seem so beautiful,* I think.

The air is dry, the flamboyants are red and the msasas have already finished rusting. I drive through their tunnels of tentacled branches.

People plod down the road in the hot sun. A security guard thumbs a lift.

'Where are you going?' I ask.

'Ah, just on the main road,' he replies.

We drive in silence for some moments. A woman crosses the road ahead of us. He gestures towards her. 'These women don't look properly when they cross,' he says. 'It's because they are wondering, wondering, wondering, where is the food coming today. They are wondering, where will I put this baby while I find food?'

The woman has a baby on her back. She looks over her shoulder. The sunlight glistens off the sweat on her forehead. Her hair is matted. The security guard smiles to reveal his diseased gums and missing teeth.

'You can drop me over here. Thanks, my friend, you have done a lot.'

He walks away with his bandy legs. And I wonder what he'd think of our madness. He'd probably look at our house and our school and our cars and search his security guard's manual for the bit that says 'What to do with rich white kids who hang themselves'. And after he'd searched in vain, he'd look at me and wonder what he could possibly say.

* * *

My throat burns. I cough up some of the sticky phlegm that lines my throat like peanut butter. In front of the mirror I open my mouth and inspect the purulent area at the back of my throat.

I tie one end of an old rope to my waist and the other to a car tyre and run until my legs and lungs burn. I run until I collapse with exhaustion on the hard ground and cough up the never-ending stream of peanut butter.

I worry that my body is slowly dying. I worry that I've developed a strange autoimmune disease.

Daylight fades and the night sounds begin. I find myself unexpectedly afraid of the dark. I sense that there are creatures in the shadows.

Mum calls me for dinner at the veranda door.

'Coming,' I shout.

Dad puffs on a cigarette and reads. I sit in front of the fire and gaze at the flames. Next to the fireplace the woodbox sits like a strange monument to Dan's last moments. Only a few days ago he rummaged through it for pine cones. I can almost see him standing on the tiles in front of me and juggling those pine cones for Miley.

Dad puts his paper down. 'I met this fellow Hipschman the other night,' he says. 'Top doctor, you know. Lovely man, offered therapy to all of us and refused to charge a penny. Educated in America. He just introduced himself to me at a function and said he was available. Sweet fellow.'

I heave and cough and stare at the fire.

'Have you ever thought about seeing someone?' Dad asks.

'I don't think it's really for me, you know.'

* * *

I sit with Kirsty in the park and stare at the dam in front of me. She puts her hand on my shoulder. 'I don't know if you can ever understand why somebody makes a decision like Dan's. Maybe everything is to blame, and also nothing.'

I look at her. 'I don't know,' I say. 'Maybe it just takes a moment to think of something like that, to do what he did. Maybe people must be careful of those moments.'

Silence returns. She fixes me with her big eyes. 'I must go,' she says. 'Let me know if there's anything I can do . . .'

Her old Mercedes fades into the dimming embers of the day.

There was an evening some time ago when Dan was still alive. Was it two weeks ago? Or two months ago? The brief seconds of that day jar my mind like a strobe light, like a blitzkrieg of memory-lightning: I walk down the passageway. A faint smell of laundry detergent lingers in the air from clothes drying in the bathroom. The overhead neon light bleaches the walls of the passageway an almost perfect white. For a moment, it's as though a ghost has sucked every sound out of the house, every molecule of air from the passageway, as though I've found myself in an instantaneous vacuum where only I, the bookshelf and Dan's door exist in the universe. I think to myself, *Would he do it? Would he do that?* And then, as though that moment were nothing, as though there had been no ghost and no vacuum and no terror, I go to my room and get into bed and turn off the light.

The night insects screech. The strobe-light memories of Dan's last night haunt me.

'I'm so glad Dan is speaking to me again,' Sarah says as she climbs into bed next to me.

Dan sits just metres away, behind a thin brick wall. Red threads creep like cracks into his thighs and calves. And all the while Sarah and I ravish each other like animals, making life while Dan makes death.

'I can't get enough of you, Hayde,' she whispers.

Did I gasp a moment of ecstasy while he gasped his final breath?

* * *

I fiddle with the chords for 'Imagine' and sing to myself. 'Imagine all the people living life in peace, you-oo-oo-oo . . .'

Distant shouting reverberates down the corridor. I stop.

'How was I supposed to know!' echoes Dad somewhere in the distance. 'I'm the one that was at work, earning a living for the family. Nobody told me what was going on with Daniel. As usual, I'm kept in the bloody dark!'

'Anthony, it's not li—'

'Honestly, you're a useless bloody mother!'

'Anthony, I tried to tell you things were going wrong at home. I wrote you that letter!'

'Oh, nonsense!' he shouts. 'I didn't see any such bloody letter!'

I slide my fingers across the black and white keys. The piano seems so simple. The keys are either black or white. There are a finite number of notes.

'. . . You may say I'm a dreamer, but I'm not the only one. I hope someday you'll join us, and the world will be as one.'

* * *

The medical campus looks like it's been battered by gunfire. Paint peels off the buildings. Greying corridors lead to a door marked 'Dr Hipschman'.

A swarthy man in a waistcoat gestures for me to enter.

'A few formalities before we begin . . . How old are you?'

'Just turned seventeen.'

'I take it you're still at school?'

'Yes.'

He asks me about my life. I tell him that the universe is much like an unwinding clock. He listens with folded arms. We sit in silence.

'Would you say that you're happy at the moment?' he asks me.

'Yes.'

'I'm just wondering if, perhaps, your brother's death has in fact been troubling to you in any way. Some people can find that sort of thing quite distressing, even devastating.'

'Life goes on, doesn't it? There's a guy I know who lost his dad in a car accident and his mum to spine cancer. He seems to be quite fine.'

'Tell me about some of your first memories. Can you reach inside and find something, anything, that was less than happy?'

I think for some moments.

'When I was about four I woke up to Mum and Dad shouting at each other. I got out of bed feeling scared and walked to the passageway. Dad was there wrestling with Mum. Mum tried to run, but Dad punched her in the back and she fell to the ground. I shouted, "Leave my mum alone!" He told me to fuck off and go to my room.'

'So what did you do?'

'I went back to my room.'

'How did that make you feel?'

'I was upset at the time. But it was nothing. I was just being a drama queen.'

He says nothing. I wonder if he thinks I'm a liar. He asks me more questions. I give him more non-answers.

'I think it's time to stop now,' he eventually says.

I walk back down the dirty corridor, along the wooden tiles and alongside the peeling walls.

Fawlty . . . I thought you ought to know, there's a psychiatrist in the building!

I open the car door. I feel somehow dirty, somehow like a terrible fraud. I turn the car radio on.

Sheryl Crow sings, 'If it makes you happy, it can't be that bad. If it makes you happy, then why the hell are you so sad?'

Chapter 18

In the middle of the night I wake, inexplicably drawn to the window.

A nuclear mushroom cloud silently erupts in the blackness, unfolding in magnificent luminescent yellows. Its beauty mesmerises me. Then I panic. Radiation from the bomb is on its way to poison us.

'Guys, we need to leave, now!' I shout.

Uncle Dale stands at the door in his hat and coat.

'Kids, we're out of here in five!' he shouts back.

The family wait for me in the car. I jump in and sit at the wheel. Mum is in the back seat with Beebs, Miley and Dad. But Dan is missing.

I shout for him and press the hooter. Anger erupts in me. I think, *If he doesn't come now then we'll all be killed by radiation.*

I hoot again.

It's typical of him to be so inconsiderate.

Then Dan floats ghostlike down the stairs doing his school tie around his neck, his eyes vacant and absent.

He starts to knot the tie, but then unwinds it and starts over, as though he's totally indifferent to the radiation rushing towards us.

He slides in next to Beebs. I yell at him, but he pays no attention. The streets clog with hooting cars trying to escape the approaching radiation. We are hemmed in.

Dad says, 'I think you'll find this is because of the Iraqis, you know.'

We're going to die slow and horrible deaths. I blame myself for taking so long to get everyone into the car. I blame Dan for wasting precious time on his tie. I sense the radiation reaching us on its invisible wave.

I wake with a thudding heart, sweating. Radiation poisoning will take effect in minutes. I want to go to Dan's room and tell him he should have been more considerate, that we might have been able to escape if he hadn't been so selfish.

Relief washes over me as I realise I've just had a terrible dream. There's no nuclear bomb on its way. Dan is sleeping soundly next door.

But then my thoughts gather further. Dan's room is empty; he isn't there to be angry with; he just isn't there at all.

*　　*　　*

Dad lies in bed covered in blankets. 'Dad, are you not going to work today?'

He slurs his words. His explanation is slow-motion gibberish. The shortwave radio crackles; it bends and hisses its BBC voices in the background, as though it's become the new soundtrack to his life.

'Anthony won't be taking any phone calls,' says Mum. 'If his work calls, just tell them he's unwell.'

Dad's face seems mummified in torment, his lips green from the Pynstop he chews constantly, cheeks sweaty from his diet of Valium. He looks more and more like a laboratory foetus preserved in formaldehyde.

He opens one eye, feels for his whisky and pills and, almost before he's conscious, is gone again.

Emily stops as she passes me. 'I know why Danny's gone,' she says. 'It is because your mother's dead brother was calling him. All your ancestors were calling for him. That is why. I am sure.'

I look into her eyes. They seem to be tired these days, as if our never-ending dramas are finally beginning to exhaust her.

'Maybe you're right,' I say.

'I'm sure. Very sure.'

'Is he eating anything?'

Emily shakes her head. 'When I bring food he leaves it there. But if I stop bringing? Ahhh, he starts to *shupa*. He says we are making him to starve.'

Dad's eyes are even paler than before, as if his body has lost the metabolic will to make pigment in his irises. And yet his eyes are somehow still human, somehow still like I imagine those of Hemmingway's Old Man. But the Old Man was a fighter at sea. He fought a mighty fish. What could Dad fight with his watery eyes? In his state he'd not even be able to fight a bream.

Dad opens a single eye, as though the light in this dim room would blind him if he opened both. 'Be a good lad and pass me some Valium, would you?' he asks.

'Dad, you have to stop doing this to yourself,' I plead. You're going to die if you carry on like this.'

The BBC still whines its doggerel.

'What I do is of no concern to you,' he says.

'Crap! We care about you!' I shout. 'You can't do this! You can't make us watch you kill yourself slowly! Do you think we want someone else in our family to die in front of us, and be asked to help them do it?'

His eyebrows contort into a frown. His voice is monotonous and measured. 'What I do does not affect you,' he says.

'So, Dan dying didn't affect you? Is that what you're trying to tell me?'

He pauses. 'No,' he says. 'It didn't.'

'You're full of crap! You weren't treating yourself like this before Dan died. I can't believe how selfish you're being. The rest of us make an effort. We all try except you.'

An unexpected knock rings out. 'Hullo, Anthony. Are you receiving visitors?'

My tears fill me with unexpected shame. I hurriedly lock myself in the en suite bathroom and curl into a ball on the floor.

At once, Dad starts to talk as though he's just woken from a short and invigorating nap. 'Hullo, Tim! Good to see you again! Long time, hey!'

Tim's guitar strums. His gravelly voice reverberates through the door:

'Just about now, I'll start thinking of you,

Just about now, you'll start to cry,

Baby I can't sleep at night,

When you're away,

Just about now, this blue turns to grey . . .'

I stare at myself in the mirror. My cheeks are stained red with tears. My eyes are bloodshot. My hair is a frizzy mess. *What'll become of us?* I think. *What'll become of me?*

* * *

Kirsty's figure forms a black silhouette against the orange, crackling flames. Music thuds into the night sky while drunken boys and girls talk nonsense to one another. Some of them seem high on drugs. I watch them as the fire crackles. Their talk seems so inane and vapid.

Those idiots, I think. *Those weak, ungrateful idiots. Are they that shallow? Yes. They are that shallow, and you are that lonely.*

Kirsty rests her head against my chest. She looks up at my face with her big eyes. I hug her. Then the lie behind why I'm here is instantly clear, and I feel dirty.

The heavens have bound Sarah and I and Dan together, I think. *We're like shooting stars: coalesced, unified. Sarah and I are meant to be. Kirsty and I will never happen.*

Chapter 19

My maths textbook lies open in front of me. A picture of Mr Pollard flashes through my mind. He's raping me up the bum with his big penis, his large frame moving over me and suffocating me.

To my left and right the library is quiet and orderly.

Why are these images haunting me? I think. *I must be mad.*

The bell rings. Chattering voices and moving chairs break the silence. I walk along the second floor balcony and stare at the concrete below. I think, *What if I were to dive over the top and smash my head open?*

Why would a voice in my head suggest that I do something like smash my head open? Maybe I'm lying to myself. Maybe in reality part of me wants to just die. Dan has shown me that the mind is its own worst enemy.

Maybe his own mind just turned on him as mine is now surely turning on me. I've begun to fear my mind. If I can't rely on my own mind, then what can I rely on? A devil has forced itself into my head, destroying me slowly with its poisonous whispers.

Mr Pollard stands outside his classroom. 'You know, Hayden, if Danny had been with me he would never have done what he did. I would have told him, don't let them get you out!'

He blocks a make-believe cricket ball from hitting make-believe wickets. He roars, 'I would have said, "Don't let them get you out!"'

His face reddens and the veins in his neck bulge. For a moment it seems as if he might cry. Then he collects himself. 'You can go in, boys,' he says.

* * *

The white door opens to reveal Dad with his head on the pillow. Machines and pipes whir next to him. A nurse stands by his bed with some pills. He sits up in bed and smiles. 'Thanks for coming to visit,' he says to me.

'I've brought these for you.'

'Oh, what's that?'

'Fresh grapes.'

His eyes follow me like I'm a vet about to put him down.

'I'm sorry about all of this, you know,' he mumbles. 'I don't know how you all put up with me.'

I put my hand on his arm and feel immediately strange, as though being close to him in this way is unwelcome.

'You're safe, Dad. That's all that matters right now.'

A different nurse brings him food. Dad thanks her and opens the foil. 'This is the first meal I've had in days,' he says to her. 'Difficult to get anyone to cook for me at home, you know.'

The nurse glances at me. Her eyes seem to accuse me of neglecting him.

She takes me to one side. 'We pumped his stomach to make sure that there was nothing untoward in there. He seems to be making a good recovery now. But keep an eye on him.'

'We do keep an eye on him,' I reply. 'It's just that we don't seem to be able to stop him from doing this to himself. And he seems to be able to convince his doctor to give him drugs. And when he can't get those he chews the over-the-counter drugs. What should we do?'

The nurse looks at me blank-faced.

* * *

I poke my head into Beebs's room. She sits at her desk with her chestnut hair neatly combed. 'Beebs, are you ready?' I ask. 'Mum says I'm giving you and Sarah a lift to school today.'

Sarah waits at the car. 'Hurry up, Hayde!'

I start the engine in a rush. 'You'll get there on time, don't worry.'

'Hayde, you need to be more organised in the morning; we're going to be late.'

'Beebs, it'll be fine,' I say.

'I'm just saying . . . next time.'

I slam on the brakes and bring the car to a skidding halt. 'Right, I'm sick of this! Get out!'

Beebs stares at me, confused. 'What do you mean?'

'I mean what I said. Get out!'

'No!' shouts Beebs. 'Why?'

'Beebs, get out or I'll make you get out.'

Her face scrunches up and her eyes fill with tears. She takes her bag and gets out. 'Hayde!' shouts Sarah. 'Please don't do this!'

'Sare, just stay out of this!' I snap back.

In the rear-view mirror I see Beebs stand at the side of the road and cry. *What's become of me?* I think. *What am I doing?*

I reverse. Sarah opens her door and gets out. I turn and watch her as she hugs Beebs. The door opens. Sarah gets in next to me. She sniffs away some tears and puts her hand on my knee. 'Hayde, it's okay, don't worry . . . everything will be okay.'

I want the fire in me to go somewhere, to go anywhere.

* * *

Dad shakes me awake. 'Be a good lad, won't you pick me up some more pills?'

I sit up and rub my infected eyes. 'No!'

'I need zhem! They're my medshin!' he says, barely able to form the words.

'I am not going to help you get your fucking drugs! I will not be part of this self-mutilation!'

'The doctor preshcribed zhem to me for a reazhon!' he mumbles.

'They are supposed to be washed down with water, not whisky, and they're supposed to last you three months and not one week. How long has the last set of drugs lasted you, hey?'

He rolls his eyes at me.

'You can't carry on killing yourself like this. It's not fair on us! And you can't keep asking us to fetch your booze and drugs. It's not right. I won't help you die anymore!'

'I'm sick,' he says. 'If I had a . . . broken leg . . . if I was on crutches, would you . . . kick it? Would you? Thatsh what you're . . . doing. Do you shink I like being like zshish? Do you shink I like shmoking sixry shigarettes a day? Do you shink I want to be zshish way?'

'We can all be like that you know,' I shout back. 'We can all sit around boozing and smoking ourselves to death if we want to. But we choose not to!'

'Zshere is no such shing as shoice.'

'Yeah, that's right, Dad.' I say. 'Choice is always something that other people have, but never you. Have you ever taken responsibility for any of your actions in life?'

Tears pour down his face. He sits down on my bed and curls up into a ball. 'My family hazsh rejected me,' he cries. 'Nobody lovsh me.'

Through the window sits the old sandpit where Dan and I once played. But the sand is long gone. In its place is a parched patch of grey. For a moment I can almost see Dan and me pushing our plastic trucks around in that sandpit. But now I begin to wonder if it was ever there, if we ourselves were ever there.

'Won'ch you be a goozh lad? Won'ch you go and gesh me shum medishine?'

I say nothing. I take the car keys from his hands.

*　*　*

The biology teacher stands at his board scribbling figures. '. . . and that, gentlemen, is what determines the start of Anaphase II.'

'What?' I want to yell. 'You talk like what you've said means something. Tell me, how do these spindle fibres you refer to magically form, then magically know where to go, then magically connect to the right chromosomes, then magically separate the chromosomes into different poles of the cell, magically knowing where these poles are to begin with, and then magically communicating the fact that they've finished separating, so that the cell can magically know when to pucker and divide itself in two.'

A boy puts his hand up. 'Sir, I don't understand. You're defining it in terms of what it isn't and not in terms of what it is.'

'Well, the thing is, Sanjay . . .' he begins.

'Hayde,' whispers Rugs, pointing to a cartoon in his textbook. 'I don't get this joke.'

He gestures to a drawing of an angry teacher confronting a student. The caption says, 'Johnny, you might blame your parents and your genes for not doing your homework, but I blame you!'

'I think it's supposed to be funny because Johnny is a product of his genes and environment, neither of which he controls,' I say. 'The joke is that Johnny's genetics teacher doesn't get this. She somehow imagines that there are genes, environmental factors and then, separate to that, Johnny.'

Mr Roscoe interjects. 'Mr Eastwood, Mr Musikavanhu. Can I continue, please?'

Perhaps someday every gene and every conceivable possible environment that each gene can be exposed to will be known to scientists. And then those scientists will understand every possible behavioural outcome. And when that happens, a rapist's lawyer will always just say, 'My client here carries this rape gene, and grew up in an environment that we know interacts with this gene to produce a raping phenotype. Your Honour, my client was predestined to commit this act through forces beyond his control.'

And how would the judge dispute this logic? On his desk would sit a fat book with information about how every human gene interacted with every conceivable environmental factor to produce every conceivable behavioural outcome.

I hate the inescapable logic of it: Dad is a product of his genes and environment, neither of which he controls. I've judged him too harshly; I've demanded too much of him; I've shouted at him, bullied him, ridiculed him. Dad has a broken leg, and I've kicked him in the shins.

The bell goes. My thoughts collapse under the weight of their own contradictions.

Sometimes it's as though everyone is a product of their genes and environment, but some are more a product of them than others.

* * *

Dad lies on his bed, eyes closed. His face is pale. Old whisky bottles lie half drunk on the floor. Unwashed clothes are strewn everywhere. There's a faint smell of old urine.

I put my ear near to his mouth to check for signs of breathing. I move his shoulder. 'Dad, Tim's here. He's playing his guitar, come and listen.'

His body flops over like a life-sized doll.

'Dad,' I say. 'I promise to try and be more understanding. I promise not to kick you in the leg.'

'Knock, knock!' calls Tim from the door. 'Anybody in there?'

He trundles in with his guitar. 'How is he?'

I glance at dad again, lying comatose with his oily face.

'Alive,' I reply.

Tim takes a seat and picks up his guitar. 'It's bloody tragic. Your dad's a good bloke. When I was here as an eighteen-year-old and got locked up for wearing a Nelson Mandela T-shirt, he was the one who came to the police station and got me out. Didn't charge me. No one else did anything for me. He's a good man. Don't let anybody tell you otherwise. These bloody chemicals are getting the better of him. And I'd know, I'm not out the woods yet, either.'

* * *

I sit bolt upright in bed, suddenly worried that Dad has drowned in his own vomit.

He lies there unconscious with an empty glass still in his hand. Half-finished whisky bottles and multi-coloured pills litter his bed-side.

His lips are bright green from the dye in the Pynstop pills. His face is contorted, like a dead rat locked in rigor mortis. His body is like an anthrax carcass, salted skin stretched across wasting bones. In recent weeks he has begun to walk like a dead man danced by a puppeteer, like his trousers are filled only by wire.

I put an ear to his chest. If he's dead I'll be relieved. The wait will finally be over.

But I sense a faint beat through his bony ribcage. I turn him on his side so that involuntary vomiting won't choke him.

Should I sleep here with him? I think.

The walls are yellow, as if someone's pissed cigarette tar against them. The cushions and sheets are covered in ash and burn holes.

I can't stay here.

I go to my room, worried that when I wake he'll have died in the night. But for how many more nights can I chaperone his sleep?

I dream that Dad stabs me in the stomach. He pulls out the blade. My blood pumps out of the gaping wound. I try to stop the flow with my hands, but it spurts between my fingers and onto the floor, like a pressure hose that can't be plugged.

* * *

I joob-joob the force diagrams in front of me. The mathematical symbols on my page lead from one to the next. They used to bore me, but now they're beautiful. Now they're the only things in the universe that make sense.

— 191 —

Dad's faint shout drifts into my room.

'I will sue the pants off that fucking Hipschman! Who does he think he is, coming to this country with his quackery? He had better watch out, I'm telling you now!'

A distant banging follows and then the sound of plates being smashed.

Mum appears at my door with a stolid and pale expression. 'What's going on?' I ask.

'I phoned Dr Hipschman and said I was worried that your father may be an alcoholic. Hipschman said he agreed.'

'And?'

'And I told your father, because I was worried. I think you heard the reaction for yourself. One moment he loves Hipschman, the next moment . . . this.'

'I don't even know how you define an alcoholic. What are the criteria?'

'I should ask Tim, really. He's battled the whole caboodle: booze, cocaine, heroin, sleeping pills.'

'What the hell went wrong in Tim's life then?'

'Who knows. Some of it has to do with his time in Matabeleland. He saw some terrible things there. People who've been there don't talk about it. Seeing those sorts of things . . . I'm sure it doesn't help matters.'

'What sort of things, Mum?'

'You know, the Gukurahundi that your father's mentioned in passing.'

* * *

Dad and I take a swim in the pool. We get out and dry ourselves. Dad's hair is still wet from the water. He tells me to follow him.

Dad says, 'Lie down over here, it'll be alright. Come on, there's a good lad.'

I hesitate but then I obey.

To my horror I discover that I am raping Mum. It has been a trick and yet the deed is done: I have raped my own mother while he has stood over me, supervising, telling me that I should have enjoyed it.

* * *

A plain middle-aged woman walks us to a room. She seats us at some chairs. The women sitting opposite us seem to eye us. I take a seat next to a humble-looking lady with sad eyes. 'What is an alcoholic, exactly?' I whisper to her. 'And what's the difference between an alcoholic and a heavy drinker?'

She puts a finger to her lips. 'Shhh, we're about to start. You'll understand the process as we go.'

'Let us hold hands,' says the leader. 'God grant me the serenity to accept the things I cannot change, courage to change the things I can, and the wisdom to know the difference.'

'Amen.'

'Who's going to begin?' asks the main lady.

A woman stands up. 'My name is Lindy and my husband is an alcoholic.' Tears fill her eyes. 'He's been dry for ten years now, but it's still a daily struggle . . .'

Someone passes her a handkerchief. 'Does anyone else want to say anything?' asks the group leader.

I put my hand up. 'Yes, though it's more a question than a statement. What exactly is an alcoholic? How do I know if I'm supposed to be here?'

The crowd is quiet. I sense people staring at me. 'We tend not to deal with those kinds of questions here . . . But you must be here for a reason?'

'Yes, I'm here because my dad's been drinking heavily and is unwell. I'm wondering to what extent his state is caused by alcohol and to what extent, wider life events.'

She pauses for a moment. 'The first stage to get over is your denial.'

'I don't even know whether he is one so how can I be denying it?'

The room goes quiet again, as though I've just confirmed my perfect denial to everyone. I want to shout, 'You idiots! If you take disagreement with your point of view as proof that your point of view is correct, then you can believe anything you bloody want! Tooth fairies, anything! Where the hell is the logic in you people?'

The group leader turns her head to the wider group. 'Would anyone else like to say anything?'

We adjourn for tea. The woman who wept stands solemnly at the window, gazing morosely into the night. I approach her slowly, like I may as well be approaching an antelope. 'Excuse me, ma'am.' I say. 'You say your husband hasn't drunk for ten years. How is alcohol still a problem in your life, if he isn't drinking anymore?'

She seems startled by my question. She answers it in a flurry, as though she's rebutting an accusation of impropriety. My brain processes her words seemingly instantly. I want to blurt out, 'Excuse me, ma'am, this is none of my business, but might I suggest that the problem with your husband is not that he's an alcoholic, per se, but a cunt. It would be better for you to join Cunts Anonymous. That way there would be no illusion about the nature of your problem. You could trot off to CA and say, "Hullo, my name is Lindy and my husband is an absolute cunt . . . I mean, last week, for example, he . . ."'

The lady looks at me. She seems to sense I will respond with something unhelpful. 'Good luck,' I finally say. 'I hope things improve.'

Mum and I climb into the car and close our doors. 'Mum, I won't be returning to this madhouse.'

Mum sits stony-faced, as though the cogs in her brain are turning and producing heat rather than thought.

*   *   *

A woman walks onto the school stage in a matron-like white dress. Our whispering and shuffling dies down.

'Morning, gentlemen,' she says with her Christian-happy smile. 'I've come to speak to you about suicide . . .'

She talks like a pocket preacher, like a lapdog barking on helium. She waves her hands about. She speaks of the correlation between sales of the board game *Dungeons and Dragons* and suicides. My thoughts wander. And then my eyes come to rest on Mr Pollard. He sits in his chair by the open door with his eyes closed, stroking his elbow as though he's listening to a Bach concert, as though her words are entrancing him with their beauty.

'. . . and remember, every time you sip a beer you are kissing the lips of Satan!'

Next to Mr Pollard sits Mr Kyle, head tilted to one side, staring into space. I sense an uncertainty in him. His world has changed. He seems like he's clinging to the sinking wreckage of the last time and place he understood. Like me.

Chapter 20

I open the fridge. There is no milk. There is no food. There is nothing. I sit on the veranda and watch the msasa leaves soak up the late afternoon sun. The borehole pump chugs in the distance.

Sarah appears wearing a beanie. She removes it. 'Surprise!' she exclaims.

Her head is clean-shaven like an American marine. 'Sare, what are you *doing*?' I ask.

'I needed a change, Hayde! What do you think? Do you like it? It's the new me!'

Rapunzel, I think. *Your hair is gone.*

'I don't know, Sare, you always seem to be a new you. Can't you just be you, whatever that is?'

'Hayde, don't be so conservative! Sinead O'Connor's beautiful with short hair.'

She hugs me.

'Your shirt smells of smoke,' I say.

She seems momentarily embarrassed. 'I've been hanging with Melinda,' she says.

Her! I think. I feel immediately alone. I want to say, 'But she's the kind of shallow idiot who thinks smoking *mbanje* makes her into some kind of philosopher queen. She's never had an original thought in her life.'

Sarah pulls away, like my brief silence already said what I was thinking. 'I'm going to play the piano, Hayde. Come find me when you've stopped judging my life.'

* * *

If a boy places a ball on a slope and releases it, will it roll or will it remain still? The textbook says that you need to know two facts to solve this problem: the force pulling the ball down the hill and the frictional force preventing the ball from rolling. The ball will roll if the gravity acting down the slope is bigger than the force of friction stopping it.

I put my hand up. 'Sir, I'm not sure about the triangle of forces in this particular problem. Can you advise me?'

'Hayden,' he sighs. 'Remember to joob-joob.'

'Sir, that's what you always say, but it doesn't help the specific case I'm dealing with.'

'No, Hayden, that's it. You just have to joob-joob.'

Another boy puts his hand up. 'Sir, I don't understand why the force acting down the slope in this problem is given by $mg(sin(a))$.'

Mr Pollard lifts his hands into the air. 'You have to remember to joob-joob. Always joob-joob!'

'Sir, I don't understand joob-joob,' says the boy.

Mr Pollard smiles. 'Teak from the tonsils up, my boy. Teak from the tonsils up.'

Two deafening bangs interrupt him. He rushes to the door. 'Ghost knocker!' he shouts, fumbling at the door to open it. 'Ghost knocker!'

His huge frame vanishes. Minutes later, the door swings open. 'Did you get him, sir?' we all ask.

He smiles demurely. 'Yes. That was Hook. I waited for him in the corridor upstairs and when I saw him I said, "Hook, was that you who ghost-knocked on my door just now?" And Hook said, "Yes, sir, it was." And I said, "Well, Hook, you know I'm going to have to rough you up now, don't you?" And Hook said, "Yes, sir." And then I roughed him up.'

— 197 —

'Well done, sir!'

Mr Pollard shrugs his giant shoulders and smiles as though he's both pleased and embarrassed.

* * *

A large group of boys encircles a shivering junior. 'Geoff, what's going on here?' I ask.

'Ah, this lightie was disrespecting a senior at the athletics tournament last weekend. Now he's getting *gotcha'd*.'

A prefect joins the conversation. 'Ah, you should have seen how we scared this lightie earlier. Blumby lunged for the lightie and I restrained him. I honestly thought the lightie was going to shit himself there and then. It was classic!'

The moment seems to be over quite quickly. The crowd starts to disperse. But then another senior arrives. 'Where do you think you're going?' he asks the junior.

The boy stops. 'Nowhere, sir.'

The runt looks like a mere child. Spectators crowd round again and eat their sandwiches. The senior holds a finger to the runt's face. 'Don't you dare do something like that again!'

'Yes, sir.'

A clean smack rings through the air. The junior boy steps back to steady himself from the blow.

'I didn't hear you!'

'Yes, sir,' repeats the boy, struggling to speak.

'You're out of line!' I interrupt the senior. 'If he's done something wrong then take him to the headmaster.'

The runt cowers in front of both of us. The senior cuffs the boy again. 'Get out of my sight,' he says. Then, 'What did you say, East-wood?'

'Do you think the punishment you gave was proportionate to the crime?' I ask.

'Eastwood, don't you ever undermine me like that again. I will beat you!'

'Did your punishment fit the crime?'

'Did you hear me?'

'Of course I heard you.'

He raises a finger to my face and breathes down at me. 'Stay out of my way.'

I wait for the blows to start. We look each other in the eye. I turn my back on him and walk away. He stands where I left him. I sense him eyeballing me as I disappear into the distance.

Geoff sits beside me in the library. 'Ah, Hayde, what happened out there was wrong. It really left a bad feeling in my stomach. You did the right thing.'

'Today it's just school, but tomorrow it's something worse, don't you think?'

'Like what?' asks Geoff.

'Like Rwanda. Like Nazi Germany. That's how it works. Thugs do what they want and normal people let it happen.'

'Hayde, you're extrapolating from this a bit too much.'

'No, I'm not,' I say. 'No, I'm not. It's the way humans work.'

* * *

Waiters bring food and drinks to boys chattering with their dates. Teachers sit with their spouses. Mr Kyle maintains an Ian Smith-like properness. He shakes my hand and mutters some pleasantries and then gazes into the distance with a half-smile.

Adrian raises his wine glass. 'Here's to life on the other side!'

Groups of boys talk and joke with their dates. Even those with little time for thought seem to notice that these last moments of our school days are precious.

Sarah wanders onto the dance floor, her hair still military. Adrian puts his arm around my shoulders. 'Hayde, you're looking into space. How are you doing?'

'Good, man.'

'No, look at me, Hayde,' he says. 'How are you *really* doing?'

His words startle me. 'Same old, same old,' I finally reply. 'The old man is going a little berserk at the moment.'

'Hayde, you impress me. Nothing seems to faze you. Those other buggers are all over the place. But you're the constant. The one person who grounds me. You should big yourself up a bit more, fly your flag a bit higher.'

'I only wish I was as together on the inside as I appear on the outside.'

'Hayde, you'll be fine. I've got faith in you. I know nobody else does, but I do.'

I want to tell him that our bond is covalent, but the words won't form in my mouth. I move to a couch and stare at the TV screen on the wall. A pretty girl with chocolate-blonde hair joins me. 'I hate music videos like these. I find them so arbitrary,' I say.

'I agree,' she says, as the half-naked woman on the screen gyrates her bum.

'People don't believe in anything anymore,' I continue. 'Life's just about drugs and distraction now.'

'It's pretty pointless, isn't it?'

'Your accent sounds English. Where are you from?' I ask.

She tosses her hair back. 'I'm not English, I'm Scottish.'

Adrian and Rugs appear. 'Come on Hayde, come dance.'

I get up. 'Lovely to meet you,' I say to the girl. 'I'll speak to you later.'

Adrian dances next to me. I shout to him above the deafening music, 'That girl's pretty nice, hey?'

'Who, Naomi? Oh yeah, Jendez's item. Do you want to put your cock in her, Hayde?'

'She's nice. Seems like a thoughtful person.'

My eyes search for Sarah, but I don't see her anywhere. A new song starts and other people join us. The Scottish girl moves to the dance floor. I hold out my hand and she takes it. For a brief moment she catches my eye and bobs up and down. And then she dances off to her boyfriend.

I feel a sudden sadness. The last moment of my last school dance registers with me. Sarah grips my shoulder. Her mascara is smudged with tears. 'What's wrong?' I ask above the noise.

'You fucking bastard, I hate you!' She punches me in the neck. I grab her. 'What the hell are you doing, Sare? Are you bloody crazy?'

'Oh fuck off, don't fuck with me,' she screams, pushing me away. I follow her across the dance floor.

'What's going on?'

'I just want to go home,' she sobs.

I grip her arm.

'Sare, I'm sorry for dancing with that girl but nothing was going on, okay? Why are you blowing this out of proportion? She's Jendez's girlfriend, for God's sake.'

She walks out the building. In the car park she buries her face in her hands and cries in the grey and yellow of the moonlight. 'I just want to go home.'

'Sarah, please tell me what's wrong?'

I wait for her to say something, but she just stares at the ground, dripping tears into the dust.

'Life isn't worth living anymore,' she finally says. 'Sometimes I just want to kill myself. I really do. And I wonder why I don't just do it.'

My heart jolts. 'Sarah, why are you feeling like this all of a sudden?'

'I don't know. I've been feeling like this for a while now.'

We sit in silence. She looks at her feet. 'Are you going to leave me for being pathetic and crazy?'

'No, don't be silly,' I say. I put my head in my hand.

What if Sarah were to kill herself? I wonder. *Should I take her seriously? Or is this just another one of her ever-changing phases?*

Chapter 21

In the old days Sarah's hair would have blown wildly in the wind. But now it's too short. It hardly moves at all in the rushing air.

She reaches over to the car stereo and turns the volume down. 'Hayde, I've got something to tell you.'

'What?'

'I don't know if I can say it.'

'What is it? You can say it.'

'I slept with Terence after your dance.'

A fresh eel slithers into my stomach. I screech the car to a halt. 'Why did you tell me? I've got my exams coming up. Do you think I need to know this now?'

'Adrian and Rugs threatened to tell you if I didn't.'

'Why did you do it?'

'I don't know, Hayde. I felt taken for granted. I was drunk.'

'That seems to be the in-vogue excuse for everyone right now.'

'You're like a zombie these days,' Sarah says. Do you know what it's like trying to communicate with someone who isn't there, someone who doesn't really look at you or engage with you?'

'So this is somehow my fault, is it?'

'No. I'm just saying I've been feeling lonely with you. You don't say anything to me about anything.'

'Well what the hell do you want me to say? How much I wish Dan was still here? How I wish I hadn't betrayed him? How I wish my father wasn't drinking himself to death?'

'I don't know, give me something. Anything. I don't feel you even care about me anymore.'

'I'm just trying to hold myself together. And moments like this really don't help, I can assure you.'

A tear rolls down her cheek. The door closes behind her. I want her to come back and tell me it was some kind of accident.

I want her to tell me that she loves me.

* * *

Rusting screws float around at the bottom of the toolbox. 'Mum,' I shout. 'Have you seen the pliers?'

'No,' she shouts back. 'Why the hell would I know where they are? Why do you need them?'

'Dad's ripped the seats out of the Nissan and left them in the driveway.'

She appears at the door. 'What?'

'You heard me. I need to put the seats back. But the pliers have gone walking too.'

'Honestly! He's getting worse.'

The canvas seats sit marooned on the driveway in a haze of soft drizzle. I search fruitlessly for nuts and bolts.

Mum and Beebs watch me, hands on hips, as my clothes darken with moisture. Then Beebs holds up a small bin from the bathroom. 'What about this?'

'What, to sit on?'

She brings it to me. 'Yeah.'

I place it in the cavity. 'Look at that . . . it fits.'

* * *

How would a psychopath behave during war? Without an emotional connection to people around him, he would likely never volunteer to fight. He'd just wait in the shadows for the good to fight and die. In the end the war would be won and he would still be alive. Or the war would be lost and he would be no worse off than those who'd fought.

And so there it is: by an accident of war, the good would kill and the evil would not. Perhaps the biggest danger in life is that good people are capable of evil for lazy reasons. Lazy thought is the mother of sin in good people.

'Howzit, bru! What are you doing?' asks Adrian from the doorway of my room.

'Thinking.'

'Christ, Eastwood, I can't leave you on your own for three minutes. Stop thinking, you'll drive yourself crazy!'

'I'm already crazy. Why are you looking so smart?'

'Because we, Flapstick, are going to get laid tonight. Put your clothes on.'

'Why are you so keen to go out?'

'Just found out Jane's been *poinking* the head boy. Who'd have thought.'

'Oops.'

'And I figured it wouldn't be fair for you to be all miserable by yourself.'

He hands me a fist of condoms. My insides feel sucked empty. 'Adrian, I don't know about this. I don't know if I want to actually clap eyes on another *Homo sapiens sapiens* female.'

'Bru? What are you talking about! This place is crawling with hot *gweel*!'

He drives us to a backpackers' lodge where rosy-cheeked girls sit at the bar. Their dreadlocked hair seems immensely cool. Shona music blares out of a blown speaker. Adrian racks the fraying pool table.

A ruggedly handsome Rasta man dances on the cement floor. His joints vibrate like rubber. Foreign-looking girls emerge from the shadows to dance with him.

'Yeah, I scheme I might not be dancing tonight,' I say.

Adrian banters with a freckly girl in torn jeans. She sounds Scandinavian.

'So bru, what's the *nyaya* with her?' I ask when he comes back.

He grimaces, 'Bru, she's arb. I wouldn't even bone her with your dick.'

The barman calls for last orders. The Rasta man saunters to the car park with a woman on his arm. 'Adrian, let's go. Nobody in this place appreciates an undercooked sausage.'

Adrian slumps onto his pool stick. 'Hayde. I don't even know who I am anymore.'

'Me neither, Aid. Me neither.'

* * *

Sarah's arm rests on my chest. I watch her breasts move up and down as she breathes.

Her clothes lie in a pile on the floor. They're different to her old ones. Hippy-looking, colourful. When she's finished in this small town I can imagine her in Paris hanging around with painters and pot-smoking artists, the kind who think taking cocaine is the same as taking philosophy. *She'll be in her element*, I think.

My clothes lie next to hers. Shorts and a T-shirt, flip-flops. An alien need only look at our clothes from his spacecraft to know that the owners are ill-suited to breeding.

Sarah seems buoyant again. But is she? Dan also seemed better before he killed himself. Maybe she's in a terrible way. But maybe I'm just thinking everything she wants me to think. Is this just one giant game that I'm losing?

She rolls over. I must stop being an amoeba. I must start being a higher-level organism. I need to step back from the machine and control it, not be enmeshed in its cogs. I need to somehow be something other than a product of my genes and my environment. Like some kind of futuristic machine, I need to learn from the learning process itself.

I go to the kitchen and open the fridge. It's empty. I go to the pantry. There's no bread, no eggs, no fruit, no cereal.

* * *

'Mum,' I say. 'There's no food in the house. Literally no food.'

'Speak to your father. He says I'm salting his money away. He's given me nothing for weeks. I don't even have petrol to take Beebs to ballet.'

Dad sits on his bed in his pyjamas. He reads the *Financial Times*. The BBC voices bend and whine in the background.

'Dad, we're out of food. You need to give Mum some money so she can go to the shops.'

His eyes meet mine. 'No.'

'Why not?'

'She doesn't need any. She's got lots. Ask her about her slush fund.'

'Oh nonsense, you're so bloody paranoid! She doesn't have a slush fund.'

At once he rises and pants his petrol-breath in my face. 'If you feel so strongly about it, go out and earn your own fucking money, hey. Think you're a smartarse, do you? Think you're going to teach your father to suck eggs? Well, I tell you now, life is going to teach you and your mother some very hard lessons.'

My body charges with electrical energy. I want to smash him through the door. I want to banish him to Lagos. With his reptilian glare, he dares me to make a victim of him.

'Your behaviour's out of order,' I murmur.

'You and your mother are behaving disgustingly! Real bloody pieces of work you are. Bloody thug, are you going to hit me?'

I hold his gaze for a moment. My fists loosen. I turn my back on him.

'Where do you think you're going? Running away as usual, are we? Bloody coward!'

* * *

'Hullo, you're new!' exclaims Mr Pollard. 'And you don't have a school uniform!'

A boy in jeans and a T-shirt holds out a note.

'Oh, I see,' says Mr Pollard, clutching it in his ape-hands. 'You're an expatriate . . . checking out some schools in the area . . . spoken with Mr Kyle.'

'That's right. I haven't yet decided which school to go to yet.'

Mr Pollard folds the note and puts it his top pocket. 'Good. And where are you from?'

'Germany.'

'Germany!' With sudden urgency he strides to the board. 'My boy, I want to tell you about the Second World War; it's very important.'

The boy watches Mr Pollard as he mumbles and scribbles, drawing convoluted arrows between chalk-strokes. The bell interrupts the history lesson. '. . . and that, finishing up, Fritzie, is why God wanted Britain to win the Second World War.'

The boy looks at him, confused and horrified. I give him a playful punch on the arm. 'Welcome to St Bartholomew's,' I say. 'Looking forward to seeing you next week!'

Geoff stands at my shoulder. He flicks his left eye like a fly's just landed on his brow, like a horse has just involuntarily flicked an insect off its rump. 'You'll find we're all quite well adjusted here.'

*　*　*

Rain splatters onto the road. Steam swirls above the soaking tar. The rich smell of red soil rises up from the undergrowth. I turn into our driveway.

Mum sits with Beebs in the guest room. There's a tray of coffee with milk and biscuits. 'Can I pour you a cup, Hayde?' asks Mum.

I notice a large suitcase. 'You've moved your stuff in here,' I say.

'Yes, I can't take the smoking and the filth of the main bedroom. It's not healthy for Miley.'

'How did you get milk and biscuits?'

'I cashed in his empty whisky bottles at the supermarket for the deposit. It'll cover groceries for now.'

Dad appears at the door in his pyjamas. 'Annette, why are your things in here?'

'I've told you, Anthony. I've asked you countless times not to smoke with Miley in the bed. I've asked you not to drink and behave abusively around him.'

'That's nonsense. You're the one who's abusive. You're the one who's withholding things from me!'

'I said I'll move back in if you improve your behaviour.'

'You're the one who's abusive. You say you don't want to fuck me anymore. You keep me from eating properly. You think you're the Queen, do you, giving me ultimatums?'

'There's always food for you, Anthony. Your soups sit there without ever being touched. But what about us?'

'What about your slush fund! How did you get the coffee and milk, hey?'

'I cashed in your empty bottles.'

'What? Annette! You are not to touch the empty bottles! Those are mine! And then you wonder why I haven't given you anything this month . . . Well, now you know! Now you know!'

'Dad, that's enough,' I say.

Dad flicks his eyes at me. 'Oh, I see. You're going to be the tough guy are you?'

'Dad, your reasoning is circular. You're using Mum's reaction to your behaviour as justification for your behaviour.'

'Oh, so now you're a smarty-pants are you?'

'It's called logic. And what you said was illogical.'

He raises his finger. 'Well, let me tell you, you've got half the brain your brother had. Half. You're just another one of these thick bloody Rhodies going nowhere in life. You like your rugby, your women. Vacuous. How could I have produced such a vile bloody son?'

Pins and needles prick at my face. I want to be the thug he sees in me.

'Dad, you need to go now. You need to go!'

'Bugger off, this is my house!'

I force the door closed in his face. He tries to resist but he's too weak. He pants and heaves with his smoker's lungs. 'Ah, Jesus!' he shouts.

Guilt overcomes me. *He's right,* I think. *How could I be such a bully? How could I be so vile?*

* * *

I pull into the petrol station. The attendant tips his hat and smiles. 'Yes, Mr Eastwood, how much today?'

'Half a tank. On the Eastwood account, please.'

'Boss. One moment.'

He dips into the petrol station office. Through the giant glass window he natters to a woman. He returns. 'Ah, boss. Sorry. The boss-lady, she said that account is no longer active.'

'Really? Since when?'

'Last week but one. Can I still fill up for cash?'

'No, thank you,' I say. 'Another time.'

* * *

Sarah's front door creaks open. She looks surprised to see me. Her hair has grown a bit more. She wears bell-bottom jeans and a tie-dyed T-shirt.

'Hayde, I wasn't expecting you. I'm about to head out.'

'I just thought I'd pop in on my way home. How's your work going?'

'Really good, thanks. I'm loving A-level French. Hoping to go to France next year to get properly fluent. Looks like it might actually happen.'

'Can we do coffee or something tonight?' I ask.

'I'd love to, but I can't. I'm going to this reggae jam session just now. Won't be back till late.'

'Who's going to be there?'

'Claire, Crystal, Celia. Angus. Simon. A few others.'

'Okay. So lots of drink and drugs then.'

'Hayde, chill out. There's nothing wrong with weed. It's natural, okay. There's so much ridiculous stigma around it.'

'I suppose it's just not my scene.'

'What is your scene, Hayde? People talking about aeroplanes and the "nature of evil"? Not everyone finds that stuff interesting.'

Her words drill into my thick skull and leave me silent. I hate myself for envying her world.

She kisses me on the cheek. 'Excuse me, Hayde, I need to finish doing my makeup.'

Chapter 22

The glider sits in pieces in a plastic bag. I glue the tail back together. I patch the holes in the plastic film. I cut the submarine-like nose off the fuselage and sand it down, until all that's left is a hollow disfigured shell of balsa. I've no right to change its form like this. But then who is to say what it should look like? Isn't the universe in constant flux? Today I'm older than I was yesterday. And over many months what seems like no difference to my cells will become a big difference. Maybe Dad is right about reality. Maybe things just change. Maybe there's no constant in this world. Maybe his undulating reality is like all reality. Maybe order is something we invent to delude ourselves. Maybe there really is no rhyme or reason to anything. Maybe Dan never existed. Maybe he's just an idea planted in my mind.

I glue layers of plywood onto the fuselage and make a flat mount for Geoff's new engine. This time the plane will have enough power. I glue coins to the rudder to balance the engine weight.

On the open field the engine kicks to life. I tune the fuel flow with the needle valve until it runs smoothly. I make pre-flight checks and then signal to Geoff that I'm ready. His skinny-ma-linky legs run knock-kneed into the distance.

The plane sails high into the big blue sky. I move the control stick to bank it. It turns slowly.

I'm a fool, I think. *I should have made the controls more responsive.*

The plane shrinks into a flea on the horizon. I bend it towards me. It loses height in the turn. Its wing trims a treetop. Like a bird shot in the wing it staggers jagged out of the sky and into the unkempt field beneath it.

I put down the controls and run towards the wreck.

I find it lying in the grass: a dismembered body with its intestines spilling out. I lift it into my arms and study it.

It's dead.

* * *

Dad stands at my doorway with rose clippers in his hand. The oil on his face is gone. He wears a freshly pressed shirt. His face is shaven. 'Why don't you come and say hullo to Bill?' he asks.

I continue scribbling equations in my notebook. 'I need to work. I'm very far behind.'

'Just come through for a moment, Hayde. He's an interesting chap, you know, might have some good university advice for you.'

The white-haired man sits in a garden chair looking out over the pool area with a glass of wine in his hand. He gets to his feet and greets me.

'Hi there, Hayden, I've heard a lot about you. Your father tells me you've just got the maths prize at school. Well done.'

His words take me by surprise. 'It's a case of the one-eyed man in the land of the blind, I can assure you,' I reply.

Dad pulls up a chair for me. 'That's not true,' he says. 'Hayde's being modest. He's very good with abstract ideas, actually.'

I flush with irritation. I want to ram the tea tray off the table and end Dad's crooked game.

'Bill lectures at Oxford,' Dad continues.

Dad's reality flaps like a flag in the wind. I can scarcely tolerate the sound of it.

'You know,' Dad continues. 'I think that fellow must be the cleverest man I've ever met.'

'Interesting you say that, Anthony,' interjects Bill. 'Because he insists that you're the cleverest man he's ever met!'

Dad cuts and jabs his hands through the air. He talks about the Soviet Union and Marxism and Africa. Bill seems spellbound, like a child watching a wizard.

I get up. 'I'd best be getting back to work,' I say. 'Good to meet you, Bill.'

'Oh, hang on,' Dad says. 'Hayden wants to go to university in Britain next year, you know.'

'Oh really, where are you planning to go?'

'Well, I don't know, it depends on my results. I'd like to do maths somewhere, I think.'

'Not Oxford?'

I swallow. 'That hadn't occurred to me.'

I return to my room. I open my textbooks and scrawl some notes. But shame crowds out my thoughts.

If Bill had a secret camera he would see the truth. He would know what really happens at Blair Road. He would know that Dad had deceived him. And that I had deceived him too.

A knock interrupts my thoughts. Bill appears at my bedroom door. 'I just wanted to say goodbye.'

I rise. 'Lovely to have met you, Bill.'

His eyes wander to my bookshelf. 'Do you mind if I take a quick look?' he asks.

What does the son of the great Anthony Eastwood have on his shelf? Will he find the great writers? Dostoyevsky? Hemingway? Perhaps a colonial boy like me will read Kipling or Lessing?

He adjusts his reading glasses. *Asterix* comics come into focus. Then Roald Dahl's *Going Solo* and *George's Marvellous Medicine*.

'If you'd like some advice about universities, just let me know. Perhaps you could just write down your predicted grades for me so I can ask around.'

'Thanks Bill, I'll do that. Take care.'

*   *   *

Adrian's class natters behind the door.

'Yes?' calls Vubu, as I enter.

'Good afternoon, ma'am,' I say. 'May I speak with Adrian, please?'

Adrian looks up from his desk. 'How's it, Flap?'

'Can you give me a lift home today? The old man has vandalised the car again.'

'Sure thing, my guy. What's he done now?'

'He's pulled out the whole distributor mechanism from the engine.'

He shakes his head and sighs. 'I'll be at the car park at lunch. Come find me there. Sorry, man.'

Hair and sellotape cover Adrian's desk. 'Dude, what's all that?'

'Oh, that? We're just making Vubu some presents.' He pulls a tuft of pubic hair from the top of his shorts and snips it off with his scissors. With dextrous fingers he takes some sellotape and wraps the hairs up like a bundle of tiny wood.

I blurt out a laugh. Vubu sits at her desk writing as the class simmers with noise, all the while unaware of the presents being thoughtfully made for her.

I think, *When she sees them on her desk she'll stare at them and wonder where the hair came from. And then she'll notice that it's suspiciously frizzy.*

'Thank you, ma'am. That's all,' I say.

*　*　*

Sarah is strangely silent. The hum of the engine and the rush of the wind are the only sounds left in the world.

'What's up, Sare?'

'Okay,' she says finally. 'I'll say what's on my mind. I think we should . . . break up.'

The eel appears instantly in my stomach. It swims and slithers around. 'Who is it?'

'What do you mean?'

'I know you too well. You wouldn't be doing this if there wasn't someone else.'

She goes quiet. 'Come on, tell me.'

'I want to get to know Angus better.'

Streetlights pass by the windows. I turn the tape deck on. John Lennon plays 'Oh Yoko!'. For a moment I feel beautiful, as if I'm stepping on the piano chords, as if I'm dancing on the musical notes, as if I'm a manikin jumping between the shapes of a psychedelic video game.

At home I lie on my bed and stare at the ceiling until morning filters into the room.

Mum puts her hand on my forehead. 'Hayde, you're looking terrible, just take some Valium for once, otherwise you're not going to sleep at all. You need some sedation now.'

She gives me the little blue pills. 'I don't want to make a habit of this, Mum.'

They seem so sinister. And yet they're just small and blue. I pop two into my mouth.

* * *

The model plane lies dismembered like elephant bones in an elephant graveyard, rotting. I finger the pieces of wood and wonder if some magic configuration exists to fit them together again.

The gardener returns on the old black bicycle with a small plastic packet.

'Noah? Is this all you can get for us?'

'Ah, boss gave me enough for milk, bread and potatoes, *chete*.'

Dad lies under the Mercedes tapping away at something. Two young men in overalls watch. 'Pass me the spanner,' he snaps.

I go to my room and open my biology textbook.

In the distance Dad shouts at Mum. 'I asked you for bloody quotes! What else was I supposed to do?'

Rage grips me. I slam my pen down on the table and stride towards the shouting. Dad stands by the car, like a serpent hovering in smoke. 'Your mother is behaving in the most abominable way,' he says.

'No, you're behaving abominably!' I shout. 'You're the one who's engineered this situation. You're the one who broke the car. You're the one who brought these halfwits here to break it more. When are you actually going to take responsibility for something you've done?'

He extinguishes his cigarette. 'The reason you're cross is because you think I loved Daniel more than you.'

'What the hell are you talking about? I'm talking about the fucking car, not about Dan!'

From his throne, he throws out his barbs. 'If you're not happy with the way I behave, you're quite welcome to go.'

'You bet your bloody life, I'm out of here!'

He follows me. 'Nobody's asking you to live here, you know!'

'You don't even know anything about me!' I scream. 'I bet you don't even know what A levels I'm doing. What are they, hey?'

He pauses like I've asked him a crossword puzzle question. 'Um . . .' he mumbles. 'Physics . . .'.

'Wrong.'

I pack my bags as he hovers over me. 'Do you have any idea what I'm interested in at all?' I ask.

Then I pick up the phone. 'Adrian, I need you to come and get me. Dad's kicking me out.'

I sit in the driveway with piles of books next to me. The world seems oblivious. Purple-crested louries swoop between the trees. Chickens root between the flowers. Adrian's old car eventually sweeps up the driveway. He jumps out and hugs me. I load my books and clothes into the boot.

And then Dad appears as if from nowhere, screaming through Adrian's open window. 'Just so you know, this is your choice!'

* * *

'Come on, lunchtime! Adrian, Nathan, James. Hurry the fuck up!' yells Meg.

One by one the boys arrive at the table.

'Kev,' I say to Adrian's father. 'Do you think the IMF and the World Bank are responsible for businesses going bust in Zimbabwe?'

'Hayde, for Christ's sake,' interjects Adrian. 'We've hardly started lunch and you're already revving Kev up.'

'Oh, fuck off, Adrian!' he shouts. 'Let me answer. Hayden, that sentiment, while popular in some circles, is absolute bloody nonsense. Why do you think these thieves went to the World Bank and IMF, hey? I'll tell you why: because they'd already bankrupted the bloody country. And why didn't they just go to a high street bank for their money? I'll tell you why: because no other institution would give them such favourable interest rates and no other institution would be mad enough to lend money to a Third World country with no history of fiscal responsibility. This government wanted the quickest, softest option, so they could carry on stealing as usual. And then they have the cheek to turn around and blame the very people who bailed them out.'

Adrian looks at me. 'Now look what you've done, Flap. Can't take you anywhere.'

Kevin Rawling shoves a sliver of roast beef into his mouth.

'But surely the reforms themselves were bad for the country?' I ask. 'How could those old Rhodesian businesses suddenly compete on the open market?'

'So,' he snaps, 'you think it's unreasonable that someone who lends you money wants some measures to ensure you'll pay it back? The world is globalising; they're going to have to compete sooner or later. A lot of people have won from those reforms. Look at agriculture. I meet guys every week exporting things all over the globe now, earning heaps of forex for the country.'

'I don't know. Everyone seems to just have very different ideas about how this world works,' I mutter.

I pick at my food and mull over Mr Rawling's thoughts. He jabbers on in the background, '. . . every fuckin' weekend we were at Domboshawa goofed out of our heads on acid. It was fuckin' amazing. When you're tripping out, those rocks are just incredible, those colours in the soil and granite, they're just un-bloody-believable.'

He talks about his disobedience at school. He talks about what a naughty teenager he once was. 'So, James,' he says, out of the blue. 'How are your exams going at the moment?'

James strikes the air with his fingers. 'All I can say is that I ploughed Shona. That's all I can say. I ploughed it *onetime*.'

The room goes silent for a moment. Then Kevin explodes, 'James, who the hell do you think you are? Do you think it's funny that you've failed Shona? Do you think it's funny that I pay all this fuckin' money for you to be educated, only so that you can piss it all away? Well, let me tell you something: it's not fuckin' funny!'

'Hang on, Kev,' says Adrian. 'Stop flexing your foreskin for a moment. First you're telling us what a reprobate you were, as though it was the coolest thing in the world and then suddenly you're yelling at James for failing a fucking exam. What the hell is that all about?'

'Adrian, I'm not speaking to you. I'm speaking to James!' shouts Kevin.

'Oh, for fuck's sake!' yells Meg. 'Why don't you all just grow up? Can't you see we've got a guest here? Grow the fuck up, will you!'

'Meg, don't mind me. Pretend I'm just like furniture.'

'Thank you, Hayde,' she cackles. 'I promise we're not always like this!'

* * *

Adrian throws a tennis ball to me. I catch it and slump back into the water. Dad's Mercedes moves measuredly up the Rawlings' long driveway.

'Fuck you, Nathan!'

'No, fuck you, James!'

The water froths. Nathan punches James. James swings at Nathan and misses. Adrian hurls wild punches at Nathan. In seconds the fight is over. James cries, 'Fuck you, Nathan, you're such a wanker. Never playing this game with you again.'

'Bru, whatever!' Nathan yells back.

The brothers lick their wounds. *There is something intimate about fighting*, I think. *If Dan were still here we'd scrap like brothers too and then forgive each other.* I find myself too sad to continue playing.

Mum stands at the pool's edge. 'Afternoon, Mrs Eastwood,' they all say.

Mum removes her dark glasses. 'Hi, guys. I'd just like a quick word with Hayde.'

I climb out of the pool and stand with Mum to one side. The brothers stand some metres away towelling themselves dry in the sun.

'Hayde, I'm not happy about you being here. There are too many distractions. It's important that you get some work done. Please consider going to Sue Hargreave's house. I've phoned her. She said she'll clear a space for you and cook for you and lend you a car.'

* * *

Mrs Hargreave's small figure hovers over the stove. She throws some bacon into a pan. 'I really wish Stephen would come back from England,' she says. 'He should never have gone. He absolutely hated schooling there. Beaten up, spat on; it was heartbreaking. I don't know what that government thinks it's doing; manners are becoming something for rich people only.'

She hands me a plate of food. 'Thanks so much, Sue. If you don't mind I'm going to eat this in my room while I work.'

Back in my room, I open my chemistry textbook and scribble some benzene reactions on a piece of paper. The scribblings make no sense. It will be a miracle if I pass any of these exams, much less do well in them.

I hear a car engine. Then Sarah's head is at the window.

'Sarah, what are you doing here?'

'I just came to see how you were. I was worried about you.'

'I need to work. You should really go.'

'I just wanted to talk for a bit. Is that okay?'

I let her in.

Hours later I wake from a deep sleep next to her. The room is dark. Sarah lies next to me. I study her as she sleeps; she seems so relaxed. *Why have I done this to myself?* I think. I glance at the pile of notes on the table. I wish they would disappear.

I sense for some moments that her lying with me has temporarily quenched a strange rage within me: the rage of invisibility. But when she's gone I'll be back to the same position in the cosmos, unable to leave so much as a ripple in the continuum of Space-Time. Was it that same rage of invisibility that undid Dan? Maybe what he did was the final protest of his suffocating sense of invisibility. Maybe he had carried that rage all his life, until the final injury proved too much. And maybe that same rage drove the African Nationalists to seek power, determined that, for once, the whites would notice that they were human. Maybe the rage of invisibility explains it all. But maybe it explains nothing. Maybe I'm just moving blank jigsaw pieces about again.

Sarah yawns and stretches like a cat. 'Hi, Haydie.'

'Sare, what's happening?'

She rolls over again and closes her eyes. 'I don't know.'

'I'd appreciate it if you would just be a support to me now and give Angus a break until my exams are over. Can you not just wait three weeks?'

I feel humiliated for begging her to kill me slowly. But it seems I'll believe anything she tells me now, anything at all, even things I know to be lies.

* * *

I get into Sue Hargreave's old orange car. The smell of the upholstery reminds me of going to church with Steve.

I pass the Blair Road house. It sits hidden behind its veil of trees and overgrown shrubs, as if radiation has contaminated it.

Adrian stands outside the exam hall. He looks me up and down as I walk towards him. 'Flap,' he says.

'What?'

'You're looking a bit sheepish . . . I know what happened.'

'What do you mean?'

'It was raining last night. The surfaces were a bit wet. You accidentally fell over and slipped your cock into her.'

I blurt out a laugh. 'No!'

He shakes his head. 'How did I know that, Eastwood? How did I fucking know that? Chop.'

The examiner comes to the door. 'Alright, boys. You may enter.'

* * *

Kevin Rawling watches the TV news. The remote control rests on his big round stomach. He lifts a beer to his mouth. 'These fucking idiots!' he shouts. 'They are just so fucking *dof*!'

'Hi, Kev,' I call from the doorway.

He glances at me. 'You can't write this stuff, Hayden! You really can't. They're calling it Black Friday.'

'What's going on? I've been too busy worrying about exams.'

'The government's just paid out the war vets! And how are they going to finance it? They're not. They're going to print money. Have you seen what it's done to the currency today?'

'No . . . Bad?'

'Zim dollar's in free fall. Lost half its value in one day. Stock market has crashed forty percent. Fuckin' unbelievable.'

Adrian walks in. 'Kev, you getting a bit hot under the collar there, big boy?'

'Oh, fuck off, Adrian. This is fuckin' serious!'

Adrian laughs. 'Okay, big guy. Just here to get Eastwood before he starts talking about some of his crazy shit.'

Meg Rawling hands me the phone. 'Hayden, it's for you.'

'Hi, darling,' says Mum. 'Your father wants you to come home. He won't admit it, but he does want you back. And so do I . . . Please come home.'

'It's a bit late now, isn't it, Mum? My exams are over. And I don't even feel like it's my home anymore. I'm just an unwanted guest that no one can get rid of.'

'Well, what are you going to do? You can't flip between Sue's and Adrian's forever. And you *are* welcome. It is your home.'

'Is there any food?' I ask.

'Yes, right now he's being good about it. I did a full shop yesterday.'

*   *   *

Adrian's engine strains up the hill. His hair has grown long and fluffy since school finished. 'How's things with Jane?' I ask.

'Ag, Hayde. She's taking the piss, man. I don't even know why I got back together with her after that whole thing with Chebwino. It's so wrong. Every time I fuck her I literally feel violated. And I can't even stop my cock. And then after it's over I'm, like, "Rawling, what the fuck did you just do that for? Why did this seem like a good idea before you jizzed?"'

'Yup. You've pretty much described my world in a fittingly vulgar idiom.'

He turns into the driveway at Blair Road. The house sits in the unkempt garden like a shack in the wilds of a Chernobyl exclusion zone. My stomach turns. Adrian turns off the engine. 'Have you got all your things, Hayde?'

I walk through the front door into the hallway. The radioactive misery of the house penetrates my skin. The stale smell of Dad's cigarette smoke hangs in the air. I feel physically sick.

I sit down at the piano. The boils and pink eye have cleared up. 'Imagine no possessions, I wonder if you can. No need for greed or hunger, a brotherhood of man. Imagine all the people, sharing all the world . . . yoo hoo wooo oooo . . .'

Dad appears at the doorway in his pyjamas. He walks over to me. I stop playing. My heart thuds. He puts a hand on my shoulder. 'I'm glad you're back,' he says.

Chapter 23

Dad sits in his green chair and cries. I want to leave him there, but my feet are somehow stuck to the ground.

'You don't show any interest in my life,' he says. 'There are all these books on the bookshelf about Bram Fischer, about my history, about my life. Have you ever read a single one of them?'

'No.'

'Why not?'

I search my mind for excuses, but I don't find any. He puts another Pynstop in his mouth and chews. The pill cracks between his teeth. He closes his eyes. I leave him in his stupor and grab the fat biography of Bram Fischer.

I sit on my bed and start to read, but before long a woman's voice calls in the distance. 'Hullo? Is anyone home?'

A spindly middle-aged woman stands at the front door. She squeezes out an anaemic-looking smile. 'Hullo, I'm looking for Anthony. Is he here?'

'Yes. He's in his room,' I reply. 'But it's probably not a good moment . . .'

Dad walks down the stairs, his hair washed and combed, his face freshly shaved, his shirt freshly pressed. 'Oh, hullo there, Angela! Why don't we have our discussion outside?'

I leave them and open the Bram Fischer biography. There's only one mention of Anthony Eastwood in it. 'Anthony recalls fondly . . .' it says.

I can imagine Dad sitting hand in hand with Bram's daughter, jabbing his other hand through the air with manic excitement as he recounts his impression of the great Bram Fischer to his interlocutor.

I look for more stories but find nothing. 'Anthony recalls fondly . . .'

I must have missed something. I search the index for references to Anthony Eastwood. The only entry links back to the page I've just read. There are no stories about the two of them together, no paragraphs saying, 'This one time, Bram and Anthony . . .' No near death experiences, no underground meetings, no brushes with military police. Nothing.

I open the fridge; there is no milk. I open the bread bin; there is no bread.

Dad and the visitor stand in the hallway. 'I think you have a very strong case,' Dad says. 'There's clearly been gender discrimination, and I'm sure we can prove that in the legal proceedings that follow.'

The woman squeezes out another smile. 'Thank you *so* much, Anthony. I feel very relieved having spoken to you. What fee would you be looking at?'

'Fee? Don't be silly. This is a matter of principle. The current structures are outrageously unfair to women.'

I want to shout the contradiction at him, to punch him until he sees the canyon between his private life and the life he shows others. Quite suddenly I feel I'm watching him like I watch wildlife, like I'm watching a rogue elephant in the moments before someone has to shoot it.

* * *

Mum sits on her bed with a towel over her head and a bowl of hot water on her lap. 'This chronic bloody sinusitis is driving me mad,' she says.

'Mum, have a cup of tea. I just made some.'

She inhales the eucalyptus steam and then pulls the towel from her head. 'Thanks, darling.'

'Have you seen Dad's new reality? The women's rights cam-
paigner?'

'Angela? Yes.'

'He literally doesn't know what reality is. He only thinks things
are real if people believe them.'

Mum puts her cup down. 'On the day of the funeral I just couldn't
believe that he went up to Mr Kyle and said, "There's not a shred
of evidence that the school is to blame for this." Why did he make
such an effort to ingratiate himself with the establishment? Why at
that moment, when it was supposed to be about Dan?'

The words I said that day linger in my mind. I stood on stage at
Dan's funeral and talked about learning from what had happened,
about making such tragedies avoidable. Why? It should have been
Dan's moment. But it wasn't. It was, instead, Dad's moment. The
funeral was the stage for the story of the undiscovered genius de-
stroyed by his own brilliance, the wunderkind sown from Anthony
Eastwood's unrivalled seed. And the tale was told without religion
because the Left are above that. The Left do good because they are
good, not because someone will reward them in an afterlife. And in
that story we absolved others of blame in the midst of our deepest
tragedy, because that's how big we were, that's how magnanimous
and stoical we could be in our darkest hour. And the setting for the
story was simple, so simple that it would show our non-materialism
and depth of character.

I feel overcome with disgust: disgust at myself, disgust that the
funeral was a Cold War Olympics instead of a tribute. Will I ever
be able to forgive myself?

*   *   *

The memory of our last family holiday in Cape Town runs through
my head: We drive along a coastal road. The wide blue ocean breaks
itself on the white sand. We stop at a rocky cove, empty except for
two lovers who splash and giggle in the sea. Dad puts the picnic

things on some rocks, all the time screaming profanities at Mum, the veins in his neck bulging like snakes.

The lovers stop frolicking. I slink into the distance to escape the embarrassment of Dad eviscerating Mum in public. A dog barks at me. I run back to the picnic spot as it nips at my ankles.

'What's the matter!' shouts Dad.

'The dog's chasing me!'

Dad picks up a stick from the ground. The dog stops instantly and whimpers away. 'Nonsense. I've never seen such a timid bloody animal!'

The lovers pack their things, suddenly silent. They pass us carrying their bags and towels. They smile awkwardly. Dad is at once calm. 'Goodbye,' he says, smiling as if he knows them quite well, as if they've just been at our house for gin and tonics.

The lovers vanish over the rocks. Dad calls to us. 'Come here, you kids. Come and eat.'

He picks a steak from the embers of the fire. 'I used to eat my meat like this when I was a student. Gives it a wonderful smoked flavour.' He hands one to me. It looks like a dead, ash-dusted slug. I bite into it and its grey-red juices flow down my hands and onto the grey rock.

In the car there is just the hum of the engine. Dan leans his torso out the window for some moments. Beebs wails, 'Hey! Where have my rocks gone?'

'I don't know,' I tell her.

'I don't know either,' says Dan.

Beebs cries. 'You guys! Where are my rocks?'

Dad yells, 'Hey, you buggers. What's going on back there?'

'Dad, Hayde or Danny has thrown my rocks out the window.'

'Oh, Jesus Christ!' shouts Dad. 'Who's done that now, hey?'

'It wasn't me!' I protest.

Dad stops the car and pulls over. 'Dad,' cries Beebs. 'I picked up special fairy rocks to take home with me and now they're gone.'

'We can just pick up some more rocks at the side of the road,' says Dan.

'Nooooo,' cries Beebs. 'Those were special rocks!'

'You bloody shitfaces,' shouts Dad. 'Which one of you did that, hey?'

'It was me,' says Dan.

'You bloody shit! Why did you go and do that, hey?'

'I just thought they were stupid rocks, that's all.'

'Honestly, what a pair of nasty buggers you are!'

Dad does a U-turn. Beebs searches the road and the grass, but the special rocks are nowhere.

That night I wake to the sound of Dan whimpering and crying. I wait for some moments to see if he'll stop. But he doesn't. 'Dan, what's wrong?' I ask.

He catches his breath in between sobs. 'Mum's so selfish. I can't believe she's having another baby. She only ever thinks of herself.'

'Dan, listen to me. Things will be better someday, I promise. We still have each other.'

My words are useless. Dan cries into his pillow. The pale moonlight casts a silhouette of his heaving body against the white wall.

In the morning Mum sits in the kitchen with a cigarette in one hand and a glass of whisky rested on her pregnant stomach.

'Mum, what the hell are you doing? You can't drink and smoke when you're pregnant!' I shout.

'I'm sorry,' she says. 'I just can't take this anymore. I'm going crazy. I'll pick myself up again later. This is the first time I've done it; I'm just having a meltdown right now.'

I walk out.

Dan plays in the garden. 'Hayde, do you want to chuck the frisbee for a bit?' He seems happy, as though the previous night never happened, as though his sobs were just some dream I had.

We pack the car and head back to Zimbabwe. Rain falls on the windscreen and leaves the windows misty. The telephone lines dance up and down through the misted windows. Dad barks at Mum without stopping. He tells her she's stupid; that she can't cook; that she's been a useless mother; that if he hadn't rescued her, she'd have been a whore in Vienna.

Mum screams like someone vomiting the last bit of bile from their stomach. She smashes her head on the dashboard and the windows, as if she were a harpooned fish battering itself against the side of a boat. And then, like a fish that's finally drowned in air and been overcome by its wounds, her twitches stop. She whimpers, perfectly motionless, her head buried in her arms. Mozart's 'Violin Concerto No. 3' plays in the background.

Dad turns to us, suddenly quiet and gentle. 'You see, kids. What did I tell you? Your mother's bonkers.'

Chapter 24

'Hullo, Hayden,' says a crackling voice over the phone. 'It's Gill Hamley here. We've got a problem: Angus is sitting in his car outside our gate. Would you please come and talk to him because he's just sitting there like some kind of madman, and he won't leave or speak to anyone. And we can't get hold of Sarah . . . Have you seen her?'

'I don't know where Sarah is, Mrs Hamley. Have you tried Simon's house? He's the new guy on the scene, I think.'

Angus's red Beetle is parked opposite Sarah's gate. He sits in it with his long Navajo hair. I knock on the window. He glances at me with blood-shot eyeballs and unlocks the passenger door. We sit in silence for some minutes. Rubber pipes snake their way along the floor. 'What are those?' I ask.

'They're connected to the beer keg behind your seat.'

I crane my neck to get a better look. 'And what's that over there?'

'The gas. Pressure for the beer kegs. It's supposed to be for the Toxic Psychosis party at Roswald's this weekend. Thought I'd start the party early.'

He puts the clear pipe into his mouth. He presses a lever. Beer tracks along it and into his mouth. 'Would you like a swig?'

Birds land at the roadside and peck the rain-soaked soil. 'I'm sorry . . .' he says. 'I'm sorry that I did to you what Simon's now done to me.'

'I understand. She has that effect on people.'

He asks me about what I saw in Sarah. The answer seems so obvious. But when I reach to grab it, it vanishes. 'I always felt that we had something special, something different . . . I felt she understood me.'

He's quiet for a moment. 'Hayde, I hate to break it to you, but she has something special with everyone.'

I feel as if he's smashed the last beautiful, intricate lie into a thousand shards. I want to cry. 'What are you hoping to achieve by being here?'

'I don't know.'

I leave him staring into the distance.

Angus's grandfather appears. But still Angus just sits there with his blood-shot eyes.

His grandfather takes a brick and launches it at the window. It bounces off and hits the ground. 'Come on, Angus, don't do it!' he shouts. 'For God's sake, don't do it!'

Mr and Mrs Hamley edge out of their gate. 'What's going on with him?'

'Ag, he's just upset about Sarah and Simon.'

Sarah's car pulls into the driveway. 'Where the bloody hell have you been!' shouts Mrs Hamley.

Sarah gets out and impatiently fumbles the gate open. 'What's he doing here? I don't need this bullshit! He needs to get the hell away!'

'Where do you think you're going!' shouts Mrs Hamley after her. 'You come here and sort your mess out!'

Sarah vanishes behind the wall. Dad's car arrives unexpectedly. He gets out and stands in his pyjamas watching the drama like a curious baboon. He turns to Mr and Mrs Hamley. 'Well, at least he hasn't done a Danny, hey.'

Mr and Mrs Hamley stand next to each other, wide-eyed and silent.

* * *

Dad sits next to me in his suit, clutching his briefcase; his black hair combed into a perfect side parting. His face is clean-shaven. He looks out the car window as if he's deep in thought. 'Watch that you slow the car down with the engine, and not the brakes.'

'I know, Dad,' I say.

'You know, I never mentioned it before, but back in the seventies I was an honorary guest of the Soviet Union. They asked me if there was anyone I'd like to meet, and I decided I'd like to chat to some-one involved in law.'

His hands cast spells in the air as he orates. 'The next thing I knew they'd organised me time with the Chief Justice of the whole Soviet Union. The chap took me off to a seaside resort. Spoke pretty good English. Stern fellow. At one stage I jokingly asked him when the Soviet state would end. Of course, as I've mentioned before, the idea with Marxist-Leninism is that the state is supposed to be a tempo-rary stepping-stone to a more idealised point where the proletariat govern themselves. When I asked the question, rather tongue-in-cheek, he just looked at me blank-faced.'

Dad breaks into an involuntary chuckle and glances at me, as though he's expecting me to laugh with him. I avoid his eyes and instead focus on the potholed streets.

I try to ignore the obvious truth: the truth that he himself knew of the canyon between what the regime said and what it actually believed; that he himself knew utopia would never be reached; that he himself knew that they knew, that he knew it. He reveals the true nature of what he wishes to achieve: nothing. He wishes to destroy that which exists and then . . . nothing. The gaping nihilism of it saps my energy. *But it cannot be,* I think to myself, *I'm reading too much into it.*

At a traffic light a street kid comes to Dad's window and holds out his hands. Dad winds his window down. The boy stands there dust-laden and snotty-nosed. 'Food, boss. Please, food.'

Dad smiles and reaches through the open window. He pats the boy on the head. 'Hi there, little chap.'

The child looks at him blank-faced. The light changes. In the rear-view mirror the boy stands and watches us, wide-eyed, silent.

Dad's hands move again. 'Africans are amazing bloody people, hey. The oppression they've endured. Hundreds of years of it. And then . . . *dup, dup, dup*, there they go, developing away. Some of the chaps I work with, so impressive.'

'Is that who you're meeting with?'

'Yes. Just a standard meeting. A few particulars to discuss.'

'If I didn't know better I'd think you were rehearsing your lines for them.'

I anticipate a rise to my challenge. But it's as though he hasn't heard me, as though his ears became promptly deaf at the moment I spoke.

The car jolts. But still he sits there, staring out of the window, locked in thought, indifferent to the potholes hammering his shock absorbers.

Dad gets out with his briefcase and walks with purpose to his meeting. His gait seems sober and confident, perhaps even powerful.

I drive past a pub and stop. 'Could I speak to your manager?' I ask the bartender.

He wanders into the back room and returns with someone. 'Good afternoon, sir. I'm looking for a job. Do you have anything?'

The man laughs. 'Son, in this economic environment? You've got to be kidding. We're firing, not hiring. But if you like, I'll take your details and give you a ring if anything opens up.'

* * *

The old plane looks like a shattered ceramic pot that was fitted together like a jigsaw puzzle. Geoff's skinny legs run into the late afternoon sun.

The plane lifts into the sky, the paint on its wings glistening bright green in the orange light as it banks and climbs. It flies delicately and nimbly.

Over and over I fly it above our heads. When I sense the fuel is running low I bring it to the field and land it gently on the grass.

I wish Dan were here to see it fly, to see the importance of patience and of fighting for what you want in life.

But maybe that was the problem: maybe what he wanted meant fighting me. And maybe he was too kind to fight me. Maybe I was too much of a monster. Maybe if he had seen this creation fly he'd have seen that life can work out for the better. He'd have seen that the universe isn't fixed, that it can change when you least expect it; that bad can become good as easily as good can become bad. *Did he just think life would always be like our planes?* I think. *Maybe it was that simple.*

Geoff and I sit on the dust and grass and watch the sun sink. The trees are like insects, like black praying mantises waiting perfectly still in the orange and yellow and purple. Sometimes I wonder if Dan ever existed, if he was ever real. Sometimes it's like what Christians say about the Earth, that it was created with a history. And today it's like that: like I was created with a history, with the memory of Dan already in my head, like he never actually happened.

* * *

Dad shouts in the distance, 'Hayden, come here! Come here right now!'

He screams his words like the day he found Dan. I rush to his room, my body prepared for horror.

His door is locked. 'Get me out of here,' he shouts. 'Your mother's locked me in.'

'I can't. I don't have the keys and I don't know where Mum is.'

'Well, bring me an axe from the shed!'

'I don't know if that's a good idea.'

I leave him screaming and walk away. 'Do you want to go to university? It doesn't sound like it to me!'

'I thought I wasn't going to university anyway. I thought you couldn't afford it?'

'Of course I can bloody afford it, you nincompoop! Now get me the axe or you're not going. You think this place is hard, do you? Just wait till you're hanging around here jobless.'

I sit in my room until the banging and shouting become unbearable. Then I fetch an axe from the shed and pass it to him through the window. I walk away and hear the sound of grunting and chopping.

* * *

I scribble some maths on a page. Someone knocks at my door. Rupert stands there in his old professorial trousers. 'Your father seems to be asleep. What in heaven's name happened to his door?'

'It had a run in with Dad . . . Would you like some tea? Hope you don't mind it without milk.'

'Thank you. That would be lovely.'

I walk him onto the veranda.

'Your garden's still exquisite, despite being unkempt.'

'Mum does her best with it.'

Rupert holds a cup of tea in his hands. 'So how are you getting on with your father at the moment?' he asks, wobbling his floppy top lip as he speaks.

'Not well. I don't think I'll be going to university. One moment he insists I go, and not just anywhere: he insists I go to a British university because the South African ones are so shit, or so he says. Then he threatens me with not going: either because he says he's broke or because he's angry I've stood up to him.'

'Why on earth are you fighting him? Bite your tongue.'

'I'm not fighting him. He's fighting us. And I can't allow him to behave the way he does. It's not right. I can't let him treat Mum like he does. Sometimes you've got to stick to your principles.'

'Bugger your principles, quite frankly. Keep your mouth shut and take the money. That's the right thing to do now.'

'You make it sound like it's possible to cooperate. It's not. Believe me.'

'Don't underestimate your father. He's very clever. He can be very lucid when he wants to be.'

'Lucid or not, he seems to have done badly in this last Asian stock crisis. I think he really is broke.'

'Nonsense. Your grandfather died with a million pounds to his name and that was back in the early seventies when a million pounds meant something. Your father got the lion's share of that. Even if he's squandered half of it he's still got plenty for your education. Take it. It's your right. It's what your grandfather would have wanted. He's the one who earned it.'

'Did you know Dad when he was in the SACP?' I ask. 'What was that scene like?'

Rupert pours himself some more tea. 'The SACP was basically a sex club,' he says. 'I suppose I can understand it. In a place where most whites were dreadful, the communist party was a good place to find different people, who, of course, were also sexually loose. They didn't believe in owning people so they just bonked one another furiously.'

His words swirl around my mind. How many times have I imagined that freedom is the freedom to indulge in my every whim? And yet, when I've given in to those whims, when I've given in to Sarah, have I been free, or have I been trapped?

* * *

Angus leads us up the cold grey rocks. We pant and sweat our way over the peaks, onto a giant plateau.

The wind blows the tall grass sideways, like my childhood visions of Zorro galloping across the plains. The sun fades and the grass turns charcoal. The sweat cools on my neck with the breeze.

'Stick to the path,' Angus says. 'There are still land mines from the war in these parts.'

We come to a thick rainforest.

'Roswald lived for days in this forest with a pump-action two-two, hunting duiker and rabbits for dinner,' Angus breaks into laughter. 'Imagine coming up here and finding a wild-eyed boy walking around with nothing but a gun and a pair of shorts!'

My feet are blistered. We light a fire and cook pasta and tuna. We shovel the food down our throats. I slouch back into my sleeping bag and gaze into the night.

'So Ang, how did you end up getting expelled from Grinham?'

He seems taken aback by my question. 'That final day . . . everything went crazy . . . we passed the point of no return.'

I look at him expectantly. 'We had just bunked a vomit-your-guts-out house athletics training,' he says. 'We returned in the evening to find that our possessions had been ripped out of our lockers and thrown out of the windows. At that moment both Simon and I realised that the situation would deteriorate, so we went to a friendly teacher's house about a kilometre away. We were halfway there when we saw torch lights in the distance, seniors hunting around for us in the dark with weapons: golf clubs, cricket bats, all sorts. The friendly teacher let us into his house. When we looked out of the window later they were there, standing and waiting for us with their implements.'

'Weren't they scared of the teacher?'

'No. They stopped short of coming in to get us, but they weren't afraid to stand outside and wait for us.'

'So what happened?'

'The teacher kept us with him and then drove us to Harare before sunrise. We returned the next day with my parents to collect Roswald. We were worried they'd kill him.'

'And was it all bad there? Did you learn anything?'

'During first team rugby matches we'd sometimes bunk by hiding out in these old drainage tunnels under the fields and classrooms. We'd put plastic bags on our shoes to keep the rotting matter off them and then hunt bats.'

'You hunted bats? How the hell did you do that?'

'We'd take an A4 piece of paper from our school notebooks and roll it into a tight tube. Into that we'd shove a pin that we'd dipped into crushed Elephant Ear. The toxins from that leaf are lethal. The trick was to balance the dart properly so that it flew pin-first.

'We tried hunting birds at first, but that didn't work. Then one day we were about a hundred metres into one of the tunnels when Roswald's torch chanced on a bat hanging from a drainpipe. That was our first kill. We kept it in the ceiling of the boarding hostel and rubbed salt into it. Eventually we hollowed it out and stuffed it with paper and pinned it to a board in a scary bat-pose.'

He goes on. 'On the weekends we'd sign out and head into the *shatine*. We'd build forts. Sometimes we'd fight bush fires. When we couldn't find any, we'd start them ourselves. One of the fires ended up completely out of control and threatened the nearby farm. We fought it and got covered in black, head to toe. Afterwards, the farmer gave us tea and biscuits and dropped us back at school. At the end of term I received two distinctions: one for music, one for firefighting!' He cracks up laughing. 'So did Roswald's brother, which was quite funny considering he wasn't even there.'

We chuckle together and then drift into silence. Angus reaches into his bag and brings out a fist of garlic and pops a clove into his mouth. 'Sweetie for you, Eastwood?'

Sometimes I wish that Dan and I had gone to Grinham. Sometimes I wish he'd been beaten and kicked so that the madness would have been outside rather than inside. Maybe then he'd have known his enemies. He'd have been able to touch them, to curse them, to plot against them. But what do you do when the enemy is within?

In the early morning we pass two Mozambican border jumpers, walking barefoot over the rocks and across the river with babies on their backs. They carry tins of *sadza* on their heads. I look into the far haze to see where they've come from. Dense bush stretches into the horizon. Their smiles fail to hide the poverty carved into their faces.

The border jumpers move slowly without a sound, like elephants choosing their steps.

After a while, I stop and look over my shoulder to see where they've got to. They're gone.

*　　*　　*

The spindly woman stands in the doorway. 'Hullo, is your father here?' she asks.

'He is fairly comatose at the moment,' I tell her.

She looks disappointed. 'I'm here to discuss my case with him.'

'Well, why don't you wait on the stoep? I'll call him.'

Dad's not in his bed, so I knock on the bathroom door. 'I'll be out in a moment,' he shouts.

I return to the woman. 'He says he's—'

Dad interrupts me as he walks down the hallway, clean-shaven, wearing a neatly ironed shirt and trousers. His black hair is combed into a slick side parting.

'Hullo, Angela!' he says with a wide smile and a vigorous handshake.

*　　*　　*

I hold my hand to my face to stop my eyes seeing the patch of floor where Dan hanged himself. I search his big wooden desk for his poem about the waterhole. It's gone. I look for his school books so that I can read one of his old school stories. They too are gone.

'Mum, where are Dan's things?'

'Oh, I think your father threw them out.'

'What? He threw them out? Why the hell did he do that? Why didn't you stop him?'

She shrugs her shoulders. 'I don't really know.'

'What do you mean, you don't know?' She is silent. I wait for her to say something, but she doesn't.

'Mum?' She looks at me empty-faced.

I go to the sitting room. The human rights woman is gone. Dad sits in his chair next to his temple of cigarette butts. 'Where are Dan's school books?'

He scarcely looks at me. 'We don't have them anymore.'

'I need them. Where are they?'

'I threw them out.'

'You threw them out! How dare you! Who the hell do you think you are?'

'He's gone now, you know. He's just worm food.'

'And where are his ashes? I don't see those anywhere. I've never clapped eyes on them. I want to see his ashes.'

'I told the crematorium to throw them out.'

'You what!' I scream. 'You had no right to do that!' My vision blurs. I pick up a chair and hurl it against a wall. I feel magically powerful, as if I'm in a video game and the tips of my fingers are charged with lightning bolts.

But he looks at me with a glint of triumph, as though I've rejuvenated his force field, as though he's merely run an insect-like proboscis into my brain and sucked out my energy.

There's a letter with my name on it by the telephone. I tear it open. My foggy eyes can hardly believe what I read. My father has paid for my first term of university tuition. Next to the letter is an air ticket.

* * *

I pack clothes into a suitcase. I want to pack my aeroplane, but I know it'd only break on the long journey ahead of me. It hangs from a hook on my wall, bent and cracked, twisted; as though the laws of physics would prevent it from flying.

I visit Dan's old hiding places and climb the tree that he fell from, the same one that haunts my dreams with his hanging figure. Mum calls for me from the house. 'Hayde, telephone. It's Sarah's sister.'

I lift the receiver. 'Hayde, I've got some terrible news . . .'

'What?'

'Sarah has cancer.'

'*What?* What do you mean she has cancer?'

'She's just had some biopsy results. They've confirmed it without a doubt.'

'What kind of cancer?'

'Something called Hodgkin's lymphoma.'

'That can't be! She's too young! And the doctor told her that it was nothing!'

She's silent for a moment. 'It's true, Hayde, she has it. The first doctor was wrong.'

I remember my fingers running over Sarah's lymph nodes. A slight swelling. Sometimes under her jaw bone, sometimes lower down on her neck.

'How bad is it?' I say.

'Stage Four. It's spread to other places. It's in her lungs and her bones as well as her lymph nodes.'

* * *

Sarah sits on the floor cutting shapes out of a magazine with scissors. Her fingers are long and elegant; she could have been a pianist. Her cheeks are red from tears.

'I'm so sorry,' I say.

She burrows her head into my chest. I clutch her in my arms. 'I'm scared. So scared.'

My head empties of words. I rock her from side to side as she cries. I find it difficult to imagine her body infected with alien cells. But it must be. Beneath my hands on her back those cells invade her blood and tissue and bones.

For a while I wonder if it's a joke, if someone might walk into the room and announce that she's actually fine. Now and again she pauses and looks me in the eye. Her gaze is unfamiliar, part vacant, part tender. Her eyes look like Mum's eyes: like they're frozen in shock.

'When are you leaving?' she asks.

'My flight's tomorrow evening.'

'I'll miss you, Hayde.'

I squeeze her in my arms. 'I'll miss you too.'

University

Chapter 25

From my desk I look out at apple-green fields and hedgerows. The sky seems so low. Somewhere in my mind I had hoped I would find Jeeves and Wooster, Gussy Fink-Nottle, Baldrick, Captain Black-adder, Lord Flashheart, Basil Fawlty. But where are they?

I walk from my residence to a pub, past trees dropping their copper leaves. I follow the winding lake alongside the Lego-like brick houses.

In the pub, nattering voices surround me. The Englishman seems to find this habit beautiful. It seems like he watches his own life from a distance, like when I'm on a train watching the green fields roll by the windows, like they're not really there, like they're just playing on a movie reel.

Students pass by me with their dead eyes and with their vacant plasticine expressions. Then, at night they are suddenly drunk, shouting and laughing, vomiting. I watch the boys trying their luck with different girls. They fail with one and then move to the next, as though rejection is nothing to them. And yet why should rejection crush them if they care nothing for the girls in the first place? Those same girls move rigidly in their identical black dresses, plastic in their thickly painted makeup.

* * *

One foot moves in front of the other. Most of the leaves are gone now. The tree trunks fork up from the earth like barren shards of coral. People in the lecture room sit to my right and left without smiling, without moving their eyebrows, without looking at what's around them.

'Quantum mechanics,' the lecturer says. 'I'd like to begin by going over the experiments by Ernest Rutherford.'

Waves are particles. Particles are waves. What does that even mean? What is the essence of a particle? What is the essence of a wave?

I close my notebook. I notice I have written down almost nothing. My head fills with sporadic unhinged thoughts, like the random noises of a Geiger counter. I pick up my bag and follow my feet to the computer room. The tapping keys seem to hypnotise me. I open an email from Sarah. Her chemotherapy is going well but causing nausea and weakness. Then I jolt. It cannot be true. I read the next line over and over again. Sarah's boyfriend, Simon, has also been diagnosed with a lymphoma. It cannot be true.

* * *

The left-wing people come to me with their message. They say that they believe in a fair world. They say that people who aren't left-wing believe in an unfair world. And so the quandary is no quandary at all. I am left-wing. To oppose Marxism, it seems, is to oppose fairness itself. And who would be so heartless as to oppose fairness? Wherever I look I see that clever people are left-wing and that left-wing people are clever. It seems that morality and reason lead to one solution, and that solution is Marxism.

I read John Pilger and Noam Chomsky. They write with blistering moral indignation, with rage, with exasperation. Their explanations are so simple, so powerful, so beautiful, so real.

Left is opposite to right. If right is bad then I am the opposite of that, which means that I'm good.

* * *

I sit in my school uniform with Dad standing over me. 'Ay, you bugger!' he shouts at me, 'Rub it out and do it again!' He slaps me across the shoulder. I lose my balance from the force of his hand but feel no pain 'Ay, did you hear what I just said?' he shouts.

'Dad, I don't know the answer,' I cry. He slaps me again. 'Yes, you do! You know it! Rub that out and do it again!'

I write something. 'Oh, Jesus Christ!' he shouts.

I worry that Mr McLaren will beat me for having a messy book. Dan stands unexpectedly at the door. He says, 'Hayde, don't worry. It's just because of Dad's sister.'

I approach Dan, but he walks away and vanishes. Lions walk on the lawn by the veranda. Noam Chomsky sits next to Rupert. 'I don't think these lions actually need to eat meat, you know. They could actually just be conditioned to eat grass.'

'Don't be silly, lions eat meat, only meat!' I protest. 'They'll never eat grass. Haven't you ever been to my school before?'

Chomsky shakes his head. 'It's because nobody's taught them how to eat grass.'

Dan says, 'They're just saying that, Hayde. They're just pretend-ing to be clever, but they don't know what they're talking about. Like Dad.'

'They must not fool the little grey cells,' mutters Hercule Poirot.

'Dan why are you here? I thought you were dead?'

'I am dead, Hayde, but sometimes I'm alive and dead at the same time.'

'Really? Like Schrödinger's cat? So can I take you to show Mum?'

'Mum!' I shout. 'I've got Dan with me, right here! We'd just been observing him incorrectly. I've discovered how to make his wave function collapse to the live state! Look, he's here with me!'

The outside light casts grim shadows on the ceiling. My heart thumps feverishly. I splash cold water on my face.

I step into the cold night and jog to the computer room, puffing steam into the air. There is an email from Mum. She confirms that

Sarah's boyfriend has cancer. The news sits in my stomach and chest.

What if there's a new virus that causes malignancies? I think. *What if a common cold virus has mutated and become a monster that damages DNA and causes Hodgkin's lymphoma?*

But if I tell people my thoughts they'll laugh at me for being paranoid. And yet, would they have laughed at the very first HIV sufferer? They'd have laughed at that person if he'd said, 'I seem to be getting sick all the time, and I'm worried that I'm infected with a new brand of virus that destroys the immune system, one that didn't exist until it mutated in my blood.'

I finger my jaw's lymph nodes. They are large and hard like small ripe grapes. Are they *too* large? Are they *too* hard? Maybe the virus that causes lymphoma is sexually transmitted. That would explain how Simon got it. And it would explain why my lymph nodes are now swelling. Because what are the chances of Sarah and Simon getting the same rare cancer at the same time?

And if that's possible, then why not three young people?

* * *

I follow my plodding shoes over the bridge and watch the ducks on the water. I push through the hinged wooden door and take a seat. The lecturer walks in. 'Today we're going to carry on from last time. What properties make a cell metastatic?'

'Professor,' I say. 'You seem to imply that cancer is a simple probabilistic mechanism resulting from the likelihood of each cell failing to genetically self-fix, so that accumulated genetic failures eventually damage enough cellular processes to deregulate the cell cycle and produce uncontrolled growth.'

'Well, yes,' he replies.

'If that's true,' I continue. 'Then the risk of developing cancer should be proportional to the number of cells in an organism. Someone who weighs one hundred kilograms should, perhaps, be twice as likely to get cancer as someone who weighs only fifty kilograms, because the heavier person has roughly twice as many cells that can go wrong. Are big people more likely to get cancer than small people? And is a blue whale more likely to get cancer than a dolphin?'

He clutches his beard. 'These are good questions. Right now I don't have answers for you. Clearly there are many things that we don't yet understand about the process.'

* * *

I press my hand against my jaw and fondle the lymph node that worries me. Is it changing shape?

'Mr Eastwood, Dr Phillips will see you now.'

A slim grey man greets me. He feels around my neck and jaw. His warm hands are somehow soothing. 'Ah yes, here we go,' he says. 'They're slightly larger than I would have expected, but they certainly don't feel sinister. They're quite hard and I'd expect a malignancy to feel soft and somewhat fluffy.'

I leave the building relieved. But when I lie in bed at night I worry that he might be wrong, like Sarah's doctor was wrong. Maybe Dad is right. Maybe all doctors are incompetent.

* * *

If each atom is dead, if each molecule is thoughtless, if each tissue is unthinking, then what am I? How have I come to be? Sometimes it seems that there must be a God, that the Left have got it wrong. The dissected mouse on the table in front of me no longer looks like a creature: it looks merely like a collection of different tissues that were once called a mouse. And each of those tissues is just a collection of cells; and each of those cells, just a collection of organelles; and each of those organelles, just molecules; and each of those molecules, just atoms; everything, eventually, just lifeless units of the universe.

I no longer see people. I just see collections of tissue that happen to have found themselves working together to produce consciousness in the shape of a person. In my mind, I dissect the humans in front of me. They start off human, but once my mind has removed their skin and peeled the flesh from their bones, they are just biological automata.

Young couples stagger to their dormitories drunk and giggling. I step into the computer room.

I open an email from Mum. She sends photos of her arms, black and blue from Dad's punches.

I immediately get to my feet and run. My lungs blow thick steam into the icy black air. I find myself standing alone in the bleaching, humming light of the gym. I attack the punch bag with my fists. I punch Dad's imaginary head until my lungs burn and my shoulders ache. For a moment I feel Sarah's deserved her fate, as though karma has only punched her back.

The neon lights continue their humming in the emptiness. My lungs heave. Guilt eats at me: guilt that I could have had such a wicked thought about Sarah, guilt that I didn't love my father more, guilt that I betrayed Dan. If I'd loved Dad more, he'd have been different. If I'd cared for him when he was weak, he'd have been stronger.

* * *

The magazine on the waiting room table has a picture of happy, pretty women on the cover. 'Dr Howard will see you now,' calls a voice.

The man puts his hands on my jaw and feels around. 'Ah yes, there they are; I've found them now. Nothing untoward about those lymph nodes.'

'What makes you say that?'

'They're quite soft. I'd expect a malignancy to be hard and mis-shapen.'

The contradiction jars me. I want to shout, 'You bloody idiot, that's exactly the opposite of what the last guy said!'

He peers at me over his glasses. 'Are you alright? The colour seems to have drained from your face.'

The cancer cells are washing through my blood, their sticky feelers clawing their way into my tissues. It troubles me that I've spawned these cells like a mother spawns a child who one day murders her. I am killing myself, much like Dan did. Only the mechanism is different.

And what does it mean that an event is unlikely? If a rare event actually happens then how unlikely was it? Once it has happened then the probability of it having happened is one. And then of what use was knowledge of the odds? It seems that there is a reason for everything, and chance is just the name we give to the absence of understanding. So who is to say that I am not dying? Who is to say I am unlikely to be infected with a new cancer-causing virus?

My sickness will be my secret. Mum and Beebs and Miles have their battles to fight. I will drop out of university and fight the battle by myself. If I win it, I will go home as though nothing bad has happened.

The lecturer interrupts my thoughts. '. . . and next week, I'll touch on cyclic AMP and how it initiates the various signalling pathways. Any questions?' The wall of students looks at him blankly. I glance at my lecture notes and find a single sentence on the white page.

*   *   *

An Internet site warns me of the dangers of using cosmetics that contain sodium lauryl sulphate. I stop using toothpaste and shampoo.

I read about the chemistry of aspartame. Chymotrypsin in the stomach breaks the molecule into phenylalanine, aspartic acid and methanol. Aspartic acid and phenylalanine are harmless amino acids. But the stomach's low pH turns methanol into formaldehyde and formic acid. Formaldehyde is a cancer-causing molecule. How can such chemicals be allowed in our food? The Left are right. Capitalists have an evil plot to poison us for fast money.

I check my bank account. It's empty.

I phone home. Dad tells me I'm living on the pig's back. He accuses me of withholding my expenses from him. He tells me I've been lying to him. 'It's not my bloody fault you can't put together a simple bloody list!' he shouts. 'I told you I need expenses before I can work out what to pay you. This is your bloody doing, not mine!'

I am in England in the lap of luxury. I should be more grateful; I should be more appreciative of the great privileges I have been given by history. I should do more work. I should get the sand out of my vagina.

* * *

A naked girl lies in my arms. She rests her hand on my chest and gazes into my eyes. My heart beats. Air goes in and out of my lungs. But that's the end of it, as if metabolising glucose is the sum total of what I've become. I return her gaze for a moment. But there is nothing in my eyes.

I sense Sarah is watching me from the ceiling, judging my embrace with this naked girl. The last photo of her won't leave my mind: the smooth head, the puffy face, the dent in her neck where they cut the lymphoma out.

I rise. 'I'm going for a run,' I say. 'Feel free to stay as long as you like.'

She looks at me for a brief moment, like she's confused, like she's wondering what just came over me. She knows nothing of my sense of disgust with her, and with myself.

* * *

I wonder what I will say to the lady behind the glass. 'Pardon me, ma'am, my father is swimming in money, but he's decided that he won't pay further for my education. Please allocate me money from your hardship fund.'

And she'll reply, 'He can pay, but he won't? Do you honestly expect me to believe that someone would waste a year of fees for no real reason?'

And I'll agree. 'Yes, ma'am, it's futile, but he seems to thrive on futility like bees thrive on nectar.'

And she'll say, 'Why should I give you money over and above those Zimbabweans who are much less fortunate than yourself?'

And I'll tell her, 'You're right, ma'am. The moral case for me receiving this hardship fund is zero.'

The lady with her bob of platinum hair casts an eye on me. 'Number seventeen!'

I make my way to her desk.

'How can I help you?' she says.

*　*　*

The *DSM-IV* lies on my unmade bed. I wish I had never read it. I move it off my crumpled sheets like it's a diseased rag, like its cruel and inhuman words would infect my bed through osmosis if I left it there a moment longer. The entry for 'Narcissistic Personality Disorder' cuts me with its descriptions: 'Preoccupied with fantasies of ideal love, success, power, or brilliance.'

Isn't everyone preoccupied with love? And what is love if not something ideal? Isn't love, and our preoccupation with it, the one thing that separates us from beasts? Should those people who wrote stories and poems and songs about love not have done so? Must I believe that in order for me to be normal, to be not disordered, that I must never be preoccupied with love, that I must never fantasise about what it might look like and feel like? Is this our Brave New World? Has it sunk to such depths of coldness that love itself, and all the daydreaming and fantasy that goes with it, is a disorder? Were Romeo and Juliet both simply suffering from Narcissistic Personality Disorder?

'Having an exaggerated sense of self-importance.' Tick.

But how would we ever measure what it means to exaggerate

self-importance? Some people would argue that Hollywood actors are important. Others would argue that they aren't. So if a Hollywood actor believes himself to be important, is he or is he not exaggerating his true importance? How can a criterion be so arbitrary, so dependent on a psychiatrist's own conception of what a fair self-conception of importance is?

'Exaggerating achievements and talents.' Tick.

'Believing that you are superior and can only be understood by, or associate with, equally special people.'

Do we not all imagine that we are somehow different from the average? And do we not choose our friends because we imagine them to be similarly above average, special, different to the common hordes they stand out from?

'Requiring constant admiration.'

Name me a person who does not like admiration, and I will name you a dog that doesn't like dog food.

'Having a sense of entitlement.' Tick.

'Expecting special favours and unquestioning compliance with your expectations.' Tick.

'Taking advantage of others to get what you want.' Tick.

'Having an inability or unwillingness to recognise the needs and feelings of others.'

This seems an inaccurate statement. There are many people who are unable to recognise the feelings of others. We call them autistic. But autistic people are not evil. The line should read, 'Recognises the needs and feelings of others, but doesn't care.' Or 'Recognises the needs and feelings of others, and works with that recognition to cause lasting hurt and pain.'

'Being envious of others and believing others envy you.' Tick.

'Behaving in an arrogant or haughty manner.' Tick.

Now that I have diagnosed myself, I think, *I should apply the same checklist to my father.*

* * *

Dan calls to me, 'Hayde, can you help me put up this rope?'

We fix the rope to a branch. The bright-green leaves brush our faces as we climb the old tree. I glance at Dan's face but his features are strangely hazy and without detail. Patrick swings on the branch next to us. 'Hey, you guys wanna play baseball?'

I find myself in the bathroom. Patrick walks in with his big tummy and curly brown hair. His adult figure towers over me. He closes the door behind him and takes his clothes off. 'Do you know what a blow job is?' he asks.

I stay quiet.

'They're really awesome,' he says. He masturbates next to me and slides my pants down.

'Wait,' I say.

He hesitates. 'Are you not comfortable with this?'

I try to say something but the words stick in my throat. My lungs are empty of air.

I sit bolt upright in bed and reach for my radio and switch it on. BBC Radio Four crackles and talks. I climb out of bed and douse my face with cold water.

I had forgotten that happened, I think. *And what if it also happened to Dan?*

* * *

Mum emails me to say that Dad has turned a corner and stopped drinking. He's been walking in the garden and looking at the birds. He's given her money to buy food. He's apologised for the hurt he's caused.

I feel at once lighter. How foolish I've been! Dad isn't a wicked man. He's just flawed and human like me, like all of us. He's wrestled with the loss of his son and has finally started winning the battle. He's realised that we love him and want the best for him. And, in any case, his moments of behaving badly were the alcohol contorting him, rather than *him*-him.

Guilt and shame infect me. How could I have been so judge-mental and wicked?

I open a web browser. The question with aspartame is not whether it's a poison. Everything is a poison in the wrong dose. I read about aspartame's chemistry and do some calculations. There is more methanol in a glass of wine than in an artificially sweetened cool-drink. It seems aspartame is not the monster I had presumed.

A fourth doctor feels my lymph nodes. 'Yes, they're bigger than I would have expected. The question is whether they've always been like this?'

'Well, yes, I think so. But sometimes I wonder if they haven't grown a bit.'

'Well, keep an eye on them but I don't think there's anything untoward. I'm ninety-nine percent sure there's nothing to worry about.'

'Ninety-nine percent?'

He breaks into a wry smile. 'Well, you can never be one hundred percent certain about anything in life, can you?'

It's like Bertrand Russell says: the problem is that the fool is cer-tain, and the wise man full of doubt. Stress drains from my body. I trust Bertrand Russell. I trust the doctor. Everything will be okay. I'm not dying. Dad isn't dying. Someday soon we'll build a new sense of family with those of us still remaining. And maybe I've read Sarah wrong. Maybe she loves me.

Chapter 26

Dad stands in the arrivals hall with a wide smile. 'Hullo, Hayde!'

He leans forward as if he might hug me. What it would be like to hug him? To smell his shirt and oily skin. His bones would feel spindly as if he were a man-sized lizard. He leans back again as though he's too shy to give anything of himself to me.

In the car he seems cheerful. I draw the air in through my nose to see if I can detect the aroma of whisky. I smell nothing suspicious. 'Things here are okay, you know. Your mother is quite well . . . been doing some of her music, getting involved in her painting again.'

People plod along the roadside in smart clothes. The colours are such a welcome change to the greys and blues of Britain. Dad takes a piece of nicotine gum from his mouth and fingers it into the ashtray. 'It seems that Blair fellow is another Thatcher,' he mutters. 'Outrageous bugger.'

He turns onto Blair Road and then into our driveway. The familiar garden smells consume me. I sense I might see Dan and me running barefoot across the lawn in our underpants, hunting leaves with our homemade spears. At the end of the tunnel of trees Mum and Beebs stand at the old wooden door entrance. They smile and hug me. Miles grips my leg with his night-ape hands.

I peer into Dan's room. Miles's toys and clothes lie on the dark wooden tiles. The room smells like a small boy.

I look at the patch of floor where I found Dan that morning. I can almost see him sitting with his clenched fists and milky face. The pull-up bar is gone, but the holes that we drilled are still there, still grey against the white wall. My heart beats furiously. My stomach feels queasy. Nothing has changed.

'Come on, Hayde,' shouts Mum in the distance. 'There's some coffee on the stoep for you.'

I wash my hands in the bathroom. The basin is big; the taps are simple, simpler than the taps I've left behind. On the veranda the winter yellows and browns sit vividly against the cold turquoise sky. 'So how is Dad really getting on?' I ask.

'He's really transformed, hasn't touched a drop of booze, been working; he's even taken us out for dinner a few times. He mentioned going on a family holiday somewhere.'

'I noticed there was food in the kitchen.'

'Yes, fingers crossed. Looks like we've turned a proper corner. And my sinusitis seems to have cleared up.'

* * *

I flick the propeller of the old scaly crocodile with its tape and glue. The engine starts. Geoff takes the crocodile and runs into the distance.

The plane whines and banks in the fading evening light. It flies back and forth, a stick-like silhouette against an icy blue sky. The fuel runs out and I bring her down gently on her belly. I wish Dan could have seen it fly. I wish he could have seen that things could sometimes turn out for the best.

Sarah sits on the car bonnet doing her nails. Her hair has grown back.

I clean the greasy fuel off the wings. The big sun dips behind the distant trees. Sarah sits next to me, gazing at the pink and orange haze fading into night. Does she see what I see? Does it touch her like it once touched me in the days when I was still fully human?

'Geoff,' I ask. 'What's the *nyaya* with you and Louise these days?'

'Ah, Hayde, it didn't work out, hey. But it's fine. It was for the best.'

'What went wrong?'

'She didn't feel the same way.'

'Eish. Sorry to hear that.'

'No, Hayde, it was good. It did something for me.'

'What did it do for you?'

'It helped me find the Lord.'

'Really? Are you kidding me?'

'No, Hayde. I was following Louise to church a lot. Then one day the preacher asked if there was anyone in the crowd who didn't yet have the Lord in their heart. I put my hand up and said I didn't. The preacher just took me to the front of everyone and he blessed me, and the Lord came into my heart. Since that time the Lord's been with me.'

'I had no idea. A lot can happen in a year.'

'It's square, Hayde. I'm still the same Geoff. It's just that I'm happier now; I'm complete. Have you ever considered becoming a Christian?'

'Briefly, but I'm still trying to understand why a deity would invent hookworm, typhoid and malaria. I'll give the big guy my vote when that makes sense to me.'

Geoff shakes his head. 'Ah, Hayde, I reckon the big guy has got answers for all that. It's easy for us humans to be proud, to think we know it all. Do you think an ant on a soccer ball knows that the soccer ball is round? *Shamwari*, we're those ants.'

I pack the aeroplane into the car. Sarah smiles and waves at Geoff through her open window. The engine hums, but my head is empty of words. I reach over and turn the music player on. The headlights illuminate the bumpy road through the cricket-filled darkness. Cat Stevens plays on the tinny speakers: 'The first cut is the deepest.'

* * *

Dad hangs his jacket on the back of a chair. His shoulders seem to fill his shirt more. He looks younger and fitter. He seats himself and downs a small glass of orange juice. He opens the *Financial Times*. 'I'm sorry about all of that misunderstanding with the money. I think, before you go this time, we'll sort out a spreadsheet in Excel, so neither of us gets confused about what's happening with you out there.'

I want to remind him that it wasn't a misunderstanding. I want him to say sorry for how he behaved. And then I fill with guilt. When will I get it into my thick skull that the money fiasco was the alcohol and drugs talking? Beneath the layer of pain and hurt there exists a kind and decent man fighting to get out. Why else would he have fought the injustice of racial oppression?

'Did your mother mention to you that we'd discussed a family holiday to the Lowveld? Lovely new spot's just opened. Breathtaking view of the Save River.'

He asks me about university. He tells me about how lonely he used to feel when living among Englishmen. He tells me about a girl called Pam who rejected him in his twenties. For the first time in ages I sense we have something in common.

'How are you doing, Hayde, hey?'

I feel inexplicably awkward and clammy. 'I'm fine, Dad. Had an exciting year at university. I learned a lot.'

'Hell, I don't know how you managed it. You have a remarkable strength. You were the closest to Dan, you know. Of all of us. Losing a brother like that, and in that way. Just appalling.'

A tear forms in Dad's eye. He opens his newspaper again. 'You've done bloody well. You really have,' he says.

* * *

Mum and Beebs sit by the fireplace. They seem unmistakably downbeat. 'Why are you so quiet?' I ask. 'What's wrong?'

Mum stares into the crackling flames. 'Your father's had a meltdown. He's accusing me of salting away his money. Sound familiar?'

— 260 —

'What do you mean? He's been fine for the past few weeks; I thought he'd turned a corner. What happened?'

'I bought him a new suit. And then he immediately asked me how I got the money to buy it. He was furious and accusatory. I just wanted him to look nice. I thought he'd look great in a new suit.'

Dad lies comatose in his bed. In his hand sits a glass of half-drunk whisky. Multi-coloured pills sprawl like a scattered sweet selection on his bedside table. Loud snores force themselves out of his gaping mouth.

Days pass by.

Now and again he wakes for a moment, reaches for his pills, and then returns to his unconscious world. Emily brings him meals. He leaves them uneaten at the foot of his bed.

I open a textbook on spectroscopy. Dad appears at my door in his pyjamas, smelling like alcohol, decaying skin and sweat. 'Why's nobody brought food to my room?'

'Because you don't eat it. And because we're out of food. You need to give Mum some money so she can buy some.'

'No.'

'Then what are we going to eat? What are you going to eat? What is going on? You were doing so well? Why are you doing this again? Just why?'

'Send the gardener to me. I'll give him some money. He can go to the shops on the bicycle.'

'Why don't you just give money to Mum?'

'Because she doesn't need any! She's got plenty! Spending it all on her bloody lovers!'

'Dad! She doesn't have any money! If she did, she'd be buying food! And what lovers?'

'She's been salting away my money for years! She's got plenty!'

'Oh, for God's sake. You're totally bloody paranoid!'

'Well, you can always go and earn your own money to give to your mother, you know. You don't need to ask me! You think I'm Mr Money Bags, do you?'

I fight to stay calm. 'You're crazy.'

'Oh, you think I'm crazy, do you? Well, I'll tell you something now. I'm not going to sit around listening to my nineteen-year-old son tell me how to suck eggs!'

I lock the door in his face. I leave him to return to his room and stare at the ceiling, to sink into his abyss with his oily mask and green lipstick.

My textbook sits on the table, but my appetite for reading it has vanished. I sink into my bed in a foetal position. I'm going mad. I'm losing my grip on reality. A hanging sense of trepidation fills my stomach. The thought of getting out of bed seems too unbearable. And what would I do if I did get out of bed? Where would I go?

Adrian and Rugs are on that cold island. Geoff is in South Africa. I'm here alone.

* * *

An aeroplane crashes into a building. Fragments of its jet engine lie in crumpled pieces at the entrance. A man lies on the floor in agony, shattered bones splintering through his shins. I want to help him, but I've nothing to help him with. I try to leave the building, but the doorways are covered with rubble. What if the building collapses? I run from door to door trying to find an exit.

Mum is shaking my shoulder. 'Hayde, you haven't lent the car to anyone have you?'

I raise my head, confused. 'No . . .'

'Well, then it's been nicked.'

In the driveway is an empty space where the old Nissan once sat. 'Oh bugger.'

'I've been telling your father for years that we need to close the carport in.'

'Mum, it's no good bringing all this up with me. I'm going for a run.'

I make my way down the driveway. Muddy tyre tracks run through a giant hole in the fence and onto the road.

The morning light shimmers through the trees. In the distant dip of the road a car sits at the side verge, lifeless in the morning sun, motionless like a ship at the bottom of the ocean.

I open the door. Wires stick out beneath the steering column. I join two of them together and the ignition lights turn red. I touch a third wire onto the circuit and the starter-engine engages.

When I return, Dad is sitting on his bed reading his paper. 'Dad, I found the car. It was abandoned just down the road. Had to hot-wire it.'

He laughs. 'I've got a good mind to thank Jim Swanepoel for doing such a shit service on it!'

'You need to hire a security guard until we get that hole in the fence fixed. They might be back.'

'Maybe.'

'Is that a yes or a no?'

'Well, I'm not in principle opposed to it,' he says.

'Well, I'd hope not,' I say. 'Because it's your asset.'

At night a thin young man arrives with a measly baton. He stands lonely in the darkness by the rusting cars. Late at night I take him some left-over dinner. Dad appears goblin-like in front of me.

'What are you doing?'

'Taking some food to the security guard.'

He makes monkey gestures, like a child in kindergarten. 'Oh, always have to be a goodie-goodie, do we?' he shouts. 'Goodie-goodie! My son's a goodie-goodie. "Look at me helping the security guard!" Goodie-goodie, goodie-goodie!'

The guard watches us, and then Dad seems suddenly self-conscious, suddenly tired of following me and like he'd rather just do a crossword puzzle.

The guard sips his mug of tea in silence, as if he's wondering how these whites manage to be so mad. 'How's the job these days?' I ask.

He shakes his head. 'Things are now too hard. With what they pay, you will never survive. Ah, my friend, you will struggle. But there is nothing else to do.'

His thin limbs move in the shadows and his eyes stare into the night and at the moon.

* * *

The ceiling is the dirty white I remember from last year. Sarah flops an arm onto my stomach. Her body seems almost healed now, as if her cancer was another peculiar episode that may never have happened. I never saw the hell she endured.

But her energy seems different now. She's thinner and less confident. She no longer talks of living in Paris. She seems to have lost the wild, untameable sparkle in her eye.

I pull the blanket from my chest. I feel dirty. How could I have allowed myself to sink back into this ether-world?

I had thought her cancer would make her less desirable to me. But for some reason I don't care that she was ill.

'Hayde. What are we doing?' she mumbles.

'I don't know, Sare. I don't know.'

'Do you think you're ever going to forgive me for how I behaved?'

'Is now the time to talk about this?'

'Well, when is a good time? You're not back for that long.'

I slump onto the bed. 'What does it mean to forgive? I don't even know anymore.'

'Hayde, having cancer changes you. I'm not the same person I was when I started treatment. If you can't see that, we shouldn't be doing this.'

I sigh. 'I don't know what I want anymore. I don't even know what reality is anymore.'

* * *

The boil on my jaw is red and angry and swollen. The whites of my eyes are bloodshot. *Are they red from tiredness or from pinkeye?* I wonder.

Dad's frame has rapidly returned to its previous state of wire and skin and smoke. 'Dad,' I say. 'It's dark already and the guard hasn't come on duty.'

'I cancelled him this afternoon.'

'What? Why did you do that?'

'We can just chain the cars to the concrete pillars outside. No need to waste money unnecessarily.'

'Well, are you going to do that? Are you going to tie them up with chains every night?'

'If need be.'

Mum and Beebs sit together on the stoep. 'Guys, please make sure you lock your bedroom doors tonight. It's not safe without a fence. They know we're an easy target.'

'Okay,' says Mum.

'Promise me!'

'I promise,' says Mum.

'I promise,' adds Beebs.

Late at night I go outside. Before I even see the cars I know what I'll find. They are bathed in brilliant moonlight without chains. And I wonder why I even bothered to check.

Dad sits in his chair, puffing smoke into the air. 'You haven't chained up the cars yet,' I say.

I expect him to shout back, but he's unexpectedly sweet. 'Oh, won't you do it?' he says. 'You're so good at that sort of thing.'

'You said you were going to do it.'

'I know. But how about you do it this time and I'll do it next time? I'm not that well, you know.'

The chains clank against each other in the cold darkness. I curse myself for being manipulated, for clinking and banging in the dark when I should be studying.

In bed I clutch a baseball bat in my hands, my heart thumping like it's lodged itself in my throat. We've brought these troubles upon ourselves.

Rustling and scraping sounds keep me awake. Is it a night breeze brushing the old msasa branches against the roof? Or are the thieves back to finish what they started?

Light blazes through the open window. The early birds screech and argue with one another. I try the handle to Mum's room. The door opens. Mum glances up from the magazine on her lap. 'Have you been out of your room yet?'

'No. About to go and get some coffee though.'

'Mum, I thought you were going to lock this door last night? You actually promised me you'd lock it.'

She looks apologetic. 'Oh, sorry. I thought I had.'

*　*　*

I sit at the piano and press my fingers into melancholic-sounding chords. I want Dad to be better. He's shown at times that it's in him. I've somehow let him slip again back into his abyss. I must try harder to help.

I close the piano lid. I will get him to move around the house and garden. If he continues to lie in his bed, he'll waste away further. And I must talk to him more. I must show more of an interest in his life.

I go to his room. He lies in his bed listening to the whining BBC. 'Dad, let's go for a walk around the block. It'll be good for you.'

'That's a good idea!' he says, sounding cheerful, sounding like he's forgotten about the mess with the cars, forgotten that his wife's been salting away his money. He puts on his socks and shoes. His shoulders and hips move like they're the components of some kind of mechanical donkey.

At the front door, he stops. 'Oh, hang on,' he says. 'I've just remembered that the heater is broken. I've been meaning to attend to it all week. Maybe you should go on ahead.'

He walks into the dining room and sits down. He picks up the heater from the carpet and taps it with his fingers as though this will somehow fix it. 'Where have those bloody screwdrivers got to . . .' he mumbles to himself.

His thin fingers clutch at the heater.

And then it seems as though the very act of his fingers moving has unlocked some coded mystery of the universe, as if before the moment he touched it, the world was a scrambled code of Morse and gibberish, and afterwards, crisp, clear BBC English. Those Nazis who believed in the Aryan dream, did they know in some dimly lit corner of their minds that their idea was all nonsense? Or did they only wake from that dream when it was beaten into them? Did they only see it when the Red Army raped them in their homes, or when they had to eat their dogs and horses, or when they had to boil their own wallpaper and drink it like soup?

I'm a German sitting in Berlin listening to someone on the radio say, 'Oh, by the way, all of that stuff we were saying about the final victory, it was all a lie. And that stuff about Aryan-*chakuti-chakuti*, it was a lie. And your leader, he's a liar. And he's dead.' It's as if I've walked outside my home to see the Red Army advancing over the horizon, leaving nowhere for my treacherous lies to hide, like I've finally fired the last beautiful lie from the last working gun.

I see Sarah's eyes in my mind. She stands there looking at me with that resting expression that I can never read. But I can read it now. She doesn't love me. She never will. And nothing I do will ever change that.

Dad attempts to undo one of the heater's screws with a butter knife. He mutters and curses under his breath.

*   *   *

Dad's lizard-carcass stares at the ceiling. A tray of cold, uneaten food sits at the base of his bed. I stand at the foot of his bed. 'The staff haven't been paid. When are you going to pay them?' I ask.

He flicks his eyes my way. 'Being paid on time is a privilege and not a right. You tell them that.'

'Why don't you tell them yourself?'

'You're the one who's the goodie-goodie, you tell them! Otherwise they can bloody well wait until I feel like it.'

'I don't believe it!' I scream. 'The fucking communist! The fucking communist thinks being paid on time is a privilege!'

'That's right, it is a privilege. They don't have to work here, you know. They can leave today if they want. It's a free country, you know.'

I point my finger at him. 'Let me tell you something!' I shout, 'I don't give a shit about any of your fucking words anymore. *Munt, kaffir, boug!* I don't care what you call it anymore. The only thing I care about is what it is. And just so you know, what this is stinks!'

The venom seems to drain from his face. He goes quiet. My face burns and tingles. The familiar electricity surges through my body, gripping me with its naked power. Tears boil their way out of my eyes. 'When Dan and I were small,' I say, 'We were playing one afternoon in the driveway. A smart Mercedes drove up the driveway. You rushed out the door in your blue suit. You turned to me and said, "I'm off to Bulawayo to monitor the elections, I'll see you next week." Do you remember that?'

'Yes, of course, I was on the Electoral Supervisory Commission.'

'You got up on national television and said that Zimbabwe was more democratic than America. That was shortly after a genocide. Or have you forgotten about what happened in Matabeleland?'

He remains quiet, almost pensive. He speaks slowly and monotonously. 'You don't understand,' he begins. 'It's not that simple. The Matabele were generally loyal to Nkomo. They were opposition. Nobody knew how serious the threat of those disbanded troops was. It's easy to talk about the government's over-reaction with the benefit of hindsight.'

'Crap!' I scream. 'They were killing civilians and you knew about it! You rubber-stamped it when they were making the Rhodesians look like the Salvation-fucking-Army! And then you complain about people using bad words over the dinner table, as if words kill! They're not the racists. You are! *We* are!'

He says nothing. 'You hate the oppressor, but that's not the same as loving the oppressed. It's not the same.'

He suddenly rises to my challenge. 'You've grown up in a different world to me, you know; it's easy to stand there, you know. You don't know what this world was like!' he shouts. 'There were some truly disgusting things happening!'

'Yes, there were, Dad. But you threw out the baby with the bathwater. Do you imagine we'll have anything left after your madmen have dismantled every single social boundary that ever existed? Do you think we're all going to run around in loincloths saying, "Hullo, my brother, can I share my cow with you?" You went to a colonial boarding school, for God's sake! You should know what people are like!'

A tear breaks out of one of Dad's eyes. I want him to make me see how I've somehow got it wrong; how the dots can somehow be joined to form Michelangelo's 'David', instead of a turd; how the awful truths searing my retinas can somehow be a rainbow.

His face contorts and shrivels. 'My family don't love me,' he moans. 'You've rejected me.'

'Oh, shut up! You've chosen this life for yourself. Nobody's rejected you; you've rejected them!'

'There's no such thing as choice,' he says, properly crying now.

'So we're all a product of our genes and environment, but some of us are much more a product of them than others, is that it?'

'And it's not just you,' I shout. 'Where were your other lefties in all of this? Silent as the night, obviously didn't give a shit either. Look at that useful idiot Noam Chomsky denying the genocide in Cambodia. Defended it till the last bloody moment, even when they were uncovering mass graves. Wow, thanks Noam! Where was he during the Gukurahundi?'

Dad sobs in his bed. He seems unable to speak.

Mum comes to the door. 'What's going on? What's all the commotion?'

I walk past her with my face tingling, my eyes blinded by fury. 'Nothing,' I say. 'I just lost my temper in a moment of sanity.'

* * *

I gather the staff in the laundry room. 'I'm really sorry, but Dad says you're going to have to wait until he feels like paying you.'

The two gardeners listen in silence, staring like statues into the distance, as if they've been turned into stone. Emily says, 'Ah-ah, I can't work here for this man! Each day I am taking him food. He doesn't eat. And then he is complaining, complaining that we don't feed him. Ahhh, he is too much *shupa*! Games, games, games. And how can I buy food now? What can I eat?'

I look at her, 'I'm sorry,' I say. 'I'm so, so sorry.'

I drive Emily to the bus station. She wears an elegant dress. I unload her things from the boot and stack them on the side of the road. 'You must come and visit me when I am black-black from working in the fields,' she says. 'Ah, I will be too black!'

She hugs me with her strong frame and then waits in the baking sun. In the rear-view mirror she stands perfectly straight with her bag by her side.

*   *   *

People meander lazily under the splendid branches hanging jagged over the road. I glance at the dashboard. It seems so benign. And yet it's the same dashboard that Mum writhed like a fish against, the same dashboard she smashed her face on over and over again during our last family holiday.

The last day of that holiday is still clear in my head: We are all standing at a black gate looking at a big white house. Dad points into the distance. 'Those houses,' he says. 'They were once all vine-yards as far as the eye could see. I used to walk through them and eat so many grapes that I got a runny tummy.'

He points back to the house in front of us. 'And that window up there,' he says. 'That's where my sister, Cynthia, convinced me to jump with an umbrella to break my fall. I hit the ground with such a crack that I lay for a long time completely winded, unable to get up. I think I might have broken a rib or two.'

He gestures to the road leading from the gate into the leafy distance. 'And along here I used to ride with my little bicycle to the school and dig booby traps in the field with my spade.'

And when he says those words my eyes fill with tears. I walk into the distance where nobody will see me and then I cry beneath the hanging branches.

I always wondered what upset me so terribly that day. But it's obvious to me now.

I had cried because I saw that the boy in there had died a long time ago. I had cried because I might have once known that boy and liked him.

At times I can almost see that boy trapped in that prison. At times I sense I'm calling for him, hoping that he'll come to the window so I can help him. I call again and again and wait. I hear the footsteps coming. Perhaps I'll see the child; perhaps I'll have the chance to help him. But it is the ogre, always the ogre. I can hear the boy screaming for help, pleading for mercy from his torturer. But I see now that I must leave that boy to be eaten by the ogre that lives in there.

* * *

From the passageway I can already smell Dad's room. I approach his closed door. Behind it the BBC voices talk and crackle. I slowly push the handle down. Dad lies in his bed. He seems pharaoh-like, as though he's already been embalmed.

I stand next to him like I'm standing next to a dead rogue elephant, like I'm studying its big dead wreck on the ground and being overcome by the futility that it ever existed, that it was ever shot, that it had ever rampaged like a mad thing when it should have just roamed in the bush. It's as if I'm looking at the waste of the carcass in the grass and studying the mountain of dead flesh in its full futile glory.

'Mum,' I say. 'You have to move out. We need to see what's in front of us. We have to stop living with this fantasy that things will change.'

She looks at me blankly. I put my hands on her shoulders. 'Stop looking for something alive inside of him. There's nothing in there. There's just nothing.'

*　*　*

The car moves its way through the streets and under the perfect sun and winter sky. Miles plays with his aeroplane in the back seat. Mum sits stony-faced next to me. The silence becomes suddenly unbearable. She pushes a tape into the tape deck. John Lennon starts to sing 'Imagine'. I reach over and turn it off. 'Please, Mum. Anything but this banal adolescent crap. *Anything.*'

The engine hums. 'When your father used to recount to me the way people were tortured during the struggle, he would convey it in such gruesome detail that it'd leave me feeling sick. A couple of times it occurred to me that he was actually aroused by it.'

'Mum, I honestly have no idea what goes on between the two of you. It sounds quite mad, whatever it is.'

I unload some boxes and carry them into the little apartment. 'At least he was never particularly violent,' I say.

'Actually, he could be downright violent sometimes, you know. There was that time he threw me down; I had a neck brace for months.'

'Jesus, Mum! I thought that was because you'd hurt your back from practising the piano.'

'And in the bedroo—'

'Too much information, Mum, too much information.'

Miles walks in with his night-ape eyes. He carries a book in his little hands. He holds it up to me and says, 'Ini!'

'Thanks, Miley,' I say, 'would you put it over there for Mummy?'

*　*　*

From the seat of the aeroplane, I watch the airport lights glow in the night. I catch the faint reflection of myself in the glass window. The boil on my neck has faded into nothing. I study my hands and clench my fingers. My limbs are working well. Some personal circumstances have cursed me. But history has blessed me. I imagine for a moment the tens of thousands of families at the mercy of a malevolent madman, blessed by nothing. *There but for the grace of God go I,*' I think.

I open the fat red book in front of me and turn to Free Energy of Binding.

'Ladies and gentlemen, we are pleased to welcome you aboard this British Airways flight from Harare to Gatwick,' says the voice on the loudspeaker. The engines roar. The thrust presses me into my seat. The plane hurtles along the runway until it finally lifts into the sky. Through the window I study the scattered lights as they fade into darkness.

Red Soil

Chapter 27

The familiar streets pass by the window.

Mum's phone rings. 'Hi, Bev . . . Uh-huh . . . Yes . . . What's that you say? . . . Great, where? . . . And is there sugar? . . . Thanks! Okay, if you join the queue for me I'll be there as soon as I've dropped Hayden home . . . Yes, just collected him from the airport.'

'Amazing,' she tells me. 'Bev's managed to find some sugar. I'm going to drop you at home and go queue.'

The Harare Botanical Gardens look unkempt and overgrown. The old stone entrance often reminds me of the story about my great-grandmother, who'd once taught French to Ian Smith.

She spotted him in the gardens with his dogs and immediately marched up to him. 'Mr Smith!' she shouted. 'Why are you ruining this country?'

And then Ian Smith stopped, and his dogs stopped. And he hung his head. 'I'm very sorry, Mrs Morgan. I'm very sorry, ma'am,' he said to her.

I take my rucksack out of the car. 'We're a bit short of space right now. Gran's house isn't quite Blair Road space-wise. I've made you a bed on the veranda,' says Mum.

*　*　*

'Miley, would you pass me the water?' I ask.

'Here you go, Hayde, but this is the last of it. Ning's going to collect more.'

'Come on, Miley, it's your turn!' says Beebs.

'Why does it always have to be me?' says Miles.

'We're so lucky to have the Williams's down the road,' Mum says. 'They've got the best borehole, and they say we can go across any time. Been there since they lost the farm a couple of years back.'

'Yes. I remember we used to ride our bikes on their old dirt roads.'

Irene hobbles in with a tray. 'Madam, where can I put?' she says.

'Ah, just over there, thank you, Irene.'

Irene slides out.

Mum leans in and whispers. 'Gosh, I heard the most shocking thing about Irene at Rupert's the other day. He said that her two-year-old son was bayonetted to death during the Gukurahundi. I'd simply had no idea. She's never mentioned anything about the eighties in Bulawayo.'

'Are you sure? How do you know it happened?' I ask.

'Well, Seymour, who works for Rupert, is Irene's cousin. She told him once. Apparently, Irene had to dance and sing pro-Mugabe songs in order to save her other children from the same thing.'

'Have you said anything to Irene?'

'Heavens-no. What does one say about something like that?'

Irene walks in again and places a jug of water on the table.

'And in other news,' adds Beebs, 'Dad's been given a Merc for, and I quote, acts of selfless kindness.'

Mum interrupts. 'Honestly, this car has to be seen to be believed. Bright silver, with *mafeecha* galore. Gas-guzzling five-litre engine or something. My new name for him is Karl Mercs.'

'You're lucky you weren't here last month,' Beebs tells me. 'We had no water and no electricity for days. The rain caused the drainage hole outside to flood and a volcano of shit just exploded out of the manhole by the gate.'

'Oh, *sis!*'

'Wait, it gets better. The dogs got covered in it and then ran inside and rolled all over the carpets. We had no water, so we couldn't clean either the dogs or the carpets, and we had no electricity, so we couldn't dry anything either. So we spent days with stinking shitty carpets until Mum managed to find somewhere to take them to.'

'Honestly,' continues Mum, 'this place is just fucked now, a free-for-all. There's no stuff in the shops. Spent hours queuing for bloody sugar today.'

'And the university, Mum?'

'Oh, a dog show. Half of the staff are just lazy Fanta-swilling idiots. Not so long ago the police came in and beat a whole lot of my students up and closed the halls of residence. Some of them call getting arrested and beaten "their education" . . . Anyway, enough of this depressing talk. Miles, tell Hayde about school.'

'It's fine. A bit boring. I got lashed last month for not knowing the verb "to be" in French class.'

'Honestly Miles,' says Mum. 'I can't believe that happened. Your mother speaks fluently. It's an embarrassment.'

'Come on, Miley.' I say. 'Just learn the verb. There's not much point in being mindlessly anti-establishment. Take it from me.'

I go down the passageway to the toilet and return some moments later. 'Alright, who left a floaty poo in the toilet?'

'It wasn't me,' says Mum.

'Nor me,' says Beebs.

'Miles, was that you?'

'Um, I'm not sure,' he says.

'*Miles*, was that you?'

'No.'

'Well somebody left a frickin' floaty poo in the toilet!'

'Yeah, but Hayde, sometimes there are floaty poos, because we hardly ever have water.'

'It's so frickin' disconcerting!' I say.

'So,' says Mum, changing the subject. 'How are Adrian and Rugs? Are they still in the UK?'

'Rugs is working in London. Seems to be fitting in. Adrian's in Afghanistan filming insurgents. He's still not quite right after that militant held a gun to his head.'

'Yes, I remember you saying last time. And what about Sarah? How is she at the moment?'

'Still in remission. Fingers crossed. She's in Cape Town. Simon and her broke up. He's playing in some band called Freshlyground.'

'And how about Max and Franz?'

'They're well. Franz is still in Ivory Coast. Max is still in New York.'

'And is Max still seeing that New Yorker girl?' asks Beebs.

'No. He dumped her. She was nuts. You should have seen what happened when he brought her out here for that canoe trip. We could hardly fit her luggage into the boats. Miles and I were in the canoe ahead of them. We would just hear these shrieks and look back to see this crazy chick waving her arms in the air and crying.'

'She was certainly hard work,' agrees Beebs. 'And now? Who's his latest?'

'I haven't met her yet, but she sounds a bit crazy too. Her name is Fanny. What kind of name is that for God's sake? Bloody Germans.'

Mum walks by and dumps a second helping on my plate. 'Let's just hope her last name isn't Kant.'

I snort my drink out my nose. Beebs and Miley shake with laughter. 'On a serious note,' says Mum, 'We're scattering Dan's ashes tomorrow at noon.'

I glance at the drinks table. Dan's ashes sit on it in a white box. It looks so ordinary, like it might just hold some biscuits. I want to open the box, but I somehow daren't.

*   *   *

My face tingles and burns like it did on the day Dan died. We huddle in the small clearing where the granite rocks are stained red by the earth. It is my moment to undo the wrong I did at his funeral.

I stand next to Mum and Beebs and Miley. Dad stands opposite us. He looks at the ground. I wonder why he came; why he left his lair; why he bothered to leave those walls, still painted with shit and ash and ants. He is still the dead man walking. He breathes. He puts one foot in front of the other. He fulfils a biologist's checklist definition of life. But I sense there is nothing much else there. Was there ever?

Mum says some words. Beebs and Miles stay quiet. I tell the story of Dan's geography project that ended in disaster. The story that was him. Nobody else in the world would have done it. I want to say more; I want to explain how Dan taught me how to think properly, how he taught me to think for myself. I want to speak about the good and the bad, about how I wished I had been able to help him. I want to speak about so much. But the words somehow can't come out, like it's impossible to say anything that would actually do him any justice.

We each dig our hands into the cardboard box holding Dan's ashes. I expect them to be a fine grey powder, like the ashes of a burned-out braai. But there is no ash. The pieces are big grey-white lumps, like broken pieces of old blackboard chalk, like dry fragments of bleached coral picked from a deserted beach. I roll the fragments in my fingers. Which parts of his body have they come from? Were they once part of his femur? His jawbone? His skull? How much of his skeleton could be remade if the pieces were fitted together like a jigsaw of bone? They are not ash. They are him, but they are not him. Where has the carbon that once formed his tissues floated to? Maybe some of those molecules have been sucked up as carbon dioxide to form part of the trees and grass in front of us. Maybe I have breathed part of him into my lungs and made him part of me.

I throw him into the grass and bushes and grab another handful to scatter him some more. I search the grassy area with my eyes for traces of him, but there is nothing.

There is only the lazy hum of the African bush and the drone of bees and screeching insects. It's as if the earth has already swallowed him with its infinite supply of clay and soil and dust.

HAYDEN EASTWOOD is a freelance software developer and tech entrepreneur working in the fields of health, education and crypto-finance. Originally a research physical chemist, he has dabbled in a variety of pursuits, including gooseberry farming, teaching and documentary film-making. He has published two Shona language textbooks. When not sipping coffee in the wilderness, he lives in Harare.